Merry Chris

Love,
Camille & John

THE 1939 TEXAS AGGIES

THE 1939 TEXAS AGGIES

The Greatest Generation's Greatest Team

by Mickey Herskowitz

Halcyon Press Ltd. ★ Houston Texas

THE 1939 TEXAS AGGIES
The Greatest Generation's Greatest Team
by Mickey Herskowitz

Copyright © 2006 by Development Fund '60

Published by
Halcyon Press Ltd.
2656 South Loop West, Ste 440
Houston, Texas 77054 USA
www.halcyonpress.com

Library of Congress Cataloging-in-Publication Data

Herskowitz, Mickey.
   The 1939 Texas Aggies : the greatest generations greatest team / by Mickey Herskowitz.
-- 1st ed.
      p. cm.
   Includes index.
   ISBN-13: 978-1-931823-39-5 (hardcover : alk. paper)
   ISBN-10: 1-931823-39-1 (hardcover : alk. paper)
   ISBN-13: 978-1-931823-41-8 (leatherbound : alk. paper)
   ISBN-10: 1-931823-41-3 (leatherbound : alk. paper)
   1. Texas A & M University--Football--History. 2. Texas A & M Aggies (Football team)--History. I. Title.
   GV958.T44H47 2006
   796.332'6309764242--dc22
                                        2006014178

First Edition
10 9 8 7 6 5 4 3 2 1
Printed and bound in the United States of America
Designed by David Raley

*To every member of Texas A.&M.'s 1939 National Champions,
and the Class of 1960, who would not let them be forgotten.*

Members of the 1939 team, taken in 1999

CONTENTS

The 1939 National Champion Texas Aggies

EDITOR'S NOTE

AT THE TURN OF THE 21ST CENTURY, an important sounding phrase right there, the writer Mickey Herskowitz spoke with Jack Rains, a member of the Class of 1960 at Texas A&M, during a lunch meeting in Houston.

It was a social lunch between long-time friends. Herskowitz has been a familiar Texas presence as a sports columnist and author. Rains made his mark as an attorney with political and sports credentials; a former secretary of state and the first chairman of Houston's sports authority, responsible for the construction of landmark football and baseball stadiums.

Both had read Tom Brokaw's book, *The Greatest Generation*. The conversation turned to the coming grid season and perennial Aggie hopes. Jack observed that A&M had its own greatest generation, the team that won a national championship in 1939 and almost repeated in 1940.

The story of these young men who came to A&M to play for Homer Norton, their hardscrabble roots, many as farm boys, was a tale begging to be told. Hardship had given them a toughness few of their counterparts in the Southwest Conference could match, and inspired in them a hunger for winning that led to a victory over Tulane in the 1940 Sugar Bowl, and a national title.

When you combined that success with the role these same players performed in World War II, and what they later achieved in business and as family men, the story took on historic dimensions. This was the story of a group of young men from a great generation, who used their talents and teamwork and discipline to win many more of life's battles.

Jack asked his lunch guest if he wanted to take a run at the story, if Rains could find the backing for the project. Mickey was hooked.

As a sportswriter and author, he knew many of the accomplishments and traditions of A&M football. Early in his career, he had ghost-written a newspaper column for Norton that appeared in several papers across the state.

As even a cursory glance at the introduction will reveal, Aggie football history is a melodrama of its own. Trying to recreate the glory of one group of champions demands a review of a hundred years of good, and less satisfactory, times. Aggie grads and fans always look to the next season as a chance to once more fulfill all their yearnings.

They have come close many times; their elusive goal often foiled by just a few inches. Any Aggie will tell you that the team never really lost a game, they just ran out of time. That attitude covers over a century of Aggie football (and long before the description was attached to one Bobby Layne during his pro career.)

The national championship will happen again, a conviction not always of comfort to Aggie fans, who want it NOW. The lofty expectations established by the 1939 championship team screams for a repeat. And the 1939 team will never be forgotten. What sports writer-slash-author could resist such a tale? Yes, Mickey was hooked.

A second meeting followed with John Lindsey, Class of '44 and years later an Aggie regent. His endorsement sealed the deal.

Jack Rains set about rallying his troops, raising the money to fund the time, research, trips, interviews and effort that would be needed to develop the story and bring it to print. His class, the Class of 1960, had already set a standard by acquiring the rights for the video distribution of the World War II film, *We've Never Been Licked*.

They had a non-profit corporation in place that could manage the funds and provide access to book stores and the alumni magazine, which they had used to promote mail order sales so successfully. It was agreed that any profits raised by the book would go back to A&M activities. Rains began calling influential Aggie grads who knew of the exploits of this championship team and wanted to see this great story told. The contributors are listed in the acknowledgments section of the book.

The Class of 1960 became the catalyst that mobilized the search for the 1939 Aggies, and a story that could no longer be neglected. Mickey Herskowitz was told to get it done. And he was hooked.

Unearthing the details behind a story now more than sixty years old was a big, big challenge. Every phone call, every interview, every foray into newspaper archives led to more stories and leads to track down. Every attempt to start the narrative led to another story and another start and more pages. From the moment an agreement was struck, until the final sentence was punctuated, Rains was the hornet who stung the donkey's rear, who kept the wagon rolling, the donors informed, and the project from falling off the rails.

There were the usual distractions and delays; status reports that kept the old grads sullen but not mutinous, summer coaches' tours that were missed. But Rains did his juggling act and a story that had been waiting for six decades to be revived found its way into the computers.

For every page printed, for every picture displayed, for every game story reproduced, there might have been two or three more. When the reader scans the biography section on the players, it becomes evident that another library of books could have been written. This, then, is the first full length attempt to tell the story of a great Aggie football team, and the great generation that spawned it.

Coach Homer Norton

INTRODUCTION

⤞⤝

A History of Aggie Football, Parts I and II

What do these men have in common: Harry Stiteler, Ray George, Paul (Bear) Bryant, Jim Myers, Hank Foldberg, Gene Stallings, Emory Bellard, Tom Wilson, Jackie Sherrill, R. C. Slocum and Dennis Franchione?

You guessed it, of course. All of them coached the Texas Aggie football team, without duplicating the success of Homer Norton, who delivered a national championship to the banks of the Brazos back in a year historic for other reasons, as well, 1939.

Of course, there is still hope for Coach Fran, still new to the job, who in his second season performed one of the major turnarounds of 2004. The mystery meat of college football, the Aggies won six in a row after an opening loss to Utah, then dropped four of their last five games and still wound up in the Cotton Bowl.

Against an Oklahoma team ranked Number 2 in the polls, they improved by seventy points over the previous season before falling, 42-35. This is a recovery of gargantuan proportions, even in defeat, because the Aggies were trying mightily to avenge the massacre of '03, when the Sooners laid on them something they did not expect—77 points.

In the entirety of 1939, A&M yielded a total of 31 points to ten opponents during the regular season.

Yes, Aggie football means having a sense of history and a sense of humor. A Houston newspaper columnist, Morris Frank, one of the country's most popular toastmasters, gave the school's former students this enduring description: "Invincible in defeat, insufferable in victory."

Although the record is spotty, its passion and unwavering loyalty long ago established A&M as a marquee program, famed for its Twelfth

Man, its marching band, its midnight yell practices, Bonfire, and the sonic sound levels at storied Kyle Field.

Through the decades, the Aggies have known almost biblical cycles of feast and famine, stretches of misery broken by seasons of stirring triumph, tantalizing their fans by coming within a win or a tie of matching that last perfect season, one ring from the bulls-eye.

After 1945, the Cadets suffered seven losing seasons out of nine, including two under Norton, whose talent had been drained by the war. Harry Stiteler, a former Aggie quarterback who had been on Homer's staff, and Ray George, a line coach hired away from USC, each lasted three years.

A&M went from no wins under Stiteler in 1948 to one in '49 and seven in 1950, when Bob Smith carried on the tradition of great Aggie fullbacks. He set a conference record with 297 yards rushing against SMU, playing in a mask welded with a shield to protect a broken nose. The Aggies were invited to play for the Presidential Cup, a short-lived bowl game at College Park, Maryland, and Smith ran back the opening kickoff 100 yards as the Aggies thumped Georgia, 40-20.

Ray George had the salt and pepper hair and sturdy build of a police lieutenant. He was a pleasant fellow who, after every loss, had a stock comment when asked about next week's opponent: "We're going to get after them."

They did just that in the last game of Ray's first season, 1951, upsetting Texas at Kyle Field, 22-21, for their only conference victory. Yale Lary ran 68 yards for one touchdown and caught a pass from Darrow Hooper for another. Hooper, an Olympic shot putter, also kicked a 31-yard field goal.

Lary went on to a solid career with the Detroit Lions, where he punted, played safety and was a teammate of Longhorn immortal Bobby Layne. It was Lary who said of Layne, "When Bobby said block, you blocked. When Bobby said drink, you drank."

The Aggies grew weary of looking for silver linings. Twelve years without a title had taken a toll and, when desperate measures are required, those who embrace the maroon and white do not think small.

They hired Paul (Bear) Bryant from Kentucky, who was not yet an icon, the godlike figure he would become at Alabama. The later Bryant had a weathered face with fine lines like a road map folded over and over, and a voice so deep it seemed to rumble like a train out of a tunnel.

Bryant was approaching his 40th birthday, handsome and vigorous and still willing, in a T-shirt and khakis, to drop into a stance and demonstrate the proper technique for one of his linemen.

Books and movies have been produced about the Bear, and his Junction Boys, and there is no need to devote reams of space to him here. His four years at Aggieland attracted a notoriety oddly out of proportion to his twenty-five at Alabama.

But there appears to be no question that the team nearest to his heart was the one that gave him his only losing season out of the thirty-seven he spent as a coach. The team that survived the scorched earth of Junction earned its only victory against Georgia, 6-0, on a day that the Aggies suited up twenty-seven players.

Before the game, his rival, Wally Butts, asked Bryant if those were the only players he had. "No," he replied, "these are the only ones who want to play." Actually, he had driven off the others, and years later Bryant would express his regrets: "I couldn't have played for me in those days, either."

But he had a mission to complete at A&M and he was in a hurry to get it done. The 1954 Aggies played hard and lost late, and the win in Athens was so sweet that in the locker room after the game Bryant and his elderly trainer, Smokey Harper, danced a jig.

Wins became a bit more routine a year later, when the Aggies finished 7-2-1. In one of the great comebacks in college football history, they scored 20 points in the final minute and 26 seconds to rally past Rice, 20-12, in Houston. Rice Stadium would not always be so kind to them.

In 1956, the players who had been sophomores at Junction—notably Gene Stallings, Jack Pardee, Lloyd Hale, Dennis Goehring, Don Watson and Dee Powell—provided the senior leadership and the Aggies went unbeaten in 10 games, with a 14-14 tie against Houston the only blot.

All dressed up with no place to go, the Cadets stayed home because of NCAA sanctions, but Bryant had given them their first SWC championship since Norton's 1941 team.

They were #1 in the nation for most of the 1957 season, and extended their streak to nineteen wins without a loss after a squeaker over Arkansas and a 19-6 victory over Don Meredith and SMU.

The quintessential Bryant moment came in the Ozarks in the closing seconds of a 7-6 classic. The Aggies had the ball at the Arkansas 12 with a minute and 20 seconds to play, and the Bear sent in a sub to tell his quarterback, Roddy Osborne, to keep the ball on the ground and run out the clock.

On the next play, the Hogs put on a hard rush and were about to bury Osborne, who looked up and saw John David Crow alone in the end zone. He said, later, he had no intention of throwing the ball, but it was as if "God had raised my arm."

The next thing anyone knew, the ball was in the air, and Donny Horton, a sprinter on the track team, maybe the fastest player on the field, cut in front of Crow and intercepted the pass at the goal line.

He had a blocker and nothing but grass in front of him. The Arkansas crowd was going berserk and many of the fans began to pour out of the stands. Only Osborne, the slowest man in the Aggie backfield, had a play, and he took an angle, fought off the blocker and made the tackle at the 27-yard line.

The gain went for 64 yards. The Hogs completed a pass to the 15, where Crow made a saving tackle, and on the next play John David picked one off in the end zone and the game was over.

That Monday morning, Bryant was on the phone, as coaches usually are, and he was describing Horton's long, frightening run to Bobby Dodd of Georgia Tech.

When he finished, Dodd said, "Paul, there's one thing I don't understand. If the Arkansas boy is as fast as you say, and your boy is as slow as you say he is, how the hell did your boy make the tackle?"

Bryant said, with feeling, "Oh, Bobby, that's easy. The Arkansas player was just running for a touchdown. Osborne was running for his life."

The Aggies were unbeaten and ranked Number 1 on the eve of the Rice game, when the story broke in the *Houston Post* that Bryant had been offered the coaching job at his alma mater, Alabama, and would accept it.

No one really knows what effect that rumor had on the Aggies, but they were playing an exceptional Rice team that had two future pro quarterbacks in King Hill and Frank Ryan. The Owls stunned A&M and wrecked its hopes of a national title, 7-6.

On Thanksgiving Day, the Aggies lost to Texas, 9-7. A 62-yard quick kick by Walter Fondren put them in a hole early, on their own four-yard line. Bobby Lackey scored the Texas touchdown and kicked the field goal that proved the difference.

The Aggies used only fifteen players, and Crow was all over the field, catching a pass from Osborne for 57 yards, making tackles and batting away passes. But the game and the season had gotten away.

Crow became the only Aggie and the only Bryant player to win the Heisman Trophy, and the Bear helped his cause greatly when he announced to the press, "If John David doesn't win it, they ought to quit giving it."

The Aggies lost to Tennessee in the Gator Bowl, 3-0 and Bryant went back to Alabama, where his teams won or tied for five national titles. But any reference to 1957 could ruin the Bear's mood—and you always knew when his mood was ruined. On a trip to Houston, ten years later, he stayed at the Shamrock Hilton Hotel, and when a friend walked in he was cursing because the desk clerk had given him a room overlooking Rice Stadium. "I can't even look out that window," he said, "without seeing THAT damned stadium and having to replay THAT game all over again. Cost us the national championship."

He went on to break Amos Alonzo Stagg's record as the winningest coach in college football history. He kept saying that he would never retire, claiming that "if I gave up coaching I'd probably croak in a week."

He did retire after a victory in the 1983 Liberty Bowl, and died of a heart attack three weeks later. "I wish people would quit writing that," said Mary Harmon Bryant, who was his sweetheart and school beauty when both were students. "Papa wasn't ready to die. Papa had lots of things he wanted to do."

A few years later, a movie about his life was released starring Gary Busey, who had been in a hit in the *Buddy Holly Story*. Mary Harmon was not pleased. "Papa was handsome," she said. "Can you imagine that buck-toothed boy playing Papa?"

The Aggies were having their own withdrawal pains, trying to find someone to play Papa on the sidelines. The athletic committee launched a national search for a successor, as did several influential former students. The result was that nearly every famous coach in America had his name linked to the job. Frank Leahy said he was "ninety-nine percent sure" he would be the next Aggie coach, then bowed out for health reasons.

The committee offered the job to Jim Myers, of Iowa State, then had to withdraw it when Eddie Erdelatz, the Navy coach, showed up on campus as a guest of the board of regents. Erdelatz backed out, and the Aggie student body sent a petition to Myers, who accepted the second time around.

Bryant left behind the core of a winning team, with Charley Milstead a rising star at quarterback, skilled players in fullback Gordon LeBoeuf, tackle Ken Beck and receiver John Tracey, and the scrappy little guards, Buddy Payne, Gale Oliver and Joe Munson.

Myers, a Tennessee lineman under General Bob Neyland, installed the single-wing, and Milstead ranked among the national leaders in total offense and punting the next two years.

But the Aggies were missing something intangible, and their defense no longer gang-tackled. After four losing seasons, Myers was out, replaced by Hank Foldberg, one of the young Aggies pirated away in the 1940's by West Point, where he became an All-America end.

Sadly, Foldberg's stay was not much longer than his first one. His teams went backward, winning three games, two and one before he was fired after the 1964 season.

All of which led to another bold, dramatic, emotional decision. The Aggies reached out for one of their own, Gene Stallings, known as Bebes, a Junction boy, then on the Alabama staff of his former coach, Bear Bryant.

At 29, Stallings would be the youngest coach of a major college team in America. Bryant was in his room at the Waldorf Astoria, preparing to attend the Heisman Trophy dinner in New York, when a phone call came from Houston.

It was vintage stuff he gave me. "I can't stop bawling," he claimed, "I'm so proud that A&M has hired Bebes, but I'm also sad because he's a helluva coach and now I'll have to go back to work."

I milked the quotes for all the familiar Bryant flavor, and thought nothing more of it, until months later when I bumped into a Boston writer named Bob Curran.

He had an interesting story to share. He had gone to visit Bryant before the Heisman dinner, and when he walked in his hotel room he saw that he was on the phone and—here was the kicker—"big ole tears were running down his cheek. I turned to one of his coaches, Dude Hennessey, and he put a finger to his mouth so I'd keep my voice down.

"I said, 'What's wrong with Paul?' And Dude said, 'He just lost one of his assistants.'

"I whispered, 'How old was he?' And Dude said, 'Twenty-nine.' I said, 'Oh, my God, that's so young, what happened?'

"Dude said, 'Oh, he didn't die. He just went to Texas A&M.'"

Thus did Stallings return to College Station, uncaring that Bryant had called A&M "the toughest recruiting job in America." The Aggies had not yet admitted coeds on more than a token basis, and were still not recruiting black athletes. The Southwest Conference was still an all-white sanctuary, although SMU would soon sign Jerry LeVias and Baylor would be close behind.

The University of Houston, still an independent, would beat them all, recruiting Warren McVea out of San Antonio.

Stallings wore the Bryant label proudly, but hoped to create his own identity. Still, he realized quickly that he would be competing with the 1954 team, not the 1939 Aggies. His seniors had learned little from defeat except how to lose.

They had three wins going into the final game against Texas, and had been shut out four times. Gene had to juggle players to shore up weak spots and few had started at the positions they were now playing. His quarterback, Harry Ledbetter, had been a halfback. He had two prime time players in Dude McLean, an end, and Joe Wellborn, at linebacker.

The week of the Texas game, I drove to Kyle Field to watch the Aggies practice and pick up an interview or two. I was standing there, chatting with Billy Pickard, the trainer, when Stallings walked over—in the middle of practice—and said, "Come take a ride with me."

We piled into his school car and I waited in a puzzled silence while Bebes pulled into the baseball stadium and parked under the stands.

Then he folded his arms across the wheel and dropped his head against them.

It looked like a case for Crisis Hotline. All sorts of wild thoughts rushed through my mind, none so shocking as the words Stallings spoke when he raised his head: "I've got a play that is guaranteed to score a touchdown against Texas—if I have the guts to call it."

I did the quick math. Before edging Rice, 14-13, they had been shut out in three straight games, out of four, and scored once in two others. They had nearly wrecked one of the school's most cherished traditions, in which the Cadets kiss their dates after each Aggie touchdown. Every mother in the state felt safe, knowing her daughter was attending an Aggie game.

Logic tells you that if a team can score, it has a chance to win. But the way Stallings described the play, it sounded like something out of burlesque:

"The quarterback bounces the ball to a flanker. Everybody acts like it was just a bad pass. They turn around as if to go to the huddle. Then the flanker straightens up and throws the ball as far as he can. Our wide receiver runs under it. Touchdown."

The trick was this: the play had to look like a forward pass, when in fact it was a lateral with the ball still alive. If you threw it a certain way, Gene insisted, it would hop right into the receiver's hands.

Of course, they had not worked out all the wrinkles. Eleven backs tried out and only one could throw the ball far enough, Jim Kaufman, a defensive back, left-handed, a junior who had played no offense in college. They had practiced the play all week. They had not yet completed it.

So Saturday rolled around and early in the second period Jim Kaufman trotted onto the field. *The ball was at their nine-yard line.* Stallings had wanted to make the call at midfield, so if it misfired they might contain the damage. But the Aggies never got to midfield. They spent the entire first quarter turning back Texas near their own goal line.

Now, in the shadow of his goal-line, Harry Ledbetter, the quarterback, took the snap and threw a long lateral that reached Kaufman on one hop. Even the Aggie linemen kicked the dirt in disgust and turned their backs to the field.

Downfield, Dude McLean stopped his pass pattern, but only for an instant. Suddenly, he took off, past relaxed Texas defenders, gathered in Kaufman's pass near the fifty and sped ninety-one yards for a touchdown.

They called the play The Texas Special. There was absolute silence in the stands until the referee raised his arms and signaled a touchdown. The fake bounce pass so unsettled the Longhorns that the Aggies scored again on a 71-yard drive and added a long field goal by Randy Sims just before the half to lead, 17-0. After the game, Darrell Royal was asked what he thought when he saw the ball in the air.

"I knew we'd been had," he said. "McLean was so wide open he looked like he had come out early for practice."

At the half, Royal gave one of the best pep talks in memory. He said nothing. He went to the blackboard and wrote in chalk, 21-17. A trick play and adrenaline could carry the Aggies only so far. Texas' power and depth wore them down and UT won by the very score Royal predicted.

There were several odd footnotes to the game. Kaufman did not return for his senior year, and the only pass he ever threw was for many years the record for a touchdown pass in the Southwest Conference.

Exactly what the moral of the story is, each reader will have to decide. There is no point in getting sentimental about the merits of losing creatively. As Stallings said later that Thanksgiving night, "I'd rather have had a sorry old play and won the game."

A Texas ex said, "I'd rather get beat by the Aggies than tricked by them."

The Aggies who played as sophomores that day went to the Cotton Bowl in 1967 and beat Alabama, coached by the man who had coached their coach. Three years later, Stallings was fired.

The play was considered by many to be a sort of tribute to Homer Norton, who had died in May of 1965. He loved the unexpected, and had jump-started the win over Texas in 1939 with a hideout play. You wouldn't expect such a gimmick to catch a well-coached team asleep, but Norton had used it effectively in other victories.

Stallings' job did not look very secure when the Aggies started the 1967 season with four straight losses, and trailed Texas Tech, 24-21, with time running out and the Aggies facing fourth-and-15 from the Tech 45.

Ed Hargett found Bob Long in a crowd of Red Raiders at the fifteen, with 11 seconds on the clock. Hargett rolled to his left to pass, but all his receivers were covered. He then tucked the ball away and darted for the red flag at the right hand corner of the end zone, and scored, to give A&M its first victory of the season, 28-24.

The Aggies wouldn't lose again. The night before the game, they had gone to a movie starring Lee Marvin, called *Water Hole Number 4*. For the rest of the year, no matter what movie they saw, the team's itinerary listed it as Water Hole Number 5, and 6, and so on.

Water Hole Number 11 matched A&M and Alabama in the Cotton Bowl. Stallings had rebuilt his offense around Hargett, Long and running back Larry Stegent. The defense featured Billy Hobbs, Tommy Maxwell, Grady Allen and Rolf Krueger, Charley's kid brother.

His old teammates were on Gene's side of the field as the Aggies upset Alabama, 16-7, with Curly Hallman's interception of a Ken Stabler pass sealing the win. One of the lasting images in Cotton Bowl history came when Bryant hoisted a startled Stallings on one shoulder. An unsteady equestrian, the Bear carried him a few feet before letting him down.

No one could have guessed that the ride would virtually end there. Four losing seasons followed, each ending with losses by big scores to Texas. He was one of theirs, but the Aggies loved Stallings much more when he won.

You had a clue to their problems when their punter, Steve O'Neal, made the All-America team in 1968 (and later set an NFL record with a 98-yard punt against Denver.) Every week was a struggle. In 1970, they played three straight games on the road, all losses, against LSU, Ohio State and Michigan. Dave Elmendorf's performance at safety and returning kickoffs landed him on the All-America team that year. The Aggies returned lots of kickoffs.

Gene went to work for Tom Landry and the Dallas Cowboys for fourteen seasons, then returned as a head coach in a dead end job with the Cardinals in St. Louis and Arizona. At last, in a second closing of the circle, he went back to Alabama, where the Crimson Tide won the national championship in 1992, stuffing favored Miami in the Sugar Bowl.

Stallings got his. The post-war Aggies were still searching for theirs.

In a throwback to the Roaring Twenties, the men in maroon decided to join an old but proven twist, Trading With the Enemy. Dana X. Bible had enjoyed eleven prosperous years at A&M, fielding three teams that were unbeaten and two unscored upon. (Granted, these records came in 1917, with an eight-game schedule that included Austin College, Dallas U. and the LSU "B" team; and in 1919, against the likes of Sam Houston, San Marcos, Howard Payne and Trinity.)

After the 1928 season, Bible bolted from Aggieland and moved to Nebraska, which hired him on a recommendation from Knute Rockne of Notre Dame. After six seasons with the Cornhuskers, D. X. heeded a call to return to Texas, to the Longhorns, where he added 62 wins and added the final flourishes to his long career as a coach and athletic director.

The Aggies signed handsome, pipe-smoking Emory Bellard, the top assistant to Darrell Royal and the architect of the Wishbone-T offense.

Bellard brought the bone with him and, after a 5-and-6 debut in 1973, his teams won eight games the next year and then kicked it into another gear. They did what no other Aggie squad had ever accomplished, with back to back 10-victory seasons and a share of the conference title in 1975.

They would beat Texas for the first time since '67, and run their record to 10-and-0, climbing to Number 2 in one poll and sending Aggie spirits into orbit. But a season-ending loss to Arkansas at Little Rock, 31-6, and a 20-0 shutout by Southern Cal in the Liberty Bowl brought them back to earth with a thud.

Bellard felt his first true exposure to Aggie mood swings with the displays of grief over that season-ending disappointment.

But A&M had rejoined the community of elite teams, and they enjoyed a true restoration on defense, with Pat Thomas, Garth Ten Naple, Ed Simonini, Lester Hayes, Robert Jackson and Jacob Green coming through the pipeline.

One of Bellard's shrewdest moves was to hire as an assistant coach a former McNeese State tight end named R. C. Slocum. After a year with the offense, Slocum switched to the other side and preached pressure defense. Although no one had yet given it a name, the "Wrecking Crew" tradition had been launched.

They led the nation in total defense in 1975, and Simonini, a prototype Aggie linebacker, was voted the Southwest Conference defensive player of the year.

They were 10-and-2 again in '76, and dumped Texas in Austin, 27-3. "That was a very emotional night," said Bellard. "Darrell was gracious as ever, and Mike Campbell came by. They were special in the coaching field, special people.

"Those were very similar teams, the same offense, fine defense, both with great fullbacks." The Tyler Rose, Earl Campbell, would win the Heisman a year later. The Aggies had the massive George Woodard, who made the field tremble when he carried the ball.

Nearly all the A&M defensive stars went to the pros. Lester Hayes intercepted eight passes his senior year, and would win stardom with the Oakland Raiders. By the end of his playing days, his most cherished pieces of jewelry were a gold crucifix he wore around his neck, and his two Super Bowl rings. The one from Super Bowl XV, a win over the Eagles, was locked in a safe. The other, earned three years later, had been auctioned off on the Internet for $18,200. It had languished in a Reno pawnshop for nearly a year.

Please do not jump to the nearest conclusion. This is not a tale of hearts and flowers, with gypsy violins in the background. This is not about a busted ex-jock who was down and out in Modesto, where Lester had made his home since he retired after 10 years with the Raiders.

This is the condensed version of what happened:

Hayes was in Reno for a sports memorabilia show. Had an abscess in his mouth "the size of a walnut." Found a dental clinic. When asked how he would pay, he reached for his billfold and found an empty back pocket. His wallet was in another pair of slacks back in Modesto.

When you are hurting with an abscessed tooth that feels as if it had invaded your right eye, you do not think with absolute clarity. He needed eight hundred dollars and he found it in a pawn shop. He removed the ring and kept the cross because "I couldn't take out a loan on Jesus."

He had four months, plenty of time to reclaim it, but a prostate problem clobbered him. He spent most of 1999 in bed and in pain. The pawnbroker gave him a final notice and when he didn't pick up the ring, it went to the high bidder on eBay. He wasn't dumb, just afflicted, as many in the perspiring arts are, with a sweet irresponsibility. He talks about Julius Caesar. He knows the story of Jim Thorpe. A lot of football players do not.

The last anyone heard, he was still trying to trace the anonymous purchaser and buy back a ring he could have recovered for the price of the loan, plus $320 in interest.

But the point is, Hayes could have covered his dental bill by hocking the gold cross, but he did not. Which reminds us that football, at any level, has a spiritual and mental and emotional side.

You can walk into any locker room before a game and feel the intensity, the edginess, the tension. Some players can't tell you the name of the guy who lines up next to them. But whatever trance they are in, to whatever lengths they are prepared to go, all of it is in pursuit of that elusive piece of jewelry, a ring for winning the conference, or a national title, or a Super Bowl. Which is what makes Lester's story funny and poignant and painful at the same time.

He was a terrific and colorful player for the Raiders, one who had at least a minor role in a decision by the NFL to outlaw a substance called "stickum," a caramel-colored adhesive widely used for a time by both receivers and defensive backs. They practically dipped their arms in the stuff.

When the league banned it, Hayes was asked what effect he thought the new legislation would have. "You won't see guys catching passes with their elbows anymore," he replied.

But we digress.

Emory Bellard enjoyed the characters on his teams, the camaraderie and the good times that were meant to be enjoyed. He had seen Royal criticized at Texas for not winning by bigger margins, or with more variety. Emory did not have the hide of a rhinoceros and he resented the second guessing that came even in successful, but not perfect, seasons.

When his '78 Aggies opened with four straight wins, then lost two in a row to Houston and Baylor, he gave the job back to them. He never appeared openly bitter, just weary, and in time he became that rare figure who could look at life from both sides now.

He never did decide which school worked up the greater passion, which crowd raised the more hellish noise, which team found the winning sweeter. "I have never found much difference," he said, "in the attitude of the two squads. They are both pretty sincere about winning. That winning, it feels pretty good whenever you get it."

Of course, no one can be neutral when the Aggies and the Longhorns collide. It is the maroon and the orange, Reveille versus Bevo, the Texas drum and the Aggie bugle, the tower and the bonfire, boots and saddles.

Somewhere amid all that symbolism is a football game with roots in the 19th Century, a rivalry so intense that loss can hurt for a lifetime, if not longer.

Bellard had a perspective on the series shared by few: he was a player and assistant coach at the University of Texas, in a different era, and then the head coach of the Aggies. His teams won big in both places. He restored the Aggies as a national power and spoiled their fans so quickly that they grumbled when he didn't deliver an unbeaten season. A proud man, who measured his words, Bellard did a remarkable thing long after he thought he had retired from coaching.

He went back to the basics, accepting the job at Westbury High, in Houston, burying like an old bone the ego that would have prevented most coaches from considering such a move. Of course, the bone he buried was not the Wishbone. He won with it wherever he went.

The move was much the same as the one Homer Norton had made, when he decided to coach Ball High in Galveston, a world away from his national championship heyday.

Tom Wilson, a onetime Texas Tech quarterback, moved up from Bellard's staff to the top job and the Aggies finished the 1978 season with eight wins, beating Iowa State in the Hall of Fame Bowl.

They struggled to stay around .500 the next three years, and by the end of the '81 campaign the Aggies were once again in the market for a head coach. Like getting out of bed in the morning, hiring coaches doesn't get easier with practice.

One more time, the Aggies sent shock waves through the college ranks, reeling in Jackie Sherrill from Pittsburgh, where he had won a national title and developed a running back named Tony Dorsett. And there was another Bear Bryant connection. Sherrill had played multiple positions on Bryant's first teams at Alabama.

They gave him the richest financial package ever offered a coach in the Southwest Conference, and maybe the nation, valued at $250,000 a year. The media had a field day over what was viewed as a display of Aggie excess, and tensions began to build even before Jackie settled into his office.

There was a good deal of gloating when Sherrill failed to create any instant miracles. His first three teams were mediocre, despite the presence of the great Ray Childress, who had fifteen sacks as a junior, a school record for a defensive tackle.

But in the last game of that third season, 1984, the Aggies turned a corner. No, they not only turned it, they did a wheelie. A 5-and-5 team and a heavy underdog, the Cadets drubbed Texas at Memorial Stadium and knocked the Horns out of the Cotton Bowl. They did it behind a scrub quarterback, Craig Stump.

In '85, the Aggies would unleash Kevin Murray at quarterback, and a pair of explosive runners, Keith Woodside and Rod Bernstine, not to be confused with the two reporters who broke the Watergate story for the *Washington Post*.

With Johnny Holland and John Roper raising havoc at linebacker, A&M would win the next three Southwest Conference titles and compile a 29-and-7 record.

In their three consecutive Cotton Bowl appearances, they encountered two Heisman Trophy winners. Twice they stopped Bo Jackson on fourth and goal at the one and spanked Auburn, 36-16, and bottled up Timmy Brown in a 35-10 rout of Notre Dame. Brown had a tantrum when an Aggie flicked the little towel from his waistband and carried it to the bench, and never quite regained his groove. In between those wins, they lost to Ohio State.

Through it all, Sherrill remained a lightning rod. Although his critics loved to picture him as self-centered and vain, the truth is he fit into no particular box. He was quite capable of being gentle and even generous. In 1988, what turned out to be his last season in College

Station, he made one of the rarest gestures the conference had ever seen and it went virtually unremarked.

When one of the state's top recruiting prospects, Conroe's 6-6 Paul Montgomery, narrowed his choices to UCLA and Texas, Sherrill urged him to sign with the Longhorns, saying, in effect, "Stay home. It will be in your long term interest after football."

No major college coach in America had shown the guts or imagination of Jackie Sherrill, in finding a way to play students on a regular basis: his Twelfth Man kickoff unit. Few coaches put more emphasis on their players getting a degree. In most of his actions, Sherrill stood with amateur football's idealists in promoting what nearly everyone claims they want: a game played by student-athletes. Yet he seldom received any benefit of the doubt, much less credit, from the big city press in the state.

Yeah, that's right, Liquid Paper breath, the media didn't give him an inch.

When Sherrill flew to Atlanta, hoping to free one of his players from the claws of a sports agent, newspapers in Dallas and Houston reacted with puzzlement. It was pointed out that the player in question might not even be a starter his senior year.

Yet the obvious answer required too large a leap of faith: that Jackie really cared about saving the young man's scholarship, his education and possibly his chance to play in the NFL.

The news reports were almost gleeful in describing Sherrill's surprise, and his rudeness, when the agent, this slimeball, showed up with writers and a TV crew.

There are figures in sports who provide writers with an endless source of copy, and we repay them by magnifying their faults. Sherrill was one of them. In time, Jackie won over the A&M faculty, but the media doesn't retreat so easily. He was resented for limiting his players in their contacts with the press. And when a newspaper and TV station in Dallas accused the Aggies of multiple infractions of the rules, Sherrill was labeled as arrogant for denying the charges.

A few months before he resigned, sparing the school an exhaustive investigation by the NCAA, the University had made him a full professor and given him tenure. It is naïve to think A&M would have reacted in the same way if his teams had not won so handsomely. But he had been sensitive to the school's traditions and to the unique character of its former students.

It wasn't enough to simply attract prime specimens. He had shown that he knew how to mold and teach and motivate them. During the week of the Cotton Bowl, a Dallas newspaper ran a psycho-profile of Sherrill, in itself a kind of bizarre compliment. An incident was related in which Jackie, coming into his own as an Alabama football star, paid back an ex-sweetheart who had dumped him in high school. He stood up the young lady and two of her friends after inviting them to the campus for dates.

Of course, this was in a more innocent time, before the movie, *Fatal Attraction*. But you suspect that the story revealed more about the immaturity of the press, than it did about Jackie Sherrill at nineteen.

For once, continuity was on A&M's side and the program would not skip a beat. The one good consequence of this turmoil was the elevation of R. C. Slocum to the heading coaching position.

He had been on the scene since 1973, less one season spent on the West Coast before Sherrill brought him back. He was a quiet contrast to his flashier boss, but that was not thought to be a disadvantage.

Tall, angular, white-haired and folksy, Slocum would hold the job for fourteen seasons. He was fourth on the list of coaches who reached one hundred wins the fastest, doing so in the eighth game of his 11th season, one game earlier than Joe Paterno and Steve Spurrier. He would leave as A&M's winningest coach, having turned out fourteen All-Americans and sending a few dozen players to the pros.

A broken ankle had ended Kevin Murray's career a season too soon, but there was no dropoff at quarterback. Slocum inherited Bucky Richardson, whose running exploits almost changed the job description for the position. Around him, the Aggies were loaded, with Darren Lewis at running back, Richmond Webb a force at offensive tackle, William Thomas and Aaron Wallace backing up the line and Kevin Smith roaming the secondary.

The Aggies repeated Sherrill's triple, winning the conference in 1991, 1992 and 1993. They won ten games or more in four straight years, going 12-and-1 in '92, their only loss to Notre Dame in the Cotton Bowl.

Slocum's 1994 team went unbeaten, with ten wins and a tie against SMU. His seniors did not drop a Southwest Conference game in four years, meaning that they never lost to Texas.

They tore down the SWC a year later, and the Aggies joined Texas, Texas Tech and Baylor in the expanded Big Twelve. With the stroke of a pen, a hundred years of college football history faded into the sand and fog, replaced by a better marketing idea.

In their second season in the new league, the Aggies won the Big 12 South, only to get crushed by Nebraska in the championship game, 54-15.

In 1998, they atoned for that misstep by staggering Number 1 ranked Kansas State, in double overtime, 36-33, with Sirr Parker scoring on a 32-yard pass play from Brandon Stewart.

They fell to Ohio State in the Sugar Bowl and finished at 11-and-3, their last season with double digit wins, through 2005.

There would be no more title runs, but easily the most heart-wrenching victory of Slocum's career came in '99, in the 20-16 upset of Texas in what is remembered as the Bonfire Game. A week earlier, twelve A&M students had died in the collapse of the wooden tower erected for the annual ritual.

The Aggies loaded their luggage on the back of Ja'Mar Toombs, who was built like a barge, and let the fullback ram the Texas middle 37 times for 126 yards and two touchdowns. But the winning points scored on a 14-yard lob pass from Randy McCown to Matt Bumgardner with five minutes left. The Aggies had trailed seventh-ranked Texas at the half, 16-6.

They listed Toombs at 275 pounds on the depth chart, but his weight was not an exact science. It fluctuated from week to week, putting him in a category with the world price of crude oil. He had a value to his team not reflected in the yards per carry. He had his biggest games against the most daunting teams.

With 23 seconds to play, linebacker Brian Gamble pounced on Major Applewhite's fumble, caused by a blitzing Jay Brooks, and the victory was assured. Emotions held in check for a week and sixty minutes burst their moorings in the stands and on the field. Gamble fell to his knees, his arms upraised, his index fingers pointing to the heavens.

If you remembered nothing else about the game, you would remember this: the twelve white doves that circled the stadium and then flew away, one for each Aggie killed in the bonfire catastrophe. And the four Air Force F-16 jets, piloted by A&M grads, doing a fly-over in the missing man formation, and the Longhorn band playing Amazing Grace.

The dynamics of the rivalry may have changed forever on a day when the two natural enemies seemed to bond. With their sympathy for the pain that engulfed Aggieland, and their respectful attitude toward the tragedy, Texas made it difficult, if not impossible, for the teams to summon again the level of loathing and anger that had always marked this series.

But you can be sure future teams will try.

Life goes on. So does football and the scoreboard always tells another story.

When the Aggies slid to 6-and-6 in 2002, only their second non-winning season in twenty years, it turned out that R. C. Slocum did not have a lifetime contract, after all. He had been an innovator, who designed the Lion Backfield to get Greg Hill and Rodney Thomas in the game at the same time. He recruited an undersized linebacker from the fishing town of Rockport, a son of Vietnamese immigrants, and saw Dat Nguyen sweep the Lombardi and Maxwell Trophies as the best defensive player in the country.

R.C. recruited so well, for so many years, that his players started turning pro before their senior seasons. It was a mistake for Toombs and Leeland McElroy, but not for wide receiver Robert Ferguson, who made it with the Green Bay Packers. Patrick Bates went in 1992, Aaron Glenn and Sam Adams in '93; they were first round draft picks by the NFL.

In a blinding snowstorm on New Year's Eve of 2000, Toombs played his last game at the Liberty Bowl in Shreveport. He plowed through the snow for 193 yards and three touchdowns. The Aggies lost, in overtime, 43-41. To Mississippi State. Coached by Jackie Sherrill. This excruciating loss dropped their record to 7-and-5. The season left their fans feeling as if the team had been put on earth to torture them.

No one can be certain what caused the Aggie skid, but they started to hit the wall just as the vigorous Mack Brown was rejuvenating Texas. The defense misplaced the fearless abandon that earned the Wrecking Crew its reputation. The true freshman, Reggie McNeal, electrified A&M fans by coming off the bench to lead an upset of Oklahoma in 2002. But too often, insulting losses followed big wins or near misses.

Slocum had been a splendid representative of the Aggie culture for thirty years, as an assistant and a head coach. In 1992, after his team went 12-and-0 and never rose higher than third or fourth in the polls, R. C. was invited to speak at the Heisman Trophy dinner in New York.

He walked around like a little kid in a museum, craning his neck to view the paintings and statues. "I've been to a few banquets," said Slocum, "and had chances to speak, but to be at the Downtown Athletic Club, with two thousand people in the audience, and seeing these guys walking around...well, I was awestruck.

"That was kind of the theme of my talk. Most of us who have played the game were average, but we always had these great players to look up to and inspire us. I can remember playing in the back yard, wanting to be Doak Walker. You wanted to wear their jersey numbers. You think about what those people have done for the game: Roger Staubach, John David Crow, Billy Vessels, Bo Jackson, Herschel Walker, on and on.

"They set a standard of excellence, something you could look up to and say, as a coach, 'That's what you shoot for, that's how you do it.' So it was a special treat for me. I kept bumping into Jay Berwanger, of the University of Chicago, the first Heisman Trophy winner (in 1935). I was thrilled. Of course, John David has been up there a bunch of times. There were twenty to twenty-five past winners on hand, and that's a pretty amazing fraternity they have."

His love of the game, and A&M, were greater than the hurt of being fired. "I do want to emphasize how remarkably positive he was," said Earl Nye, the chairman of the board. "He is naturally disappointed, but he doesn't seem to be angry. He doesn't seem to hold a grudge. He wants what is best for the university."

At most places, a coach gets fired and he wants to blow up the science building. At Texas A&M, some of them try to comfort the guy who broke the bad news to him.

So the newest knight to try to remove the sword from the rock was Dennis Franchione, a salvage specialist who turned around programs at New Mexico, TCU and Alabama in their second seasons.

It should be noted that this was not part of A&M's original plan, mainly because no one expected his first season to be such a disaster, four wins and eight losses, and a defense that allowed an average of 46.5 points a game.

But the even-tempered Coach Fran isn't the type to throw chairs or kick Reveille or file a lawsuit after a few defeats. He and his staff had misjudged how thin and young the Aggies were, he said. They went back to work, recruited a strong freshman class and hauled in some junior college prospects, and put on the field the least experienced team in the Big 12.

After opening the 2004 season with a tough loss to an ambitious Utah team, at Salt Lake City, the Aggies turned the ball over once in seven games, including six wins in a row. The season would have gone from splendid to spectacular if they had not dropped a crazy one to Baylor, blown a 14-point lead three times against Oklahoma, and closed with losses to Texas and Tennessee, in the Cotton Bowl.

They should have beaten Oklahoma, then ranked Number 2 in the land, because twice they tricked the mighty Sooners for touchdowns, on a fake punt and a fake field goal. (Shades of Homer Norton.) Punter Jacob Young was nearly an Aggie hero forever, after the senior passed to Earvin Taylor for 71 yards and a 28-14 lead in the middle of the second quarter.

With two minutes gone in the final period, with A&M facing fourth and goal at the four, holder Chad Shroeder straightened up and fired to Joey Thomas in the end zone, tying the score, 35-35.

OU won it on Jason White's fifth touchdown pass with just under seven minutes to go, but the Aggies still brought the game down to a failed Hail Mary pass on the last play.

So you do the math, and find that Coach Fran's kids improved by three games over the previous season. In 2005, they had another year in his system, and a wiser team still led by McLean, with Courtney

Lewis, Jaxson Appel, Jason Carter, and Red Bryant in leadership roles.

But the year would end in disappointment and disbelief, with four straight losses, their misery compounded because they had Oklahoma on the ropes and played Texas tough. The Longhorns would go on to win the national title, while A&M saw its defense vanish, finished 5-and-6 and again missed going to a bowl. Sadly, the career of Reggie McNeal, the most gifted quarterback they had ever recruited, had been wasted.

Meanwhile, the Aggies are still paying tribute to the idea of winning everything. No matter how much we try, you can't live in the past, although it would be a great way to reduce the national debt. The clock is ticking in Aggieland.

Coach Homer Norton

John Kimbrough (39) and Bill Jeffrey (28)

Chapter 1

YES, WE HAVE NO COLLATERAL

೮ﾐﾐﾍ౦

THIS IS HOW THE BUILDING OF A NATIONAL CHAMPIONSHIP TEAM BEGINS: The football stadium is heavily in debt—by nearly a quarter of a million dollars—an amount of money so humungous in the 1930's that the players feared the bank would repossess it.

The coach has known since his first day on the campus that a hard core of influential alums did not want him; yet he would dodge the executioner's blade for fourteen years.

Most of the team's hopes rest on a player who, at midseason the year before, was their fourth-string fullback.

These were the Texas Aggies, who could not afford to pave the dirt under the stands in the north end zone. The coach, Homer Hill Norton, the son of a Methodist minister, did not tolerate profanity by either his assistants or his players, a distinct disadvantage in hard times. Still, the Aggies were heavy on potential, as typified by John Kimbrough, who had raw power and speed, so evident that as a freshman they worked him out at guard.

These were the 1930's, and the Great Depression still choked the land with its bread lines and boxcar hoboes and 'brother, can you spare a dime' desperation. "For most of us," said Jim Thomason, the rarest of athletes, a blocking back who became a star, "football was the best way out. It gave us a chance to get an education."

They had no way of knowing, not Norton nor Kimbrough nor Thomason, that so many factors would come together in the year 1939 for the everlasting glory of Aggieland. Nor did Edwin Jackson Kyle, the Dean of Agriculture for 34 years, and head of the athletic council, whose primary task was to worry about the stadium debt.

One day Dean Kyle came upon Howard Shelton, a backup center, tutoring Marshall Robnett, soon to be an All-American guard, on the front row of the north end zone, scuffing their shoes in the dirt.

"You boys could go a long way toward reducing our mortgage," implored the dean, "by having a good season."

After he walked away, Shelton and Robnett just looked at each other. "We were kids," said Howard. "We didn't know what a mortgage was."

This was the year Homer had projected that the goal of the Aggies would be to win the Southwest Conference title, which seemed a bit of a stretch right there. They were coming off a .500 season, four wins, four losses and a tie, and in the preseason polls for 1939 had been picked to finish fifth—in the conference.

It did not occur to the players to aim any higher. Most of them were country boys, just out of their teens and only two or three years away from fighting a war. They were glad to be in the Cadet Corps, which was then mandatory for every Aggie the first two years. They had two uniforms, assuring them of at least one change of clothes, not counting their football togs.

The bonding of the Aggies has taken on a special aura in academic and football lore. The military tradition dominated the campus, and for six or seven decades the student body was for men only. The train stopped in College Station, but their world was an insulated, colorless, womanless world. Their pride, spirit, loyalty, tradition and legendary stubbornness have been maddening to rival schools, if not a source of envy.

This era and this mystique were immortalized in 1942 by a motion picture produced on campus by Universal Studios and directed by Walter Wanger, called *We've Never Been Licked*. Yes, it may be true, in everyone's life there is a summer of '42.

To the hip and self-indulgent viewers of recent vintage, the title may sound slightly pornographic. But the basic plot of the movie is how the Aggies used their training as farm agents and engineers to infiltrate the Japanese Air Force and win the war. The script was enriched by footage of the football team, with Bill Stern providing the play-by-play.

The film marked the screen debut of actor Robert Mitchum, who boasted years later that he had never seen it. Too bad about him. He missed his own contribution to humanity, a movie so bad it became a cult classic.

A poster shows two Aggies, played by Noah Beery, Jr. and Richard Quine, in their brown, belted coats and olive drab trousers, with the senior boots reaching just below the knee, marching proudly toward the camera, with a blonde beauty on each arm.

The Aggies had the last laugh and then some. The Class of '60, at the urging of one of their own, Tom Wisdom—an apt name if we ever heard one—acquired the rights to *We've Never Been Licked*, and raised a quick $100,000 by selling and renting videocassettes to Aggies around the globe. The money has gone to scholarships and causes dear to A&M.

But it was the 1939 team, not a movie, that gave the Aggies their first sweeping national exposure. One could argue, and we do, that the Southwest Conference offered the strongest brand of ball in the nation—three national championships in the same decade. SMU broke through in 1935, behind The Little Red Arrow, Gerald Mann, and TCU finished first in the 1938 polls behind another vest pocket quarterback, Davey O'Brien.

Of the three champions, A&M was the most dominating, led by Kimbrough, a Herculean running back who never wanted or accepted the credit.

The Aggies prevailed at the end of a history-book year. In September, of 1939, the start of football season, damned inconsiderate of them, Germany plunged Europe into a war that would last six years, embroil most of the world and cost the lives of more than sixty million people.

The civil war in Spain had ended. Russia invaded Finland. Italy occupied Albania. War overshadowed most events, but in the United States life went on, as life so often does. There were World Fairs in New York and San Francisco. Joe Louis retained his heavyweight boxing title by knocking out 'Two-Ton' Tony Galento, and others. When President Roosevelt moved to strengthen U.S. defenses, the Republicans denounced him and argued for neutrality. Times change.

In Rome, His Holiness, Pope Pius XI, born a peasant and once an ardent mountain climber, died in his bed at eighty-one.

The literary world celebrated the publication of two powerful novels, James Joyce's *Finnegan's Wake* and John Steinbeck's *The Grapes of*

Wrath. Movie lovers swarmed to see Judy Garland in *The Wizard of Oz*, and Clark Gable and British import Vivien Leigh in *Gone With the Wind*. The wild new campus fad was goldfish swallowing, but not the kind that would catch on at Aggieland, where a Fish was a freshman.

In May, Lou Gehrig, the indestructible first baseman for the New York Yankees, took himself out of the starting lineup for the first time in 2,130 games—covering fourteen years. In July, he was diagnosed with the disease that would kill him, and in time would carry his name.

Against this backdrop, the '39 Aggies may have been the least publicized national champion of all time. "Really, it was just a bunch of country boys from little West Texas towns that you couldn't even spell," said Tommie Vaughn, the starting center. His teammates might jokingly claim that there were a lot of words Vaughn couldn't spell, but he was a terrific center, and went on to become a successful car dealer in Houston.

"We really didn't care that much about the national championship," Vaughn added. "A lot of us didn't know there was such a thing. But we were undefeated, we won the conference and we won the Sugar Bowl. We knew we had a team."

The defense gave up only 18 points in the regular season and 763 total yards. The offense was built around Kimbrough, who had shoulders as wide as New Hampshire, and measured—for those times—an unheard of 6-foot-3 and 220 pounds. In every recollection of the '39 team, Kimbrough is the focal point.

After the Aggies stormed their way to their eleventh win and the title, before a then record, standing room crowd of 73,000 in the Sugar Bowl, a *New York Times* reporter wrote: "Every word of A&M prowess was true. This is the best all-around football team in years, and Mr. Kimbrough is the best football player since Jim Thorpe."

The Aggies entered the game ranked Number 1 after recording six shutouts and whipping national powers Santa Clara, Villanova and the defending champs, TCU, 20-6, in consecutive weeks. The Aggies allowed only two first downs in defeating Texas, 20-0, to wrap up the regular season—having yielded two touchdowns in ten games.

Tulane, ranked fifth and playing before a highly partisan crowd, equaled that total on New Year's Day in losing, 14-13. The Green Wave managed a total of 101 yards. The *Chicago Tribune's* renowned

Arch Ward later would write that he regretted giving his 1940 Heisman vote to Tom Harmon instead of Kimbrough. "Only a truly great team could have beaten Tulane on that day," Ward reported. "You couldn't escape the impression that you were watching one of the greatest groups of athletes the game has seen…and the greatest piece of football flesh this writer ever saw. He (Kimbrough) is too much football player for one team to stop."

Kimbrough, Joe Boyd, and Robnett became All-Americans. Six others, including Vaughn and Thomason, earned all-conference honors. Eventually, the entire starting lineup of the 1939 team—and four back-ups—were voted into the A&M Hall of Fame.

"We had our heroes and All-Americans," said Vaughn, "but everybody on that squad made a difference."

The roster was put together under the strangest of circumstances.

As unlikely as it may sound today, many former students, on the heels of the Depression, were calling for the college to drop football in 1934. The Aggies had not won a conference title since 1927 and, worse, they owed $210,000 to banks and borrowed $30,000 more from the college's general fund.

The regents hired Homer Norton and gave him five years to shape up the program or possibly be remembered as the man who buried Aggie football. They did so without consulting some of their more prominent former students and contributors, and Homer arrived in College Station to a mixed reception.

His record at Centenary, in Shreveport, resisted criticism. In eight seasons, his teams went undefeated three times, at one point winning 20 games in a row, and fourteen shutouts.

But Norton was not a marquee name, nor a showman. And at A&M he was following three coaches who would become legends: Uncle Charley Moran, Dana X. Bible and Matty Bell.

Moran put the Aggies on the football map in the halcyon years leading up to World War I. He was a handsome, ambitious rogue who may have been a pioneer in the art of hard-nosed football. His critics accused him of bending the rules and of pushing his players with a harshness and tenacity that quickly weeded out those who were unprepared to give their all. Moran had one losing season out of six at

Aggieland, but left under pressure (Texas refused to play A&M from 1912-1914 while Moran was coach).

In accounts of his success, he comes across as an early day Bear Bryant. Decades before Junction, he hauled his players off to training camps away from the campus, at LaPorte and Seabrook.

He also appeared to take advantage of eligibility rules that were less than rigid. Students only had to attend one day of class before they were eligible. When he accepted the Aggie job, he "recruited" Victor (Choc) Kelly, a Choctaw Indian who had played three seasons at A&M in a backfield with the esteemed Joe Utay, before transferring to the Carlisle Indian School, where Jim Thorpe had launched his epic career. Kelly played one or two seasons for Carlisle, and one more for the Aggies.

Moran brought along other players with unusual credentials, who were rejected by the faculty. His teams had won 80 percent of their games when he left, and he stayed close to that percentage for a career that spanned 18 seasons. He was later closely identified with Centre College, whose nickname, "The Praying Colonels," was a gift of the eloquent Grantland Rice.

It became a college football joke that whenever he spotted Rice covering one of the team's games, Moran would announce, "Down on your knees, boys, here comes Grantland Rice."

Two years after Moran moved on, the Aggies hired Bible, who would compile the third longest tenure of any A&M coach, 11 seasons, winning 76 games and fielding two teams that were unbeaten, untied and unscored upon in 1917 and 1919.

In 1922, in the Dixie Classic in Dallas, the predecessor of the Cotton Bowl, the Aggies faced Moran and Centre College in a game that would become historic. With his squad depleted by injuries, Bible summoned E. King Gill from the press box, where he was spotting for Jinx Tucker, the sage of Waco.

Gill had dropped football for basketball, but Bible had him suit up under the stands, putting on a uniform that had been worn by one of the injured Aggies. He remained on the bench for the remainder of the game. Although he wasn't needed, his willingness to come out of the stands gave birth to the tradition of the Twelfth Man.

Bible won the last of his five conference titles at A&M in 1927, with a team that featured the resourceful Joel Hunt, who would be inducted into the College Football Hall of Fame in 1967. Bible resigned a year later, after Knute Rockne recommended him to Nebraska, one more stop on the road that would lead to Austin and greatness at Texas.

Matty Bell was the coach who opened up the passing game and made the state known for its "aerial circuses," but his stay at A&M was notable mainly for losing the close ones. He was fired in 1933, and two years later led SMU to a classic victory over TCU, earning a trip to the Rose Bowl and a claim to the national title.

The Mustangs lost to Stanford on New Year's Day, but at the time bowl games were not considered part of the championship process. In truth, the Associated Press did not start soliciting ballots for the national rankings until 1936, launching the poll that became the most accepted.

In the early 1900's, and through much of the Twenties, the national champs generally were picked by Walter Camp or Grantland Rice, who would check out Yale and Harvard and maybe Princeton and toss them a crown. These selections were greeted mainly with indifference around the rest of the country.

For the most part, people were too concerned about where Khartoum was, and the 80-hour work week, and whether the Wright Brothers were crazy or if there was really a future to planes that could fly 200 yards before they crashed.

In 1934, Homer Norton arrived in College Station, a town even smaller than Shreveport, and it must have occurred to him very quickly that he had not researched his new job with the proper diligence. He surveyed his material and quickly concluded that his talent was short and his budget low. His first two or three seasons were going to test his patience, his humor and his health.

After the Aggies finished spring training, he piled into his car and made a tour of the A&M Clubs around the state. He spoke honestly to his audiences, telling the old Ags that the team would be lucky to win a couple of games in his first season, and 1935 would be no better. He hoped there would be some visible improvement in 1936.

"We need to offer more scholarships and get some of the better high school players," he said. "Then, perhaps, by 1937 we should be able to compete and—"

A voice from the crowd cut him off at that point. "Never mind telling us about 1937, Homer," the man shouted. "If you haven't started winning by then you won't be around to worry about it."

Norton proved to be an unhappy but accurate prophet. The Aggies won two games in '34 and three in '35. But in the latter year there was a major breakthrough that spoke to better times. Norton won the biggest recruiting prize in the nation, signing Dick Todd, who had broken the national high school scoring record at Crowell, in West Texas.

During his first two seasons, Aggie football tickets were marked down to a buck and a half, and the team's revenues were not enough to make the interest payment on the large note at the bank in Dallas. Joe Utay, by then an important figure in state politics, had to get a special bill passed to allow the A&M financial office to lend the athletic department $30,000.

That kept the loan from being called, but the bank now had to approve any expenses. Norton had to explain why the players needed more than one pair of shoes and why, with 6,000 male students to pick from, he needed scholarships?

Homer developed a severe case of ulcers and checked into the Mayo Clinic for surgery. He was worried about winning, about the money problem, and constant harping from some of the old grads about his coaching style.

He was an innovator whose ideas were copied by coaches whose reputations were enhanced by them. But his critics objected to the fact that Norton liked to sit in a scouting booth in the press box, where he could observe the line spacing and how the backs were positioned. He had a telephone hookup to the bench to relay plays and defensive adjustments.

But this struck some of the alums as detached and lacking the kind of involvement that had been part of the game forever—a coach with his hand on a player's shoulder, or slapping him on the rear.

Norton did not enjoy confrontations. He assigned an assistant to the scouting booth and moved back to the field. In the meantime, he had a mobile tower designed so he could observe practices with an overview. He had his groundskeeper strip an old Ford, taking it down to the frame and wheels. Then in the middle of the chassis he had a 12-foot wooden tower with a ladder and a platform constructed.

There was a seat and a small desk and a public address system so his instructions could be heard all over the field. He asked the press to keep any reference to the tower out of the papers, but the practices were open to the public, and the complaints soon came pouring in.

Homer climbed down from his tower, but when he mentioned the idea to Frank Leahy a year or so later, the Notre Dame coach jumped on it. There soon appeared photos of Leahy coaching from high above the field, the master of all he surveyed, and the praise flowed like communion wine for his imaginative approach to coaching.

Although no coach enjoys, and few would accept, having his authority challenged or compromised, Norton had less ego than most. He made these concessions, and waved off the absence of any credit, because they were not life-or-death decisions. He was driven by an urgent need to win. He loved the school, loved the atmosphere, and had to let go of the money and other issues so he could concentrate on the 1936 season.

The varsity debut of Dick Todd and the shift of Joe Routt from fullback to guard had raised expectations for the team. They were stamped as contenders for the first time under Norton.

Todd was a sensation as the Aggies rebounded to an 8-3-1 season. The 12-game schedule was the result of the pressure Norton felt to generate funds to meet the annual interest payment to the bank. Greed, need, and a fluke of timing led the coach to accept an impromptu game on a few days' notice.

The Aggies were en route to the west coast by train to play the University of San Francisco on Saturday. Aboard the train, Norton received a telegram from the University of Utah, begging A&M to help bail them out of a jam. The opponent they expected to play in a special Armistice Day observance in Salt Lake City on Tuesday had suddenly canceled.

Since the Aggies were in the neighborhood, meaning less than a thousand miles away, would they accept the extra date and keep the program from being ruined? After officials with both schools consulted by phone, the game was approved, the Aggies receiving an attractive guarantee without rolling up serious expenses.

They would sleep in their Pullman cars to avoid hotel bills, and the extra cash would be helpful. This reflected the financial shape the Aggies were in; they were a proud school reduced to barnstorming for a payday. They were not quite ready to start fishing for quarters through a manhole cover, but it was a triumph of sorts that their fortunes on the field were turning around.

The Aggies drubbed San Francisco, 38-14, and spent the night sight-seeing. They handled Utah with ease on Tuesday, 20-7, with Norton getting every member of the traveling squad into the game.

They returned to College Station Thursday, in plenty of time to lose to Centenary Saturday, in Beaumont, by 3-0. When he was coaching the Gents, Norton made a habit of beating the Aggies and other Southwest Conference teams. "I may have taken that tradition too far," he lamented, after the game.

A&M had opened the season with four wins, beating TCU for the first time since 1924, by a score of 18-14. The game was memorable for the duel between Dick Todd and Sammy Baugh, the greatest passer of all time.

Todd had a 76-yard run and a 51-yard kickoff return and scored two touchdowns. That was enough to offset Baugh's artistry. Three years later, they would be teammates on the Washington Redskins, and best friends. Sam named his son Dicky after Todd.

A key to the season, and Aggie prowess still to come, had been the willingness of Homer Norton to engage in a stare-down with the pugnacious Joe Routt. For all of his physical gifts, Routt was temperamental, and had offended most of his professors.

Norton had been displeased with his attitude during the Centenary loss and benched him for part of the game. During the team meal at the hotel, Norton ate slowly, and when he looked up he and Joe were the last ones in the dining room. Norton could see in his eyes that Routt, who was on the Aggie boxing team, wanted to fight him.

"Go ahead, Joe," he said, "do whatever you want, but I'm going to run this ball club my way." Routt began to think it over, and Homer kept talking. "I got him around to my point of view, and I talked him out of trying to whip me. After that he was easy to handle."

Routt's attitude on the field improved and so did his performance in the classroom. He graduated with honors.

Suddenly, the future was now. Norton had told the Houston Aggie Club that the team should be in a position to recruit the blue chip high school players by 1937, and he was obsessed with finding a way to fulfill that pledge.

He hit upon a rather strange plan, under the circumstances. The Aggies would compile a list of the forty players in Texas they most wanted to recruit, and—here was the cute part—they would go to the banker in Dallas and borrow another $25,000 to recruit them.

If they landed even twenty-five, the scholarships would cover $250 per player for four years.

He immediately contacted Bert Pfaff, a powerful former student who made his pile in oil and construction. Bert agreed to meet Homer and Lil Dimmitt, his trainer and ace recruiter, at the bank. Lil had the list and he knew the background and credentials of every boy on it.

The banker was flabbergasted when Homer announced that they were not there to make a payment, but to take out another loan, "so we can recruit a team that will win, and in winning attract a gate that will pay off our debt."

Norton had never wavered from his earlier judgment: to succeed, A&M first had to provide full scholarships to convince the state's best players to enroll at the all-male campus on the banks of the Brazos. Now they needed to act.

Norton, Dimmitt and Pfaff targeted the high school senior class of 1937 as the group that could resurrect A&M football. In that class were Kimbrough, Tommie Vaughn, Marshall Robnett, Jim Thomason and virtually the entire team that would win the national championship.

Dimmitt carefully screened players across the state and came up with the state's top forty schoolboys, a group that some called the "Forty Most Wanted." All but a few were poor, many literally came off the farm. None could go to A&M without a full financial aid.

But, considering the debt already in place, the Dallas banker resisted the arguments of his three visitors, up to the moment Bert Pfaff threatened to close his account—estimated at more than $100,000—unless the bank made the loan.

By lunchtime of the day Pfaff made his threat, the Aggies had their money, and Dimmitt had driven off to sign his first player, quarterback Marion Pugh, in Fort Worth. By the end of the day, Thomason, Vaughn and Bill Miller were signed. And by the time fall practice began, 23 members of Lil's "Wanted Forty" were ready to play for the Aggies.

"We were all there when the Depression hit," recalled Roy Bucek. "We weren't a lot of rich boys. Most of the time, all we knew to eat was what we had on our farms—milk that we milked ourselves, corn and farm hogs.

"There was a real bond between us because we were all on the same level. We all knew the only way to make it to college was to play football and use that scholarship."

Said Kimbrough: "We were just lucky to all come together the way we did. In those days, a coach would tell you, 'If you can't block that man, step back and let somebody else do it and you can go back to the farm.' They could take your scholarship away in a day, or give you one in a day. And anybody that ever chopped cotton didn't want to go back to it."

By 1938, the talented group of recruits were sophomores, but the old grads were restless for wins. Finally, with the Aggies losing, 34-6 to TCU, that year's eventual national champions, the fans caught a glimpse of the future.

Norton, who earlier in the week had inserted sophs Robnett and Vaughn into the starting lineup, called on Kimbrough to enter the game. "When I got in there," he said, "it was like a Chinese fire drill. In the huddle, the linemen were saying, 'Don't run over me again because I can't block those guys.' And the backs were saying, "Don't give it to me. I don't want to get hit anymore.'

"So I just said, 'Hell, I'll run it.'"

On the first play, Kimbrough plunged into the line and bulled his way for nine yards, putting a TCU defender on the bench with a bloody face. When Kimbrough went back into the huddle, he said quietly to give him the ball again. This time he ran for 14 yards and left a defensive back writhing on the ground. When the trainers helped the TCU player to the sideline, Coach Dutch Meyer rushed onto the field and got in Kimbrough's face.

"He said, 'You big $*&%, we're trying to win a national championship here and you're putting my guys out," Kimbrough remembered. "Then he grabbed my jersey and said, 'You keep that up and we're not only going to break both your arms, we're going to break your legs, too.'"

We pause to inject a reminder here that college football, in the '30s, was not policed by the NCAA and did not always observe the rules of conduct recommended by the Marquis of Kingsbury.

Kimbrough just grinned and said to the Dutchman, "Look, little fella, you're too small for me to punch. Get somebody bigger out here."

From that point on, Kimbrough started every game. By 1939, the Aggies were poised for an extraordinary run.

They lined up with Herb Smith and Jim Sterling at the ends; Ernie Pannell and Joe Boyd at tackle, with Robnett and Charles Henke at guard. Vaughn was the center. Cotton Price and Marion Pugh shared time at quarterback. Bill Conatser and Derace Moser shared time at tailback. Thomason was one of a kind as the blocking back. John Kimbrough was in a league of his own.

Of the players who had been targeted, 37 signed—a remarkable number. And too good to be true. Other schools picked off a few and the stark landscape of College Station may have discouraged others. But twenty-three reported as promised and were on the varsity in 1939. Fourteen were still alive in 2006, all in their eighties. Members of the team are proudest of one statistic that doesn't show up in the record book: all but two earned degrees, in spite of the interruption of World War II.

And of all the players who eventually married, only one was divorced.

"That says something about commitment," observed Shelton. "That's what the team was all about."

Six of the 23 were named to the All-Conference team, while Kimbrough and Robnett—named after a famed French general in World War I, Marshall Foch—won All-America honors. Joe Boyd, the tackle who later became an Evangelist of some renown, also made the

All-America team but had been recruited a year earlier. Eighteen of the original prospects earned letters and 14 of them did so three times.

The Aggies had finished with five wins, two losses and two ties in 1937, with Joe Routt inspiring a wicked defense and Dick Todd bringing the fans to their feet with his exciting, weaving breakaway runs. The Aggies were starting to draw sellout crowds. Among those rooting for their success was a happy banker in Dallas. They had started paying back the loans.

Their celebrated freshman team was undefeated, but the real revival was still two years away. Homer Norton was in charge of his own budget for the first time, and Dean E. J. Kyle had silenced some of the rumbling by extending his contract another five years.

After more than sixty-six years, a depression, a world war, countless changes in the game and the culture, the surviving '39 Aggies remain close. They still have their reunions, and they still see each other on at least two traditional occasions—funerals and the wedding of someone's grandchild.

And when they visit at these events, or return to the campus, they talk about that year, that special, incredible, historic year, and that national championship season.

The original Reveille (1931-1944) and unknown cadet

John Kimbrough

Chapter 2

Q. & A. WITH JOHN KIMBROUGH
൦ೲಲ

(His wife, Barbara, and Howard Shelton, a teammate and longtime friend, joined the acclaimed Aggie fullback for this interview.)

Q. Tell us your memories of Homer Norton, good or bad?
A. I don't have a bad one. You can write any damn thing you want and put my name to it. But make sure anything you write about Homer that I say is good. He was a good man, a damned good man.

Q. Your father was pretty much against you an your brothers playing football. Is that right?
A. Oh, you bet. There's no need to talk about it. It's come and gone. He didn't like it in high school.

Barbara—He was very against football. John has told me the story about how he once made he and his brother, Jack, build a fence before they could go play football. Well, he and Jack went out there and worked on the fence all day before they could go play football that night. Dr. Kimbrough went out there and said he accidentally backed over the fence just so they would have to start all over again.

John—He was a good man, and you knew where he stood every time. And you knew you would rather be standing with him than riding in a damn car with him. It was pitiful (the way he drove).

Q. What are your memories of beginning your college career at Tulane?
A. Well, I didn't like it. They were going to make me a guard or tackle. Everywhere I went, they wanted to make a tackle out of me. I

don't really know or remember how I ended up at fullback at Texas A&M. I guess I just walked over there on the first day of practice and stood where I thought I should stand. Homer was a good man and a good coach in my estimation. As far as I know, Homer was the first coach to ever utilize a tower to get above everybody and watch practice. It actually had wheels on it, so he could roll it around and see everything. He was one of the first to ever do that. Homer was a good man as far as I'm concerned.

Q. Because of the bad experience at Tulane, did you feel like you had something to prove at A&M?

A. I never did try to analyze anything. I just thought I would go out there and do the best I could. As far as I was concerned, if it was not good enough, hell, send somebody else out there. I never did know I was any good. My attitude was always, "Give me the damn ball and let's go." I've forgotten the coach's name at Tulane.

[The name of the coach was Lowell (Red) Dawson, whose only loss of the 1939 season would be a 14-13 upset in the Sugar Bowl at the hands of the Aggies. A former Tulane quarterback, Dawson was a relentless recruiter, whose 1939 team included players from 13 states and the Panama Canal Zone.]

John continued: He was a good coach. But it was extra special that we won the national championship against Tulane. I guess I was just another player to them (when they signed me).

Q. Really? You were pretty well regarded as a prospect.

A. Hell, I don't know about that.

Barbara—He was well known by the time they played the Sugar Bowl. The police stopped their car one night, and John was in the back. The other players were trying to get John to tell the police who he was. Well, finally he said, "I'm John Kimbrough." The police officer said, "Yeah I'm Bronko Nagurski." The policemen didn't care or didn't believe him. The more they talked, the worse the ticket was.

Howard Shelton—After John became known as a great football player, he was a big figure on the campus. Students would drop by just to say hello. That's the way John was regarded. He was really modest about it. He still lived in the dorm in the E company infantry and was with the Corps and all that. He was very humble.

Q. After that '39 season, you finished second to Tom Harmon in the 1940 Heisman Trophy balloting. Was it disappointing not to win it?
A. Hell, no. Hell I didn't know what it was. That's the truth. I had never even heard of it.

Howard—This is more my idea, but the fact that Davey O'Brien won the Heisman Trophy in 1938 was somewhat of a disadvantage to John and others, because I don't think they wanted to give it to another guy from Texas and the Southwest Conference so soon after O'Brien won it.

Q. That 1940 season was a great one, too. But is it true you felt that more Aggies back then remembered you as the team that lost to Texas in '40 instead of the team that won it all in 1939?
A. Yeah. That's true.

Barbara—One of the Houston writers, George Fuermann, wrote that Texas didn't defeat A&M; two Rice co-eds did. John and Tommie Vaughn came down to Houston the weekend before the game, and there was this tremendous rain. We started back to College Station on Sunday—John and me, Tommie and Tommie's girlfriend—and we got to Hempstead and there was standing water.

They wouldn't let any traffic through. It was over the bridge. People were turning around and had to go back. They tried to get back, but the train wasn't running, the track was washed out. It was bad. They said, "Maybe tomorrow it'll be fixed." Well, they had a football meeting that night. John and Tommie called and said Homer's pulling out the last two hairs on his head. Anyway, I have a picture of them all dejected about not being able to get back to practice. They are sitting down and you can see these sad faces all around the table. They got back on Monday night, I think.

Q. John, you didn't miss too many practices. What are your recollections of practices under Homer?

A. I remember it was tough. We had this Coca-Cola cooler where they kept soft drinks for after practice. But back in those days, the coaches didn't think you were tough if you were drinking water in practice. So, you would dunk your head in this tank filled with ice to keep the drinks cool, and while we were down there dunking our heads, we would go, 'gulp, gulp, gulp.' The coaches wouldn't let us have water, but we would steal a few drinks that way. That was before the days of letting people get hydrated.

When we came in from practice, there would be Old Sarge, who was our equipment manager. He'd give us two halves of an orange. We'd eat that orange, and that was our primary refreshment after practice.

Barbara—John doesn't like oranges to this day.

Q. What was Texas A&M like back in those days?

A. Not a lot to do. But we knew before we went down there what it was going to be like. We didn't complain. We just made the best of the situation, and we waited for the girls to come on weekends.

Barbara — My mother wouldn't let me go to the boys' school without her. She and I went a couple times. John had other girlfriends during the time we knew each other. One time when he was in Houston, he told me to come on up to school some football weekend. I said, 'When?' He said whenever you'd like to come. I said, 'OK, what about for the TCU game?'

Well, he had a date for that game. He said another weekend. I called an old friend of mine, Sam Wheeler, and said, "Sam, would you want to invite me up for the weekend for the TCU game?"

He wrote a letter to me and invited me up to the TCU game. Mother went with me and stayed at the hotel in Bryan. We were going up in the elevator and who should get in the elevator but John and his girlfriend.

Anyway, we had a dance that night and ate in the dormitory on Sunday. Coming out of the dormitory, I saw John again with his girl.

Cute girl. We said good-bye out there by the dorm and left. But my mother told me to drive around and come back around. I said, "What for?" She said, "Just do what I tell you." So we drove around; I guess it was the parade ground or something, and came back and there stood John waving us down.

He had already told his girlfriend good-bye. He said, "I'll drive you to Houston." I was in my car. So he got someone to follow us down there to bring him back. And he drove us back to Houston.

Q. Could you take us through your career path after A&M?
A. Hell, I'm an old man. I'm lucky if I could tell you what I did yesterday.

Q. What about going into the service after your career at A&M? What were your thoughts about the unrest in the world?
A. I didn't give it much thought. You either went or you didn't.

Barbara—He played one year with the New York football Yankees in 1941. And then it was 1942 when he went in to the service. Actually, he made a movie (*Lone Star Ranger*) and then went in [the service]. His brothers, Jack, Ernest, Bill and Frank were already in the service. He made one movie in 1941 and one in '42. He said he had never even been in a high school play. He also read a book a day when making the movie because of the waiting around and wasted time. John was never one of those people who liked to waste any time.

Q. You also had a major advertising deal with Chesterfield cigarettes, right?

A. That's true. I didn't smoke, so I didn't know how to dangle the cigarette in my mouth. They took the picture and painted in the cigarette to make it look more natural. That picture was on billboards. It was on the subways in New York. It was in national magazines. It ran longer than any ad that Chesterfield had at that time.

Q. Is it true that you were once the highest-paid player in pro football?

A. Something like that. Don't pin me down to exact numbers.

Q. Where were you in World War II?

A. I was commissioned as a second lieutenant in the infantry, then went through flight school in Albuquerque. Got my wings in 1943 and served some time in the Pacific. Was the personal pilot for a colonel at one point. It sure was nice to call in and say, "This is Q-0-1 requesting landing." They'd say, "Come right in Q-0-1," and make everyone else go around. That was because it was the colonel's airplane.

Q. How did you end up back in Haskell?

A. We own these 22 acres here. When we got ready, it was so expensive after the war that we decided we would just build a little house, which we did. In fact, one Saturday night Barbara sketched it on a piece of paper. When they built the bedroom, she said, you left a window out. I said, I didn't know that was a window there.

Barbara—We had owned a house in Houston. After World War II, my grandmother said, I'm going to build you and your sister a house. We bought these two lots in River Oaks. We had ours in the poor side of River Oaks, on the east side of Kirby Drive. Anyway, we built the house and John said we can't live in Houston. Our son, Johnny, was about 2-years-old and he never got to see him.

John said, "When I leave in the morning, he's not awake and when I come home in the evening, he's gone to bed. I don't spend any time with him." John worked for Earl North Buick Company, probably in about late 1945 or '46. Earl North wanted to build a second Buick place because he had been told they had to have more than one Buick dealership in Houston. He wanted John to run the new one. But John said, "No, I want to go back to Haskell."

When he played pro ball, we lived in a little house before we built this one in 1947 or '48. He gets a check from the NFL for playing 11 years. They counted the years during the war and from him playing in the other league. He was in the All-American Conference. They took all those teams into the NFL. I guess it was retroactive.

Q. What all did you do after you retired from football?
A. We had a couple of farms. We had some cows at one time. Worked for the Gulf Oil Company, selling products to the farmers. That was about the time I ran politics into the ground. Served one term in the 51st Legislature and just commuted. Didn't care for it much. I liked everything black and white. Everything in Austin was gray.

Q. When you were in the Army, didn't you play for an all-star team against the Washington Redskins and Sammy Baugh out in California?
A. Yeah. We had an Aggie reunion. Wallace Wade was the coach, and he brought in Marion Pugh, Jim Thomason, Bill Conatser and me. Then Dog Dawson and Joe Routt showed up. Baugh and Dick Todd were with the Redskins. Sam said, "They're paying to see me throw the ball, not to see me get tackled, so don't tackle me. I took it easy on him. He'd get up and say, "Thanks." Sam still lives out in Rotan.

Barbara—Sam and Dick Todd and John used to meet at Knox City, which was kind of in between them all. I went up there one time with John. Sam would say, "Dick, I was going to have you for one of my pallbearers, but you dropped everything I ever threw to you. So I'm not going to have you."

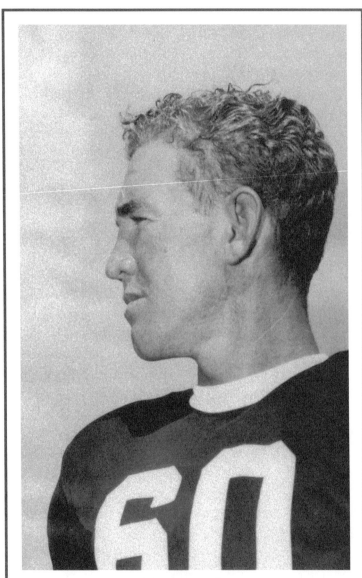

Tommie Vaughn

Chapter 3

THE TIMES

THE ONLY ARGUMENT ABOUT THE 1939 TEXAS AGGIES was whether they were stronger on offense or defense. Those who saw him compared John Kimbrough to Red Grange and Jim Thorpe. But the defense put some serious hurt on opposing teams, not allowing a touchdown in eight games and yielding a total of 18 points in conference play.

It was a team composed largely of juniors, some of them still in their teens, two or three years away from going off to fight a war. Of the starters, two died during World War II in plane crashes, Herbie Smith—even now a member of the all-time Sugar Bowl team—and the dashing Derace Moser. Marshall Robnett, their All-American guard, died of cancer in 1967, the week the Aggies upset Bear Bryant's Alabama team in the Cotton Bowl.

Tommie Vaughn, who for fifty years owned and operated a car dealership on days when the Aggies were not playing football, was the team's center and holler guy. He was redheaded and spunky and he never wasted words.

He was asked if it was his job to get on the fellows who made a mistake.

"Always."

Did you really chew them out?

"Raw."

Was it as great a team defensively as people have said?

"Eighteen points."

How good was Kimbrough, really?

"As great a back as ever played the game. He was big for that time, 6-foot-3 and 225, and he had a long stride. He looked like his feet didn't touch the ground."

How good a coach was Homer Norton?

"Twenty years ahead of his time."

Vaughn recovered the fumble that set up the touchdown by Kimbrough in A&M's tightest win, 6-2, over SMU. The 1940 Aggies were an extension of the team before it, and their 19-game winning streak was achieved in the cauldron of hard times and an approaching war. They had most of the same players, the same coaches, the same no-nonsense approach, the same sha-boom.

In both seasons, fifteen players saw the bulk of the action. They didn't have free substitution and they wore leather helmets without a face mask. They played hurt because they didn't know any other way.

Other heralded defenses stopped teams. The Aggies sent them in reverse. In 1939 and 1940, Texas A&M was a terrific place to be because, as the pros once said of Green Bay, there was nothing to do there except win.

Aggieland was one of the few places in America that did not have a street that served as an off-campus nerve center. Yes, there was a short block across from the North Gate, but none of the surviving '39ers remember much about it. Most of them have been back to the campus many times for football games, but some were not even sure the street was still there.

Of course it is, but none of the national champions would recognize it, partly because you need a compass to find the North Gate. The campus is now surrounded by shopping malls, three large ones within a mile, all with nice eating places like Bennigan's and Steak and Ale and, heaven help us, a sushi bar or two.

But in the Thirties, there was no drag or strip, just a drug store, a barber shop, a dry cleaners and a movie theater. The White Way Café had a nice plate lunch, but it mostly attracted old grads and working folk, not students.

There were no Gucci stores, either.

The Aggies were the Greatest Generation's greatest team because, as a practical matter, they were Number 1 when the war actually broke out, in 1939. When it ended, in 1945, the GeeGees had to come home and finish school, or make living, or try to assemble the barbecue pit in the backyard of the home they financed with a G. I. Loan in a place called suburbia.

By then, the legend was complete. They had survived the Great Depression and defeated the Japanese and Nazis and saved the world.

Those who were on the cusp of manhood in the Thirties remember those years as a wistful time, when practically everything seemed better than it does today, except air conditioning. Or so observed another noted Texas writer, Dan Jenkins, who made his bones in Fort Worth and Dallas and *Sports Illustrated*, before gaining renown as the author of "Semi-Tough" and other best sellers. Here's Jenkins on the glory of their times:

> *Even gangsters were better in the '30s, because you could tell them apart from the politicians. Gangsters put black shoe polish on their hair, wore pinstripe suits, packed heaters and talked about C-notes as they slapped their women around.*
>
> *Cars were better because they were flashy roadsters with rumble seats and all kinds of wraparound chrome, and you could drive from College Station to the Hill Country on ninety cents' worth of gas.*
>
> *People could dance to the music of the '30s without hopping around like Siamese cats, and they could listen to the music without screaming at a teenager to turn down the heavy metal or put on earphones. Music was definitely better.*
>
> *Food was better. You could almost always open the packages food came in. Or you could pull food out of the ground, or wring food's neck in the backyard and then roll it in flour and pitch it in the frying pan. You could also get food at drug stores, which, if they were good drug stores, sold comic books and chocolate milk shakes.*
>
> *Comic books were better because they were serious. It was a sad day for America when comic books got funny.*
>
> *Movies and novels were better because they had good guys and bad guys in them and they frequently had endings. Movies were also better because the leading men were taller and pretty terrific sword fighters. In a '30s movie, Dustin Hoffman wouldn't get the girl. He would get the luggage.*
>
> *Staying home was better even if you didn't read a book. You could listen to the* Amos and Andy Show *and* One Man's Family *and* I Love a Mystery *on the radio instead of hurling your house slipper at the TV when American Idol comes on; and then switching to the telethon on public broadcasting where several phone lines are always open.*

All in all, trains were better in the '30s, and so were newspapers,
swimming holes, cafeterias, shade trees, bicycles, corn bread, drive-ins,
doughnuts, candy bars, picnics, oceans, skies, parades, dust storms,
rodeos, Christmas and tap dancing.
    And football.

Thanks, Dan.

Football was better because college football was the major league.
Pro football consisted largely of a group of second class citizens wad-
dling around in the baseball parks of blue collar cities.

The pros were already astute in the art of offensive holding, but
they were pushovers for a Sam Baugh, fresh out of TCU. He led the
College All Stars to victory over the Green Bay Packers and then he
became the All-Pro quarterback in his rookie year. Until Sam Baugh
lit it up, pro football in Texas was a one-paragraph story on the third
page of the Monday sports section.

Meanwhile, college football was glamorous, mysterious, important.
College teams had mascots, not dancers. Reveille, the Aggie dog, is one
of the game's best known and most functional, along with the Army
mule and the Navy goat and the Texas cow, or steer, whatever he or she
happens to be.

Every team in the country had its own look, and the players dressed
properly. If a player had shown up for a game in a fishnet jersey cut off
at the rib cage, he'd have been thrown in the slammer for indecent
exposure.

Nobody wore a face mask, and the gladiators were expected to play
offense and defense, quite often for sixty minutes.

No two college teams ran the same offense. Their coaches had
names like Dutch, Jock, Tiny, Pappy, Bernie, Bo, Biff, Stub, Clipper
and Bear, except for the ones named Amos or Clark or Homer. They
all developed a variation of the single wing, double wing, triple wing,
spread, short punt and box formations.

They used shifts and men in motion, unbalanced lines, tricky
reverses, daring laterals, statues, flea flickers, shovel passes, button
hooks and long passes, which weren't called "bombs" yet because
World War II hadn't started.

And they quick kicked on first down and got away with the hide-out play, even though everyone in the stadium could see it except the other team.

It's true, dammit, life hasn't been the same since they outlawed the hideout play.

Elsewhere, the world was turning violent, as the world often does. For those tempted to think of football as mock combat, the real thing would be available for comparison.

On the first day of September, 1939, the phone rang at the White House at ten minutes before three in the morning. The Ambassador to France, Bill Bullitt, was calling President Roosevelt from Paris. He had just received an urgent call from Ambassador Anthony Biddle in Warsaw.

World War II had begun. Adolf Hitler's bombers were dropping death all over Poland. A radio station in Warsaw played Frederic Chopin's *Polonaise* every thirty seconds to show the world that the nation's capital still resisted. After eleven days, the station went off the air.

The first shots were heard on the Western Front, as Britain and France entered the war against the Nazis. Winston Churchill, the British prime minister, announced that the Royal Navy was hunting the U-boats day and night.

Meanwhile, the Russians and Germans signed a non-aggression pact. The last diplomat to sign the papers stole the fountain pen.

In December, Russia attacked Finland, sending waves of planes to bomb the cities, but their aim was wretched. In Helsinki, the Russians tried to wipe out the railroad and freight yards, but leveled an apartment house several blocks away, shattering the windows of their own embassy. They also hit the new Olympic stadium.

Finnish anti-aircraft guns and fighter planes downed a dozen Russian aircraft, whose pilots had been told it was safe to bomb any-where. Three fliers who fell into the hands of a mob of women and children were killed with axes, pitchforks and shotguns.

On the domestic crime front, Al Capone was moved from Alcatraz, where he had served six years of a ten-year sentence for tax evasion, to San Pedro, Calififornia, to make it less likely that other inmates would kill him.

Gangster Lepke Buckhalter, high on the FBI's Most Wanted list, turned himself in to gossip columnist Walter Winchell, who led him to a black limousine. Waiting inside was J. Edgar Hoover.

In Iraq, King Ghazi crashed his sports car into a light pole, crushing his skull and killing him within the hour. The British announced that a regent would rule the country until his three-year old son, Feisal, came of age. In Mosul, rumors that the British had done away with their king inspired a mob to drag the consul-general out of his office and stone him to death.

In Hampton, England, Sigmund Freud died at 83.

In California, a court declared Amelia Earhart, the famed aviatrix who disappeared over the Pacific eighteen months earlier, officially dead.

In sports, Lou Gehrig, having benched himself after 2,130 games, returned from the Mayo clinic with the grimmest possible diagnosis. He suffered from a rare, creeping disease that slowly laid waste to all muscles controlled by the spinal cord. "I guess I have to take the bitter with the sweet," said the Yankee first baseman. "If this is the finish, I'll take it."

'Two-Ton' Tony Galento got his wish to fight heavyweight champion Joe Louis. After biting the cap off a bottle of beer, Galento had predicted, "I'll flatten the bum with one punch." Referee Arthur Donovan stopped the fight in the fourth round and dragged Tony back to his corner. When he came to and had his mouth stitched, Galento said, "That bum is way overrated."

In his first All-Star game, 20-year old Bob Feller of Cleveland took the mound with the bases loaded in the sixth and one out, and got Arky Vaughn to bounce into a double play. He gave up one hit, in the ninth, then struck out Johnny Mize and Stan Hack to protect a 3-to-1 win for the American League.

On Broadway, the hit shows were Lillian Hellman's *The Little Foxes*, starring Tallulah Bankhead, and *The Philadelphia Story*, with Katherine Hepburn in the leading role.

Time Magazine judged Thornton Wilder's play, *The Merchant of Yonkers*, as silly and giggly and soft as a pillow fight. Later, the play was turned into a musical and renamed *Hello, Dolly*.

In Chicago, John Barrymore was drawing packed houses to see him act, sick or drunk and unsure of his lines, in *My Dear Children*. The doorman of the theater paid him this tribute: "Yep, he arrives every night, dead or alive."

In December, the two most popular selling records were "Beer Barrel Polka," and "South of the Border," the latter a song about Mexico written by two Irishmen living in London who had never seen the country.

Turning his attention briefly away from his several wars, Adolf Hitler announced that the revolutionary new German car, the Volkswagen, five years in production, would reach the market in 1940.

The five biggest box office stars in Hollywood, in a poll of 10,000 independent theater owners, were in order: Shirley Temple, Clark Gable, Sonja Henie, Mickey Rooney and Spencer Tracy.

Bette Davis won the Oscar, her second, for her role in *Jezebel*, and Tracy for his performance as Father Flanagan in *Boys Town*, also his second.

Zane Grey, 64, a former dentist and ex-baseball player, who hit the jackpot with *Riders of the Purple Sage*, died of a heart attack in California.

John Steinbeck had the year's most talked about novel, *"The Grapes of Wrath,"* the story of the Joad family in the Dust Bowl era, Okies who lost their farm to the bank, sold their possessions for eighteen dollars, bought a jalopy and headed west, looking for the land of plenty.

For many in Texas and Oklahoma, that was not a history lesson but life close at hand. For strong young men who were born in those states, football was their ticket to ride.

Roy Bucek

Chapter 4

Q. & A.—In the Pits
WITH ROY BUCEK

ℰ✺೦

Q. How did you wind up at Texas A&M?

A. Well, I'm from Schulenberg. That's where I graduated from high school, the Schulenberg Short Horns. At the time, we didn't have as good a ball club as they had in other years. But I had an opportunity. I had a scholarship to go to Texas. T.U. talked to me first about going to school and, hell, I wanted to go to college somewhere. The reason I came to A&M was because I liked my high school Ag teacher. My daddy didn't have a car, so my high school teacher drove me to College Station. I did get a full scholarship. That was the fall of '38. But then I was also a track man. When it came to the time of the track meet, I had four or five other schools try to get me to go to college there.

When it came time for the high school regional track meet, I won the high and low hurdles. At the state meet, my foot was sore as it could be. So the University of Texas man packed it up real good. This is how much I wanted to go to A&M. Lil Dimmitt was there, the Aggie trainer for A&M, and he put something on there that wasn't worth a damn. But I said, "Oh, that's wonderful." I did everything in my power to get a scholarship up here.

I was the high point man at the state meet in 1938. If it hadn't been for track, I think maybe they would have kicked me off the football team. The thing I remember most, I was a lineman and my coach was Uncle Bill James. By the way, we only had three full-time coaches and two part-time coaches. Of course, when I say full-time, I mean the backfield coach (Marty Karow) was also the basketball and the baseball coach. The end coach was also the track team coach. Uncle Bill James had a motto, 'Let's Go and Go Hard.' Every time we'd go out there to practice, all the players would mimic him, 'Let's go and go hard.' In my career, when I was running my business, I always remembered that. Let's go and go hard. I kind of got my crew to do the same thing.

I remember when Uncle Bill James was buried. I went to his funeral in Hunt, Texas. He was buried out on his farm underneath a large live oak tree. There was no cemetery there. That was his wish. We called him Uncle Bill because he had no children. Everybody called him Uncle Bill. He had a camp up there, Camp Stewart. It was a boys and girls camp in the summer time. Of course, in those days, as soon as the football season was over with, the coaches left. I think Homer, the head coach stayed, but Bill James didn't hang around. He had nothing else to do here. He was an outstanding person.

Q. What are your memories of Homer?

A. I had a different point of view than some of the players. I thought that Homer Hill Norton wasn't as good of a coach as he was a psychologist. My thinking is, that guy had Aggies from Houston, Austin, Dallas send us telegrams. We had a big blackboard in the locker room. In the room where we sat down and studied the film—maybe the training room—there was a blackboard full of telegrams. They showed up when we were playing a good team.

When we played the University of Texas, the head man over there was D. X. Bible, and they put up a telegram from Bible on our blackboard. It said something like, "We'll beat the hell out of you Aggies." Things like that. Now, they weren't from Bible. They got some Aggie from Houston and so forth to send them to get us fired up. We never did wire things to other schools. But we didn't know at the time that Bible wasn't just sending them to us to cut us down. So, dumb as it may sound now, hell, yes, that fired us up. I think it fired up everybody.

Q. So, the rivalry with Texas was as big back then as it is now?

A. Oh, yeah. The thing that irks me is that I was on the '39, '40, '41 teams. In three years, we lost three games, and we lost two of them to Texas. That sticks out to me. That hurt the hardest. The other loss we had was in the 1942 Cotton Bowl against Alabama. But that was an outstanding trip. I remember they had us eat at *Antoine's* after the ball game. [*Antoine's* is a New Orleans landmark].

We were country boys, we just had a fork and a knife to eat with. I think we had spoons at home, but not very many spoons. Spoons were used for soup and if we had ice tea. Anyway, we were country people. I think we had 12 pieces of silverware to eat with at that *Antoine's*. We had lots of forks and knives and so forth. We didn't know what the hell to do with them. I asked somebody, they said, you start out from each end and go towards the middle. We were just country boys, and we experienced all kinds of new things by playing at Texas A&M. And I mean all kinds of different things.

Q. Give me some other examples.

A. Well, for one, we were all white back then. And we played against all white teams, except when we went out to UCLA (in 1940). They had two black players on the team, both great running backs. When I was growing up, we didn't know anything about race. Back then we called them colored. I didn't know that was bad. We picked cotton together and ate lunch at the same table.

Well, this one back ran pretty good that first half. To start the second half, Marshall Robnett kicked off to him and he made the tackle. Think the UCLA player injured a knee and didn't come back into the game. That back's name was Jackie Robinson. And, of course, he broke the color line in baseball with the Brooklyn Dodgers. [The other back was Kenny Washington, who led the nation in total offense in 1939.]

Q. The team was on such a roll in 1939. Did you ever feel the pressure to win?

A. There was probably some pressure before we ever got on a roll. We were going through two-a-days in the fall of '39. E. J. Kyle was the Dean of Agriculture at that time. Of course, the football stadium was named after his family. I'll never forget it. Jimmy Parker was our manager. He'd go and get one of those insect sprayers and fill it up with water and he'd pump it full of air. He'd go around and spray your face. He'd spray until you cooled off.

Dean Kyle was standing there. About the same time that Parker was doing that, the Dean was telling us, "You fellows have got a burden on your back. You know, we haven't made a principal payment on this stadium in three years. If we don't make a principal payment on this stadium this year, the bank is going to foreclose on us." Well, hell, what did we know? We're 18, 19, 20-year old kids. We didn't know what the hell he is really talking about. The principal was more than most of us could have ever imagined.

I thought maybe they'd take the stadium away from us if we didn't put more people in the stands and make money. And he said they'd foreclose on us. Hell, (in 1937), they had an average of 5,000 people come to see the game or less. Sure, we didn't have anybody. We only had 4,000 kids in school. Of course, all of them were in the Corps. Ninety-nine percent of them came to the game unless they had an excuse to go home. Other than that, we didn't have hardly any paid attendance on the other side. Tickets cost $2.50.

The reason I remember is that at every home game we'd get two tickets. Other guys might have gotten more than I did, but I got two. I sold those two tickets. We were supposed to ask our folks to come to the game. I'd sell them. The athletic department would buy them back from us for $5. We didn't have but four or five games at home, it wasn't but 20 or 30 dollars for the whole damned year.

Q. You guys had it pretty rough. But you were pretty rugged, tough guys, weren't you?
A. Yeah, I guess we're still pretty rugged and tough. Here's my tough-guy souvenir. (HE PULLS HIS EYE OUT)

Q. How did that happen?
A. I was in the infantry in World War II. Somebody along the way said, "Why don't you get into the infantry? It's easy." That's why I got into the infantry. I went overseas and I had a little problem. I lost this eye from shrapnel. That's a marble eye. I was the company commander at the time. I replaced a dead man. I was a

replacement officer. We were in the Battle of the Bulge. I hadn't had any sleep for at least two days. Actually, the Battle of the Bulge was the prettiest thing that I've ever seen in my life. I don't ever want to see it again, but it was beautiful. The bullets were going like fireworks at night. Just beautiful. Every now and then a big explosion here or there. That was the best damn fireworks show I've ever seen.

I was in the Seventh Army, but they transferred us to the Bulge to help out General Patton. We didn't sleep for a long time. The battalion commander told me to go someplace. I guess he showed me wrong or I went wrong. I heard a popping noise. I got behind this big tree. The noise was a machine gun. I was behind that tree. I decided I better crawl away from there. I got on my belly. Of course, it was in the mountains, we had snow on the ground. I crawled up 300 or 400 yards, waited 30 or 40 minutes. Then I looked again to see if I could see anybody. They saw me. I didn't see them.

So the first time they shot a round one of them landed about three or four feet from me, made all that snow come up. It knocked me over, knocked my helmet off, my gun off. So I shook myself and got up and before I put my helmet on, the next round went off in the tree. What happened is that tree, the shrapnel went through my eye, cut my eye in half, went behind my nose, now it's in this cheek. I have a piece of metal in this cheek that's seven-eighths of an inch long. The doctor gave me an option if I wanted to remove it, but they said, if it don't hurt you, don't remove it. It don't hurt me.

Q. Were you thinking about the war when you were at A&M?
A. Not so much. We were just thankful to be at A&M. We were all so damned hungry and tired of farming that it was a joy to be an Aggie. I never did leave campus. The economic conditions of that time ... Joe (Boyd) and I were both farm boys. Tommie Vaughn was from Brownwood. I'm not sure if he was a farm boy, but there were a lot of farm boys. We didn't have it very good. When we got up here and, hell, we went into the mess hall, that food was pretty

damn good. I heard some people griping about mess hall food, but that's the best food we had.

We worked for it. They fed us; we worked. That's the way I felt about it. I never did want to leave. I think it was tough as hell. A&M, at that time, they were teaching more agricultural courses, so they attracted more students from the farm. That's the reason I think we had so many farm boys, but I think that made us a special team. I think farm boys worked harder on the farm and longer hours on the farm than these boys did in the cities.

Kimbrough was a farm boy. Let me tell you a little story about how good he was. I was a guard. Kimbrough was a fullback. I was next to Vaughn, and I was supposed to lead the blocking over to that side. But what I did, when the ball was passed to Kimbrough, I went that way and Kimbrough hit me, not intentionally, but I got the damned signal wrong, and his leg came up like that in my face. That was the only time I was knocked out. We didn't have any face guards back then. Nothing but your nose. He was a hell of a good runner, a straightaway runner who could bust through the line and run people over.

Q. The game has changed a lot since then?
A. Yeah, and so has College Station. Hell, we had the Aggieland Inn. That's the only thing that's really the same. There wasn't much around here. We had the post office. The post office was built in 1938 or '39 on University drive. There wasn't much to do, so we made our own fun. I remember ol' Robnett used to make his own fun.

Robnett and I roomed in the summer time in a housing project. We paid $2 apiece, and we had one bed. I paid $2 a week and he paid $2 a week. This lady rented a room in the house so she and her husband could make some extra money. Robnett and I went out one day, and he said, "Let's go fishing." He had a car, so we bought us a quart of shrimp and we went out there to fish. Of course we had a case of beer, too. After about 40 or 50 minutes, we didn't catch a fish. He said, "Dammit, let's go into a restaurant and have them fry these damn shrimp." That's what we did. Took the case of beer into that little ol' restaurant and left every bottle on the table. I think there was about 30 bottles before we left. He drank two to my one. I wasn't that big of a beer drinker, but he could drink it.

Q. You must have thought you were on another planet when you went to New Orleans for the Sugar Bowl?

A. That's right. I don't remember how many fans were there that day for the Sugar Bowl, seems like 70 or 80,000. I know that they were pretty damn noisy. Ninety percent of them were for Tulane. We didn't play a very good ball game. We were lucky to win.

Q. Did you know early on that you had a special team?

A. No, we didn't. We didn't know anything until the Baylor game; then we thought that we had a good team. We played Oklahoma State—back then it was Oklahoma A&M—in the first game. I got to play quite a bit in that game and I dislocated my shoulder and it's still dislocated. It hurts like hell. They put skin toughener on it. That was the best they had. But we played Baylor, which was about the fifth game of the year, that's when we found out we had a good ball club.

Q. What is skin toughener?

A. Shoot, we couldn't live without that stuff. It was a fluid of some sort, it would toughen up your skin. Basketball players put it on their feet. It didn't help much, but they had no money. The A&M Athletic Department was in bad financial shape. I think the head coach was making $10,000 and I'm sure that was a hell of a lot of money if he was making that. Ole Sarge, he wouldn't give you a jockey strap either, unless you turned one in. Things like that. Pair of socks. You didn't get nothing.

Coach Norton (left) speaks to the team

Chapter 5

THE COACH

❧

IN THE DUSTY, HALF-FORGOTTEN ARCHIVES OF TEXAS A&M, there exist two rare and priceless letters. Dated in the late summer of 1937, they represent a short, but fruitful, communication between Homer Norton, then the Aggie football coach, and a recent high school graduate named John Alec Kimbrough.

Norton had visited Kimbrough at his home in Haskell, in West Texas, and attempted to persuade him of the rich advantages of an Aggie education, which included free khakis, because membership in the Cadet Corps was at the time mandatory.

But Kimbrough declined with thanks, saying he intended to study pre-med at Tulane and become a doctor, like his father.

John had been on the Tulane campus for two weeks, just prior to the opening of classes, when he had a change of heart, which moved him to contact Norton by mail. You will detect in the text a certain plaintiveness:

"Dear Coach,

"You were right. I'm unhappy here and plan to change schools. Would you still have a spot for me at A&M?"

And Norton replied:

"Dear John,

"Enclosed please find one railroad ticket..."

Surely, one can only admire Norton's deft literary style, his clarity, his economy of words. It had the desired effect. Kimbrough transferred to A&M, and two years later led the Aggies to the crest of college football, a national championship and on to a streak of nineteen victories.

After the Aggies fought off Tulane in the Sugar Bowl classic on New Year's Day, of 1940, there were whispers out of New Orleans that the Green Wave had let Big Jawn walk because he had asked for the equivalent of his own medical school. The truth was, he wanted a job for his brother, Wallace, who was crippled.

Coach Red Dawson refused. The Aggies were happy to find a spot for Wallace, as a tutor for the team, and John, the youngest of six Kimbrough boys. Five had found their way to Aggieland: Ernest, who became a doctor, Bill, who won his football letter, and Jack, who dropped out of school for a year but was his teammate in 1939 and '40. Only Frank, who made his mark as a coach at Hardin-Simmons and Baylor, escaped A&M's grasp.

To this day, many believe that John had no equal as a fullback. He ran with speed and power and he put a big hurt on people who tried to tackle him. He was not the franchise. But he became the marquee player on what may have been the greatest team the greatest generation ever knew.

At this point, a confession is in order. I never saw Kimbrough or those 1939 Texas Aggies play, never watched them on television, which did not yet exist, heard them on radio or read the newspaper accounts of their games. Yet I probably know their deeds and dogged faith more than those who played in that era.

* * *

For the better part of a dozen years, I was the ghost of Homer Norton—in the literary sense, that is.

I didn't know Homer when he was developing good and great football teams at Texas A&M. I met him in the third and last stage of what was really a kind of classic life pattern: public acclaim, obscurity, elder statesmanship.

In the late 1950's, Coach Norton authored a series of football columns for the *Houston Post* and other Texas newspapers. I provided the spelling and punctuation for these essays and Homer enriched us all—me, my typewriter and the readers he soon attracted.

He had welcomed the chance to return to the Southwest Conference scene; to talk football and breathe the smell of autumn. He even enjoyed being a part of the press box confusion, greeting old friends in the media whose names he could never remember.

It was as though he had never been gone, had never been fired by the Aggies, had never taken a high school coaching job in Galveston, so he could at least touch the sleeve of the game he loved. It didn't matter to him what people thought, or even what they said out loud: "Poor Homer, he really has slipped."

I don't want this to sound like something condensed by the *Readers' Digest*, but he had values; values that today might be regarded as old fashioned or un-stylish. He could compare football to the Game of Life and preach about character and tell you that winning isn't everything, and you would nod your head and feel guilty because maybe your thoughts were not that pure.

Homer was a gentle and unselfish man with a quiet sense of humor and an absolute horror of offending anyone. For years I tried to convince him that if he would predict the outcome of the games he would please his readers, and harm no one, except possibly those who bet money on his predictions.

He steadfastly refused, on the theory that somehow this would put an additional pressure on the coaches, whose jobs he considered already difficult enough.

Finally, before an Aggie-Texas game on Thanksgiving Day, with a conference title on the line, I renewed my appeal and he agreed within limits to risk an opinion on the game. I wet the tip of my pencil and waited eagerly for his prophecy.

"It could go either way," he said, firmly, "and I wouldn't be surprised if it did."

It would be pointless for me to rave about what a great coach Homer Hill Norton was. I never saw him react under pressure, and that is what coaches do, and besides it is all there in the record book for anyone who requires convincing.

He held the Aggie job for fourteen years, no small tribute in itself, and he gave the school three conference championships and one national crown. He developed half a dozen All-Americans, and he acquired a reputation as a creative intellect, an innovator, a gambling man.

He came along in the heyday of razzle-dazzle, everything goes football. It was a happier and more romantic time, when people were still trying to figure out how the sound came through a radio. In his day, other coaches knew they could always borrow a cup of ideas from Homer—and he wouldn't scream about it.

Some credit him with designing the blitzing defenses now so popular with pros and amateurs alike, and he had a passion for trick plays.
His favorite was the hideout pass, in which an end would camouflage
himself against his teammates on the sideline. It gained many a yard
for the Aggies and enraged opposing coaches, until the rule makers
outlawed it.

He also introduced such techniques as the sky buggy—observing
practices from a tower—and at least advanced the use of the press box-
to-bench hotline.

None of that, of course, remains his monument today. The legacy
of Homer Norton is his 1939 team, his pride, his treasure and his one
enduring vanity. What a fierce ribbing he suffered in later years about
those frequent, irresistible references to that squad. Homer seldom
delivered a speech, or so much as held a conversation, without men-
tioning the '39 Aggies.

He did it in the spirit of a father telling his son how far he walked
to school as a child. He repeated himself because he was afraid someone might not have listened the first time, and because the subject was
one he loved.

"As long as I'm alive and kicking," he vowed, "I don't intend to let
anyone forget that team." No coach ever remained closer to a group
than Norton to that one. They were middle-aged, some grandfathers,
when the old coach died in May of 1965. Then, for the first time, really, Homer Norton's boys were on their own.

The '39 Aggies won eleven straight games, shut out most of their
opponents and defeated powerful Tulane, 14-13, on New Year's Day in
the 1940 Sugar Bowl, one of the great muscle games ever played.

Homer was to outlive four of his greatest players. Joe Routt, from
the '37 team, died a hero in the Battle of the Bulge. Herb Smith and
Derace Moser were killed in plane crashes during the war. Bill
(Jitterbug) Henderson was felled by the same disease that struck down
Lou Gehrig.

Norton's eyes would moisten when he told about mounting a
speaker's platform at a football banquet in San Francisco, in late
December of 1944. He was one of the coaches in the East-West game.
Just as he started up the steps, someone slipped a telegram into his

hand. He ripped it open because those were the war years and telegrams meant bad news.

The words blurred as he read that Captain Joe Routt, his bristling All-American guard, had been killed leading an infantry advance against German tanks. His company commander called him "the most courageous man I ever met." Some of the bloodiest skirmishes of the European campaign were fought in the area, near Bastogne. It was said that the ground was lost and gained by the Allies and Germans at least eight times.

Because he didn't know what else to do, Homer apologized to the crowd for the tears that glistened on his cheeks, and then he told them that one of his boys, Joe Routt, was dead. "A lot of people who were there, who didn't even know Joe," he marveled, "were crying, too."

Of course, they wept for all the brave young men, swept up in a world of carnage, who would never come home.

Norton's mood was seldom maudlin. He was no Pollyanna, either, but he had an unshakable faith and adversity made him strong. Each new push and knock became a bugle or a snare drum to which he responded.

Over and over, he retold the story of the 1940 Aggies, when Kimbrough and Jim Thomason and Marshall Robnett and Jim Sterling were seniors, and he thought THAT team would be his Mona Lisa. They oozed with talent and physical clout and confidence. In a continuation of the 1939 script, their winning string had reached 19 games. They were so good, in fact, the idea that they might lose had not occurred to them. It had only occurred to the Texas Longhorns.

"We had one foot in the Rose Bowl," Homer would lament, milking his punch line, "and one foot in Memorial Stadium. And Texas chopped off that other foot."

Texas scored right after the kickoff and made it stand up, 7-0, in what would become the most famous of all Southwest Conference upsets. The loss cost the Aggies a second straight national title and a trip to Pasadena. Norton actually had a written invitation in his coat pocket.

Typically, in the somber, silent, tear-stained Aggie locker room, Homer chose to make them a sermon. "Boys," he said, "if you'll remember what happened this day, what you had and what you gave away, what you lost by not paying the price, then in later years this game may have done you some good."

In truth, I have never encountered an Aggie who thought a defeat made him a better person, but you give Homer a few points for trying. In looks, he was a cross between Pat O'Brien, who played Knute Rockne in the movies, and was more convincing than Rockne himself, and Edmund Gwynn, the character actor who played Santa in the film, *Miracle on 34th Street*.

Homer considered coaching the noblest of professions, though hazardous, on the order of being a missionary in some unexplored, God-forsaken jungle. He was a moralist, but he admired a certain amount of roguery.

He once had an enlightening conversation with Paul (Bear) Bryant, the most famous of all Aggie coaches, though the fame was totally out of proportion to the years he spent there—four out of thirty-eight.

During his first recruiting drive, after a late start, Bryant was shaking every tree in Texas looking for talent to build a winner at A&M. "I ran across a boy the other day," Homer told him, coach to coach, "who would make you one helluva football player. Biggest, fastest, strongest kid I ever saw. But you wouldn't want him, Paul. Mean. A bad apple. Always in trouble."

Bryant whipped out a ballpoint pen from his coat pocket and asked, "What's his name and where do I find him?"

His faith in the old-fashioned virtues must have seemed almost prudish. He had the work ethic of a Cambodian rice farmer. He had tunnel vision on game day, setting up a card table in front of the bench, on the 50-yard line, to keep his charts and diagrams and substitutions.

There was a game when he sent in Bill (Big Dog) Dawson to kick a field goal. An end in football and a center on the basketball team, at 6-9, Dawson's place-kicking was a source of fine suspense to his teammates. He had a habit of stubbing his foot on the turf, which did not lead to a high percentage of successful kicks.

But he converted this one, and as he trotted past the coach's card table, Homer took a puff on one of his Chesterfield cigarettes and called out, "Nice going, Doggy."

As he sat down, Dawson said, "F%&* you, Coach. You didn't think I could make it." Norton fired him on the spot. "Go on in, Doggy," he said, "you're off the team."

Early that Monday morning, Howard Shelton was one of a few players who observed the scene at the door of the athletic department. "He was down on all fours," recalled Shelton, "and he crawled from the front of the office to the coach's office in the back corner. He knocked on the door, crawled up to Coach Norton's desk, and started begging. 'Coach, I apologize. I didn't mean to say that. I was just excited over kicking the field goal.

"'Please, Coach, forgive me. I don't have anything at home. We don't even have anything to eat. I can't go home.'

"The coach said, 'Okay, Doggy. You're back on the team.' Homer didn't make a big thing of it. He didn't have to take him back, but Coach was a good guy."

Unlike many in his profession, he believed in the basic goodness of people. He also had a bit of the absent-minded professor in him. Decades later, when I would sit across from him to talk out his next newspaper column, he would often call me "Jimmy," confusing me with his student manager in the '30s, Jimmy Parker.

Sharing a typewriter with Coach Norton was an adventure. He had a terrific memory for everything except names, dates and scores. I made up for his lapses by being young and inexperienced.

Once, he dictated a story to me about how he had finally out-maneuvered cagey old Dutch Meyer, as the Aggies rallied in the second half to beat Texas Christian, in 1938. It made an interesting yarn, and it didn't occur to me to check the year.

A few days later, a postcard landed on the sports desk of the *Houston Post*, and typed on it was this message: "I didn't think anyone would ever beat that undefeated, untied, national championship TCU team of 1938. But I see where Homer Norton finally did it in Friday's paper."

A minor misstep; the true significance was the fact that Kimbrough, a sophomore, left the bench to raise havoc with the TCU defense and provide a glimpse of the great times coming.

THE 1939 AGGIES WERE COMING.

These were Depression-era kids working on family farms and living on a diet of beans, greens and cornbread. There was an entire country on the mend from its own financial meltdown, and a world war bullying its way onto the horizon. Rich and poor were hungry for any diversion they could find.

So twenty-three farm boys and future war heroes, by circumstance and clever planning, came together in the dusty Brazos Valley for coach Homer Norton. And there was a moment in football history that would take on a mythical aura.

Norton never felt underrated, never needed more recognition than he received. In time, he would be inducted into the College Football Hall of Fame. He built a national champion, but rarely rated a call when the elite coaches of his era were hailed.

He was not an orator or a phrasemaker or a showman. He did not patronize his players or use sarcasm as a tool. The son of a Methodist minister, he may have struck some as a soft because he never swore. He had another habit that did not serve him well with the old grads and poll-makers: he would not allow his team to run up a score.

What made his success all the more rewarding was the fact that he didn't crave it. Baseball was his first love, over football, although he had been an exceptional end at Birmingham Southern, a receiver who could block and play defense. He lettered in four sports.

He earned his bachelor's degree in 1916 and played three seasons of minor league baseball, before he accepted an offer as line coach for Bo McMillan at Centenary. When Bo moved on two years later, the school offered Homer the head job. He turned it down for a reason that would not have discouraged most other candidates. He wasn't ready to be a head coach.

In 1926 he decided that he was. In the five times the teams played, Centenary shut out the Aggies of D. X. Bible once and Matty Bell twice. When A&M hired him, over the protests of those who wanted a bigger name, the regents knew what they were getting.

Norton was on the brink of building a dynasty in 1939, the first of his three straight Southwest Conference titles, a feat no other school had achieved. Yet he was the instrument of his own undoing. His loyalty and unselfishness cost him dearly.

Homer had a reputation for developing great players, starting with Routt, the first Aggie to make the All-America team, and the brilliant Dick Todd. When the war came, West Point had first claim on the most talented athletes, in the interest of national morale.

Colonel Red Blaik, football coach at West Point, called and asked Norton for a list of his best players and recruits, so he could have them transferred to the military academy. Typically, Homer held none of them back. He sent Blaik a list that included Hank Foldberg, Marion Flanagan, Goble Bryant, Milt Routt and DeWitt Coulter. The first three had already lettered at A&M.

Blaik took them all, and a year or so later added Charley Shira, Dan Foldberg and Bill Yeoman. Five of the Aggies won All-America honors at Army. Most of them played on Blaik's greatest teams, the ones starring Glenn Davis and Doc Blanchard.

Three went on to become head coaches: Hank Foldberg, who returned to A&M in the '60s; Charley Shira and Bill Yeoman. The curly-haired, youthful looking Yeoman spent twenty-five years at the University of Houston, and changed the game with his version of the triple option.

The talent pool at Aggieland was so dry that Norton literally called on the Twelfth Man to fill out his roster in 1943. He played 17-year olds and his lineup changed every week, but the Whiz Kids, as they were known, posted a 7-2-1 record, losing to LSU in the Orange Bowl, 19-14.

When the war ended, and the veterans came back to get their degrees, all were older and slower and some were disabled, but a scholarship was waiting for every one of them.

"When my boys went off to war," said Norton, "they knew they could come back and I would honor those scholarships. I didn't regard them as scholarships to play football. They were meant to enable them to get an education. When they started coming back in 1946, some had families and some had lost their zest for football. But there was never a thought to not keeping those commitments. They were entitled to them.

"I knew what I was doing. That used up all my scholarships and I had none left to give to . . . beef up the squad. But it was the right thing to do. Nevertheless, it got me in trouble with the alumni."

In the first two seasons after the war, the Aggies slipped to four wins and then three, and a tie. Norton threw in the towel, letting the exes buy out the remaining two years of his contract. Harry Stiteler, his line coach, succeeded him, but sadly so.

"If they had left him alone," said Harry, "Coach Norton would have been back in there winning. He had so much integrity, he honored the scholarship of every one of those boys who went into the service. Some of them could no longer play, but he refused to take away their scholarships.

The last victory, in his last season, 1947, saw the Aggies beat Baylor with the help of the hideout play, one of Homer's oldest tricks. Frank Broyles, who as a coach and athletic director would become an institution at Arkansas, was then a 21-year old assistant on the Baylor staff.

He relished telling the story. "Early in the week," said Frank, "we called in Buddy Crews, who wasn't a starter. So his job would be to watch both sidelines to check for an A&M player hiding out. That taken care of, we forgot all about it.

"On the first play, Stan Hollmig took the snap and turned and passed to Barney Welch streaking down the sidelines. Barney had to lunge for the ball at the seven-yard line, and fall, or else he'd have gone all the way. Before the play was over, we started looking for Crews to find out how it happened.

"'Coach, I didn't see a thing,'" he said. "When we got the films, they showed that the hideout man was standing right next to Crews."

The Aggies went on to win, 24-0, for Homer's last hurrah.

It was a heartbroken Norton who left Texas A&M. He had loved the job, the school, the campus and the kind of athletes he believed were attracted to the discipline at the center of Aggie life. He vowed that he would not consider an offer from another university. As far as anyone knew, he did not.

With the money from his buyout, he went into the motel business in Galveston and there he yielded to an appeal from local football fans and, for a season or two, coached the team at Ball High School. One can only guess at what kind of idealism it takes for a man who once coached the Number 1 team in college football to accept the task of teaching schoolboys, in a town where most people would rather work on their sun tans than attend the games.

Later, he bought a motel in Rosenberg and, a few years before his death from a heart attack in May of 1965, he built and operated a popular restaurant across the road from the main entrance to the Aggie campus.

From his front door, he could see the lights of Kyle Field.

Joe Boyd

Chapter 6

Q. & A.—All the Way
WITH JOE BOYD

ᏋᎳᎳᎦ

Q. What are you doing now?

A. I haven't done a thing in the last 61 years but try to get people into heaven. That's all. I live in West Virginia, and I built a youth camp (Mt. Salem Revival Grounds in West Union) that is probably worth $1.5 million today. We have more than 60 buildings, and we have one of the best youth camps in the world.

Q. Why did you first decide to come to A&M?

A. Well, that was the college that would have me. I made all-city in the Dallas area and we were city champs. Then I went to Paris Junior College. We didn't have a very good ball club at Paris, so I left and began looking for some school that would take me and let me play football. SMU wanted me to live in my home, and I didn't want to do that. I tried Baylor, and they already had their team. Then I tried A&M, and they said they would take me and that if I made the ball club I could stay. But they said that if I didn't I would have to leave. Well, I made All-Southwest Conference for three years and also All-American.

I was playing strongside tackle on defense. Grantland Rice really wrote some nice things about me. In one story he wrote that I would be "sorely missed around Aggieland, where he has been one of the most popular athletes ever to attend the College Station campus." Grantland Rice really gave me nice write-ups, and so did the *Dallas Times-Herald* and the *Dallas Morning News*. I made about five or six All-American teams in 1939.

Q. What was special about that 1939 team?

A. We had a good man named Faulkner, who was a scout, and he

brought in so many all-state men from Texas. He got the cream of
the crop. We had John Kimbrough, the greatest fullback ever to
come through the Southwest. Kimbrough was just tremendous.
Our quarterback was Marion Pugh, who was cool under fire. And
then, of course, we had an outstanding defense that allowed only 18
points that year in the conference. The boys also loved one another. Homer Norton, our coach, was loyal to us, and we made a pact
to him and to each other that we weren't going to be coming out
of the game unless we couldn't walk. We had really good fellowship
on that team.

Q. Who was the best leader on that team?

A. I'll tell you the truth. There wasn't any special one. We just worked
as a unit. John Kimbrough was the tough fullback; Marion Pugh
was the cool quarterback. Tommie Vaughn was an excellent defensive man and center. We had good ends. Little Herbie Smith was
the hero of the Sugar Bowl game. It was just one of those teams
that comes along every once in a while.

Q. How about the most unselfish player? Is there one that sticks out
in your mind?

A. Little Herbie Smith. He didn't weigh but about 150 pounds. He
wasn't very big at all. He liked to play with a chaw of tobacco in
his mouth. He was tough, unselfish and ready to make plays. I
remember we were playing against Baylor one time. Baylor had
this tailback named Jack Wilson. He dropped back to throw a pass,
and Herbie and I arrived at him at the same time. Herbie just took
the ball out of his hands and said, "Thank you, sir."

Q. Who was the funniest or most witty player on that team?

A. I don't remember anybody really being witty or funny. Everybody
was just dedicated to winning those ballgames. The Blue Boys (the
scrubs who scrimmaged against the varsity) were more of the guys
who may have put on a show.

Q. Did you go into the war after you left A&M?

A. No, I went to the shipyards (in Galveston) because I was so beat up.

I had a cracked vertebrae in my neck, and the doctors advised me not to play. The Washington Redskins had drafted me, but I didn't play because the Todd Galveston Dry Docks Incorporated came to me and asked me to go to work for them. I did. And I got to where I was in charge of all the accounting, payroll, bookkeeping and auditing for the shipyards.

It was down there when I got right with God. I was a terrible man and I had strayed from the Lord. It was the Todd Dry Docks in Galveston. We were controlled by the Rockefeller family. It came out in the paper that they were training me to take over a shipyard on the west coast. We dry-docked many, many ships. Most of them were oil tankers. We sent them down to the Panama Canal or to the east.

Q. When did you crack your vertebrae?
A. I was knocked out in the last game of the 1938 season. I cracked some vertebrae and broke some ribs. I had time to get back in shape before the 1939 season, but I played the whole season with a cracked neck. It absolutely bothered me. They hired a big, strong woman to massage my neck in between games and absorb the chips that came off that break. Then I would go back in and play on Saturdays, but yes, I played that whole year with a cracked neck.

Q. That sounds horrible. Did doctors ever say your life might be in danger?
A. No, they never said that. They took me to Houston to get X-rays after I got knocked out and I began to fall and stumble around. Both of my legs had some temporary paralysis. Anyway, the man came out of the X-ray room and told me my neck was broken. I said I knew there was something wrong with it. I guess I was just a tough old bird.

Q. So, how did a tough, old bird like you get called to the ministry?
A. My mother prayed for me and got me right with the Lord. I just got called to preach. So I went to the Todd Dry Docks and I resigned. They thought I was nuts. I started doing city, area and county revivals. I'm still preaching revivals, and I still preach a full

schedule. I work out of Hyles-Anderson College in the Chicago area, where I have an apartment. They like me up there, and I teach there.

I have a home in West Virginia, but I do miss Texas because Texas is the greatest state in the world. But I have been preaching for 61 years. I have held revivals all over Texas. I have held revivals in Jerusalem. I've been in every state in the union and I've been in many foreign countries holding revivals. I'm a member of the Spanish-speaking evangelism team, and I have been in almost all of the Spanish-speaking nations. We preach to so many people in Mexico—5,000, 4,000, 6,500. It's been a real blessing.

In Jerusalem, they told me I couldn't baptize my converts. I asked them why, and they told me that the Arabs—the Palestinians—would kill them if they were baptized. So, I didn't baptize them, but I had a great many people saved. God has been good.

Q. So, did your experiences at A&M help to shape the man you are today?

A. Absolutely. It taught me how to work with people. I've got six boys with me right now. They are top-notch soul winners. I have taken as many as twenty with me. I take boys and train them how to do evangelistic, pastoral and missionary work. These boys are good. It's almost like a college on the road. But I think back on those days at A&M, learning how to get everybody on the same page. I've managed to get many thousands of people saved because of my experiences at A&M. It taught me to be dedicated, and it taught me to never, ever give up.

Q. What has been the most special honor for you from football?

A. I think it would be the fact that I made the All-American team, and that *Sports Illustrated* put me on a 25-year All-American team. I had a lot of nice honors through football. But most of all, I just loved to compete. I loved football. I also was a heavyweight boxing champion and the heavyweight wrestling champion at A&M. I never lost a bout in either one of them. I went to the top in athletics.

But I looked in the Bible to see how much credit I was going to get for those things, and I found out it wasn't anything. But I thank God that He has allowed me to preach for 61 years. I am 86 now. If I get to where I can't preach standing up, then I will preach sitting down. And if I can't preach sitting down I will preach from the bed. God called me to preach and I intend to end my life on this Earth preaching.

Q. Can you elaborate a little more on how you were called to preach?
A. My mother cried and prayed for me all during my football career. She would tell me that God loved me, but I had gotten so hard and tough that I would say, "No, God don't love me." But she just kept it up. I once had a hurricane come down on me and the roof went off of my head at the shipyard.

When the roof went off, God spoke to my heart. I had never heard such a voice in my life. He said, "Son, I'm going to take you if you don't straighten up." I tried to straighten up and reform, but reformation won't get it. I fell back in my sins.

But my mother kept praying and crying for me. She gave me the scripture, Isaiah 1:18—Though your sins be of scarlet, they could be as white as snow. But I said, "No, God couldn't forgive me." I was tough, rough and no good. Then I left a poker game about two in the morning—I was fascinated with gambling—and I had a car wreck. I got out of the car and got down on my knees, but I couldn't find God. My father, who was a Baptist preacher, had given up on me. My father told my mother that I was too wicked to come to God. I had gotten so sorry that I had tried to whip him, and I had liked to gotten killed.

Q. You tried to fight your father?
A. Yep. I was only about 16 or 17 at the time. He put me on the floor before I could even get a swing in. I was going to fight him in the kitchen, but I wound up on the floor real quick. He pinned me with his foot, took off his belt and began to beat me with the buckle. I was bleeding, and my mother came running. She said, "Sam, you're going to kill him, you're going to kill him." He said, "I'm trying to, but he won't die."

I was mean and no good. I was a member of a tough gang. Dallas had a lot of bad gangs—the West Dallas Gang, the Fair Park Gang and so forth. The city actually organized them into sports teams, and I played on one of the gang teams. I played football for them for a couple of years, and it was so tough and rough that we drank wine at the half and all the games wound up in free-for-all fights. By the time I got to Crozier Tech High School I was already tough, and I thought I could whip my father. I was definitely wrong.

My mother was still praying for me. I finally got a Presbyterian preacher to come to my house, and I asked him, "Does God have anything for me?" He quoted Isaiah 1:18—the same verse my mother had told to me. I fell on my knees and began to cry for mercy. God gave me mercy. My wife had never seen me as defeated. She had always seen me as the champion, the one in control. She came and knelt beside me and she got saved and I got right with God. I have been going in his name ever since. That was 1943.

Q. So, you were pretty bad?

A. Oh yeah, I was bad. I was drinking, gambling, whatever. The higher I went in sports, the more I thought of myself and the less I thought about God or anyone else. I bought into all the good publicity I was getting for boxing, football, wrestling and whatever.

Q. You were quite a legend back then?

A. Oh, I don't know about that. I got some good write-ups. But I hoped the boys on the team liked me. I loved those boys. I witnessed to some of them. But I couldn't do much with them because I had set such a bad example.

Q. What do you remember most about Homer Norton?

A. He was a dreamer. He was definitely a dreamer. He dreamed of accomplishing big things. He also dreamed up plays. He would dream up a play, take the first team over and try to run those plays with us going against the second team. Good night. Some of those plays were more nightmares than dreams. He finally settled in with about 30 plays that everybody knew backward and forward. But he was a very good man.

Q. How many times do you tell stories about that team to kids, grand-kids, great-grandkids?
A. Many times. I have actually preached a lot of the stories. Many of my sermons have come from boxing, wrestling and football.

Q. Tell me about your family.
A. My wife (the former Edith Alice Cocke) and I were married 51 years. She died three years ago. She is in heaven waiting for me. She was a good wife, and she really sacrificed for me. We were childhood sweethearts. I proposed to her when she was 14. I said, "If I ever get a job and I ever get out of school, would you marry me?" She said, yes. We had to wait a little while, but I held her to her promise. We got married during my last year at A&M. That was 1939.

I have two children, four grandchildren and four great grand-children. They are such a blessing.

Bill Conatser (49) and Jim Thomason (47)

Chapter 7

THE TEAM

ᏬᎷᎯᏬ

The temper of friends, the love of your life,
Or the favored conference member.
Which of the three will survive the strife
Of a frenzied Texas November?

APOLOGIES ARE IN ORDER, of course, to Rudyard Kipling, whose original verse dealt with a subject more romantic than college football. In truth, he never saw a game, although he did witness a polo match played with a human skull instead of a ball, which you must admit is awful close.

The part about strife and the frenzied Texas November, that part spoke to us as through the years.

This is the way it once was, and will never be again, because the Southwest Conference disappeared in the mid-1990's. Some thought of it as a mercy killing. Others, the purists, the traditionalists, were not thrilled to see 80 years of history swept away by the dust broom of change.

But the Fab Four, A&M, Texas, Texas Tech and Baylor, were gone, off to see the wizard, off to search for Dorothy and Toto in Kansas—not to mention Nebraska, Iowa, Missouri, Oklahoma, and Colorado.

We wished them packed stadiums and television dollars that fell like raindrops upon their heads. We wished them happy trails. We accepted the reality that this was sports in the 1990's and beyond. It looked suspiciously like big business, but then most of us had realized long ago that Frank Merriwell didn't live here anymore. Even the most innocent of football players no longer went to college in hopes of earning a letterman's sweater, and the Rose Bowl queen wasn't judged by the quality of her fudge brownies.

Still, they came oh, so close in the Thirties, when we viewed Davey O'Brien and Sammy Baugh, Bobby Wilson and John Kimbrough, among many, as real heroes, with no flaws in them.

In that decade the Southwest Conference was king. SMU and TCU introduced the aerial circus, and the Aggies all but invented smash-mouth football. Those three teams won the national title in 1935, 1938 and 1939. Logic tells you this was the most dominant conference in the country. The Aggies were arguably the best of the best, based on their record and a schedule that did not include a weak sister (no sexism intended.)

The Associated Press, the most authoritative of the ratings services, did not officially adopt the Top Ten and a recognized national champion until 1936. But one year earlier, the two North Texas schools, the erstwhile religious schools, the Texas Christians and the Southern Methodists, met for what was truly a mythical national title.

In a piece for Texas Football, Steve Perkins, my friend and onetime writing partner, who worked for newspapers in Austin, New Orleans, Houston and Dallas, recaptured that day:

About 4:20 p.m. on November 30, 1935, Mr. Ed Wilkerson, a Dallas insurance man age 56, announced to his family that he had just heard, over the radio, the greatest football game in history. Mr. Wilkerson then turned off the set, got up from his chair and dropped dead on the living room floor.

It's entirely possible that in Mr. Wilkerson's tragic demise, truer words have never been spoken.

He had just heard SMU beat Texas Christian, 20-14, and like the last fluttering page on Mr. Wilkerson's calendar, there could never be a game quite like it again. It was a day and time when The Game on New Year's Day, the one and only classic game of football in America, was the Rose Bowl game. No team west of the Mississippi had ever been invited—and wouldn't have been in 1935, either, had not Fate conspired to tumble Notre Dame, North Carolina, Dartmouth, yea even NYU into the leprous ranks of the beaten.

And there you have it. The Horned Frogs had rallied from 14 points behind to tie the score in the fourth quarter, on an eight-yard pass from Sammy Baugh to Jimmy Lawrence. But with nine minutes left in the game, SMU's Bob Finley faked a punt from the TCU 37 and passed to Bobby Wilson, flying down the right sideline.

The pass was thrown to Wilson's wrong side, and he had to twist in midair to catch it over his right shoulder, and fall into the end zone for the winning touchdown. "It took a great athlete to make that play," said Dutch Meyer, the TCU coach. "But, of course, Wilson was a great athlete."

Meyer blamed himself for the loss. He had sent his players onto the field after giving them "a fight talk to end all fight talks." He called it, "The most grievous mistake I ever made in coaching. I shouldn't have made a speech."

Sam Baugh agreed. "You don't need anybody to get you up for a game like that," he said. "Dutch's talk got everybody tight as ticks, and we dropped some passes."

But Meyer would not repeat himself, to the greater glory of the Frogs. "The mistake I made before the game," he said, "helped me in 1938 when we went to play A&M. I kept the boys calm and we won with ease."

That 1938 season was TCU's year to reign as national champs, and the Aggies returned the favor a year later. Homer Norton didn't believe in pep talks, in Win-One-for-the-Gipper appeals. He gave his team its space, and did not attempt to pump up their emotions. He thought it would be like playing the death scene from Carmen.

In '39, the Aggies beat TCU comfortably, 20-6, on their way to a perfect season.

That last day in November, of 1935, would echo through the rest of the decade because the Aggies would have their own close and ago-nizing brush with the Rose Bowl.

"TCU and SMU suddenly had the only contest in the country that meant anything," wrote Perkins. "It meant everything—the national championship, the Rose Bowl oh holy bid, All-America recognition for its stars. And they came. Grantland Rice and Joe Williams from the east and Maxwell Stiles from the west, and even coaches named Bernie

Bierman from Minnesota, Pappy Waldorf from Northwestern, Dana Bible from Nebraska.

"The cold and dreary depressing years of the '30s erupted for one extended burst of regional pride. Texas held the stage. Not for 30 years, until Texas met Arkansas in an epic showdown in Fayetteville, would there be another Southwest Conference matchup to challenge it."

There is not much room for debate here because in their quests neither the Aggies nor the Horned Frogs had to stake their hopes on the final game of the season against another, unbeaten conference foe.

The Frogs were so good in '38 they breezed through the schedule without a scare, behind the passing and running of little Davey O'Brien, who looked not much bigger than a hood ornament at 5-7 and 150 pounds. He performed his artistry behind a fearsome line led by I. B. Hale and Ki Aldrich.

Davey won the Heisman Trophy, an honor that eluded Kimbrough. The award was created a year too late for Baugh.

But the rest of the country was discovering the brand of high voltage football played in the oil and cotton belt. SMU's most deadly weapon was the buck-and-lateral, with Bobby Wilson winding up with the ball as a runner or receiver.

Baugh was simply the greatest passer the game has known.

SMU and TCU were so acrobatic, throwing the ball around like rugby players zipping in echelon formation down the field, that the efficient Aggies went nearly half of their championship season before the headlines grew large and the applause deafening.

"Coach Norton was ahead of his time," said Kimbrough. "We were running a pro offense in 1939. We had two talented passers in Cotton Price and Marion Pugh, and we lined up with wide receivers, the way they do today. We also used a lot of open blocking, one on one, instead of double teaming at the point of attack."

Jarrin' Jawn had missed most of his freshman season with a knee injury, and had to work his way into the starting lineup from the fourth string. Norton eased his path by moving Marshall Robnett and Bill Audish to guard and Odell Herman to center to back up Tommie

Vaughn. Jim Thomason, another power runner who felt at home as a fullback, had been switched to blocking back.

Norton had a gift for moving a player from one position to a needier one, and watching them turn into stars. He put a priority on speed and quickness in the line, and these moves became the key to A&M's splendid line play, opening the holes and hounding opposing backs.

Their average of allowing 1.71 yards per play was still standing as a national record more than fifty years later.

The Aggies were two and three deep at the skill positions. Homer did not substitute frequently, but alternated his quarterbacks and his two halfbacks, Bill Conatser and the sophomore Derace Moser, both triple threats.

There was one personal oddity related to Marion Pugh, out of Fort Worth's North Side High. The writers of the time insisted on printing his nickname as "Duke." Actually, it was "Dookie," a play on his last name, as in the cartoon character, Peppy Le Pew. What can we say? It passed for Aggie humor.

The preseason polls picked TCU and SMU to fight it out for the title, no surprise, and the Aggies to finish fifth. There was a sense among many that the Aggies had lost their best shot at a conference title with the graduation of the dangerous Dick Todd.

Norton could only lament the faulty timing. If Todd had come along two years later, joining Kimbrough in the backfield for their junior and senior seasons, the Aggies could have charged the other teams admission.

Homer called Todd "the greatest broken field runner I have ever seen. Possibly, the next best is Red Grange."

Grange, known as "The Galloping Ghost," had been considered an all-timer at Illinois, and was a box office attraction in the pros. His agent was a flamboyant and creative character named C. C. (Cash and Carry) Pyle. Red stayed in the public eye as one of the first football analysts on TV, where his grammar may have set college standards back several years. He was fond of offering such insights as, "Chicago are using a seven-diamond defense."

But Todd was gone and the Aggies had an additional worry when Cotton Price suffered severe burns in a gasoline fire during the summer. But Price, a senior with blond good looks and an easy poise, put himself through a difficult therapy and reported in time for fall practice.

After shutting out Oklahoma A&M (now State) in the opener, the Cadets blanked Centenary, as seven members of their Most Wanted list started and twelve more played as subs. Norton and his staff, Marty Karow, Dough Rollins and Uncle Bill James, were doing a slick and prudent job of feeding these anointed players into the lineup.

Santa Clara had won the last two Sugar Bowls, and the Aggies were no longer a mystery team when they rallied in the fourth quarter to beat the Broncos, 7-3. They had trailed by the margin of that field goal for most of the night, a defensive tug of war. They won it on a 19-yard touchdown pass from Pugh to Jim Thomason.

The coaches were still experimenting with the lineup as the Aggies prepared to meet Villanova, unbeaten in 22 games, in the Rose Festival at Tyler. They had met the west and prevailed, but many of the players were nervous about this next test, against a beast from the East. To compound the fears, the Aggies had been banged up in the hard earned win at Santa Clara, and both Kimbrough and Moser were listed as doubtful starters.

Both played, but for less than two quarters.

In the locker room before the game, Thomason decided to try and lighten the mood by injecting a regional bias. "He stepped up on one of the benches," remembered the future reverend, Joe Boyd, "and announced, 'Fellows, the granddaddy of those old boys shot my granddaddy right through the nose. Let's get 'em.'

"It was so ridiculous to bring the Civil War into a pregame pep talk that we all rolled off our benches and broke into laughter. It relaxed the team completely."

The Aggies were so relaxed that their starters could have showered at halftime, and perhaps some did. Blowing open what had been tabbed as a close contest, the Aggies scored all of their points in the first half of a 33-7 romp, with Kimbrough scoring twice on short runs, Pugh hitting Moser for a 49-yard touchdown pass, and Bill Conatser dazzling everyone, including the Wildcats, with a weaving, 70-yard punt return.

As the game wore on, the players exchanged insults and threats and, at one point, an irritated Thomason kicked a Villanova player in the seat of his pants. Out of the corner of his eye, the A&M blocking back saw a flag fly and one of the officials racing over to eject him.

He turned the player around and gave him an invitation he could not refuse. "Hey, kick me," said Jim, as he bent over. The Villanova lad obliged, and the official picked up his flag and called offsetting fouls.

"He almost made a field goal, with Jim as the ball," noted Joe Boyd. "But Jim was able to stay in the game. That's what I call quick thinking."

The Aggies had not yet allowed a touchdown in four victories, but no one could have imagined the circumstances surrounding their trip to Fort Worth. TCU, the defending national champion, had been staggered by injuries and were winless after three games.

Jack Odle, the successor to the beloved Davey O'Brien, was on the shelf and his backup, the promising Rusty Cowart, would start.

Yet the Frogs had not lost at home to A&M in twenty years, and the situation appeared ripe for an upset. The Aggies had their own wounded. Kimbrough and Moser were again on the injured list, along with both quarterbacks, Boyd and end Herbie Smith.

But Homer Norton belonged to the coaching ministry that preached the miracle of self-healing, also known as the Throw-Away-Your-Crutches- and-Walk school of coaching. Somehow, the injured Aggies always seemed to play.

The Horned Frogs were primed to pull it off. In the first three minutes, Cowart found Earle Clark with a 30-yard touchdown pass, and they clung to a 6-0 lead for most of the half. The touchdown was the first scored on A&M in five weeks.

In the closing seconds, Kimbrough caught a pass from Cotton Price in the flat and bulled over one defender to score from eight yards out. Neither team kicked the point and at halftime the game was tied.

In the third quarter, the Aggies controlled the ball with Kimbrough crashing into the line. Moser scored the go-ahead touchdown on an sweep for 12 yards.

With the issue still in doubt, Bill Conatser put the game away, 20-6, with another of his cross-country runs. He picked off a pass at his own eight, and for the next 92 yards followed the blocks of Kimbrough and Thomason, and outraced the TCU pursuit to the end zone.

On any other team, Conatser might have been treated as royalty, but in a backfield as loaded as A&M's he sometimes had to dig down to the 10th or 12th paragraph to find his name.

Kimbrough gained 84 yards on 23 carries and completed a 30-yard pass to Moser. Big John was tackled once behind the line for a two-yard loss by Don Looney, the rugged TCU end. The crowd stood and roared, as if stuffing Kimbrough might be the highlight of their day.

Looney would gain a secondary fame as the father of a remarkably talented but puzzling halfback, Joe Don Looney, a star at Oklahoma and a source of endless frustration for the Detroit Lions and other pro teams.

Joe Don had a habit of skipping meetings and practices and the Lions dispatched Joe Schmidt, their Hall of Fame linebacker, to reason with him. Schmidt found Joe Don stretched out on the covers of his bed, listening to music. He began by telling the younger player that he, Schmidt, had not missed a practice or been late to a meeting in 13 years.

Looney jumped out of bed and yelped, "God damn, Joe, have a nap. If anyone deserves a rest, it's you."

On another occasion, during a team practice, Joe Don lifted a towering punt almost straight up, a brown speck against a clear blue sky. "How do you like that one, God?" he shouted.

You can dig through many an Aggie football archive, and not find a truly eccentric member of the second generation. The '39 team had most of the shared experiences of players at other schools: the financial and emotional damage caused by the Great Depression; parents without jobs or decent wages; a sense of desperate times.

As most teams do in a full and competitive season, the Aggies got up close to moments of laughter and tears. If the players were more serious than at other places, the explanation may have been obvious. Most of them, by far the majority, came from rural Texas.

They had country kids and poor kids on the campuses in Austin, Waco, Houston and even Dallas, too. But A&M was the university built for farmers. For the most part, football was their best way out, their best escape from the scorched earth and living off the dirt.

In itself, none of this should have guaranteed the Aggies any kind of edge. Talent isn't usually improved by the fear of an empty stomach or bare feet. But determination often is.

As they prepared to face Southern Methodist, the other preseason favorite, the Aggies were ranked fifth in the national polls, moving ahead of Notre Dame. The four teams ahead of them were, in order, Tennessee, Michigan, Cornell, and Syracuse, all undefeated and untied.

It may or may not strike you as weird, but of the surviving Aggie players, only three or four admit to being even vaguely aware of this lofty status. True, few of them read the out-of-town papers, and the *Bryan Eagle* was not exactly a wealth of information.

"We just didn't think about it," says Jim Thomason, "and I don't remember anyone talking about it. Our goal was to win the Southwest Conference. We were focused on that. And Coach Norton kept reminding us, you have to take it one game at a time. He never let up: *one game at a time.* That was how we went about it."

Baylor was up next, at Kyle Field, not a snap but a win with a twist. In the opening minute, the wispy Herb Smith tore the ball out of the hands of Jack Wilson, as he searched for a receiver, and sped 29 yards for the game's first touchdown. That was all the Aggies would need, even though Baylor kept the score right there, 7-0, for the rest of the half.

After the intermission, A&M added a touchdown in each quarter on short runs by Kimbrough and Moser, and the Bears were turned away, 20-0.

A week later, the Aggies would raise their record to 7-and-zip. Sub quarterback Marlin Jeffrey gave the ailing Price and Pugh a rest, starting the scoring with a 60-yard pass to Herb Smith. Bill Conatser rushed for one touchdown and caught a 46-yard pass for another from Moser, in a 27-0 pasting. The shutout was A&M's fourth.

On Armistice Day, the Aggies would survive their closest call of the season, in the rain and slop at Kyle Field, against an SMU team blessed with a great punter in Preston Johnston. The Mustangs had lost only one game, to Notre Dame, by a point, 20-19.

In the second quarter, the Aggies caught the break both teams had been craving. Johnston fumbled trying to get off a punt and Tommie Vaughn recovered at the SMU 11-yard line. Norton had given Jeffrey, his only healthy quarterback, another start, and the sophomore needed no signal from the bench to know what to call.

He called Kimbrough's number three times and on the third Big Jawn barged into the end zone. That touchdown lead hardly looked secure, as both teams struggled on the slippery field. Bill Conatser had a 74-yard quick kick and a run almost as long called back by penalties.

Then, in the fourth quarter, a goal line stand kept the Mustangs from scoring, but forced Conatser to punt from his own end zone. Roland Goss, rushing from his end position, blocked the punt and a scramble followed, with Conatser pulling the ball to his chest for a safety.

That was how the game ended, by the odd score of 6-2. With their eighth win in a row, the Aggies moved up to third in the land, which might have excited them if they had known about it.

Between them the teams scored a total of eight points, but the game was so tense, the bounces so odd, the mistakes so frequent, that the venerable Jinx Tucker needed 17 pages of copy to describe it for the *Waco Tribune-Herald*. All through his story, the grizzled Tucker referred to Kimbrough as "Big Jim." Which only goes to show that even 65 years ago, writers and editors were not catching all the errors.

Rice (19-0) and Texas (20-0) were victims of the Aggie whitewash in the final two games, but the stubborn, sophomore-laden Longhorns made it a struggle for a half. And therein hangs a tale.

Norton always feared the Longhorns, in good years and bad, no matter what the scenario, or the point spread. He did not take the Owls lightly, either, but he knew the Aggies were a much better team and against Rice that was usually good enough.

But for more than a century, stunned A&M coaches have been baffled by the ability of Texas to play better than they were capable of playing when confronted by a maroon jersey. The great philosopher, Bear Bryant, once pondered this mystery and finally concluded, with disgust: "They just hate us more than we hate them."

Coach Norton was determined not to leave the game to fate, and for certain he would not rely on his team winning on merit. Homer spent a good part of the week in practice rehearsing the Aggies on the gimmick so dear to his heart: the hideout play.

Texas won the opening toss, leaving the Aggies with the option to start the second half. When the teams went to the locker room,

Norton was miserable because the scoreboard was blank, and the Horns were playing the Aggies even, as he knew they would.

Only one thought offered him comfort. He was practically dry washing his hands as he entered the visitors' quarters, looked around and told his team: "Okay, boys, it's time to try the hideout play."

Earl (Bama) Smith was A&M's fastest back, and he was subbed into the lineup to start the second half. When Cotton Price brought Longhorn Jack Crain's kickoff back to the Aggies' 30-yard line, Smith hid out near the sideline, with fellow squadmen forming a backdrop to shield him. On the snap to Price, Smith sprinted down the sideline, caught the pass, which was slightly under-thrown, and made it to the Texas 26 before Gilly Davis caught him from behind and made the tackle.

Four plays later, from the 16, Price passed to Jim Sterling in the end zone for the tie-breaking score. The genie was out of the bottle.

A 37-yard completion from Price to Herbie Smith set up the second Aggie touchdown by Conatser. A monster break set up the third. On a punt, the Longhorns' David Thayer was guilty of a "disqualifying foul" on an Aggie player while the ball was still in the air.

Thayer was ejected and A&M took possession at the point of the foul, the Texas 14-yard line. On third down, Kimbrough banged across for another touchdown, and Rock Audish kicked the final point as the Aggies closed out their 10th win, 20-0.

The touchdown gave the conference scoring title to Kimbrough, who played 59 minutes, even though he injured his leg in the third quarter and twice was forced to call time. He refused to come out until just before the final gun.

Although they had to sweat for the win, the swarming Maroon defense, sparked by the inspired Marshall Robnett, held Texas to a net total of 24 yards.

The headlines the next day, December 1st, touched on events far removed from College Station:

"FINN CABINET RESIGNS, MOSCOW SURRENDER DEADLINE PASSES."

"ROOSEVELT CALLS ON RUSSIA AND FINLAND NOT TO BOMB CIVILIANS."

"HELSINKI IS AFLAME FROM AIR ATTACKS."

Although they would be involved in it far sooner than they could have imagined, the A&M players were blissfully unaware of the Russian threat to Finland, or the German invasion of Poland in September. Finland and Poland were not in the Top Ten.

In more ways than one, Homer Norton and the Aggies had paid off all their creditors. The perfect season was their first since the 1919 team, under D. X. Bible, was undefeated and untied. That team polished off a 10-game season with a 7-0 victory over Texas.

But those Aggies had no bowl invitation, partly because there were no bowl games available to them. [The twice-beaten 1921 team appeared in the first Dixie Classic, in Dallas, later the Cotton Bowl. The Aggies whipped Centre College in what became the historic E. King Gill, Twelfth Man game.]

Twenty years had elapsed between flawless seasons, and the Aggies finished Number 1 in the Associated Press poll. As the national champions, they had the right to be insulted when the Rose Bowl invited Number 2 Tennessee to play Number 3 Southern Cal.

That left the Aggies to accept a bid from the Sugar Bowl to meet Tulane, ranked Number 5. But the post-season action unfolded to the total benefit of the Aggies.

USC would hand a 14-0 thumping to Tennessee, coached by General Bob Neyland, who had played his freshman year at A&M under Charley Moran before receiving an appointment to West Point.

The Aggies were in awe of New Orleans, and the French Quarter, and the elegant ladies who leaned out of windows to show off their cleavage, and make promises of heavenly delights. It is safe to say that few of the players had been to the Crescent City, had sampled the kind of exotic drinks served in the bistros on Bourbon Street, or tasted French cuisine.

But even before they arrived in town for the game, their hot streak continued. A monsoon had struck College Station while the players were on the Christmas break, turning the field at Kyle Field into a swamp.

Coach Norton made a quick decision to take his team by train to Biloxi, Mississippi, and it proved to be a master stroke. They practiced for a week on a field that had lush green grass, in a town isolated from all the commotion of New Orleans—and even the slight distractions of

College Station. On the day of the game, they dressed, boarded two buses and drove to Tulane Stadium, arriving two and a half hours before the kickoff.

Only one problem was disconcerting. All three quarterbacks were ailing. Young Jeffrey was out with a sprained and swollen ankle. Marion Pugh was still weak from a bout with the flu. And Cotton Price was favoring a trick knee that bothered him through the latter part of the season.

Price had been fitted with a brace and would start the game, while Coach Norton prayed. If the worst happened, Homer's emergency plan consisted of having Jim Thomason call the signals.

The Aggies would do what Aggies always did in a crisis. They would soldier on.

A crowd of 72,000 filled the stadium as the Aggies threatened first, but were stopped at the Tulane two-yard line. On their next drive, they reached the three and this time Kimbrough jammed it across. Price kicked the point and the Aggies led, 7-0.

That remained the score until the third quarter, when Bob Kellogg returned Derace Moser's quick kick 76 yards for a touchdown. To the joy of the hometown crowd, Tulane had tied the score and would soon go ahead.

Early in the fourth quarter, the Green Wave took advantage of a fumble at the Aggie 38. Halfback Monette Butler—no relation to Rhett—rushed for the touchdown and Tulane led.

Now came one of the plays of the day. Herbie Smith blocked the extra point attempt to keep the score at 13-7, and the Aggies began a long, clock-consuming comeback.

After the kickoff, they drove 70 maddening yards, in seven plays, with Kimbrough powering his way for most of it. From the Tulane 26, Cotton Price passed to Herbie Smith to the 10, and Smith flipped a lateral to the Aggie fullback for the final dime.

As the stadium dissolved into bedlam, Price's kick sailed through the uprights. The Aggies had won, 14-13, in the game that would be voted the best of all Sugar Bowls. The win gave them the undisputed national championship.

The post-game praise and headlines belonged to Kimbrough, who drew raves from such renowned scribes as Grantland Rice and Arch Ward. Number 39—a number he was given randomly, but now seemed so symbolic—won the Most Valuable Player Award. But the storybook hero had to be Herb Smith, the little fireball who had been treated for flu symptoms and nausea only minutes before the kickoff.

In the Aggie game plan, the 150-pound end had been assigned to double team Tulane's All-American tackle, Harley McCollum, with help from Ernie Pannell.

The Aggie team doctor, Henry Harrison, tried to ignore the pleadings of the little man, but finally relented and gave him permission to enter the game. Herbie immediately checked in as a sub for Dog Dawson and played the final 59 minutes. After a few plays, Smith decided he could handle McCollum without help. Turning to Pannell, in words that even today sound brazen, Herb said, "Ernie, you go for the linebacker. I can take care of this big s.o.b. all by myself."

He did so thorough a job that McCollum was yanked from the game after just twenty-two minutes. And, of course, it was Herb Smith who went airborne to block what would have been Tulane's 14th point.

Kimbrough got the trophy, but Smith went home with the souvenir of victory—a Tulane helmet. He had made a wager with Tulane's Harry Hays, a halfback who had been Herbie's teammate at San Angelo High School in West Texas. They had bet their headgear on the outcome of the game.

Three years earlier, Homer Norton had been a patient at the Mayo Clinic, after surgery to remove a few feet of his intestines, a remedy of last resort for ulcers. The team outlook was grim, and the school had been unable to pay down on a stadium debt of a quarter million dollars.

Now Homer was the coach of the best college football team in America. The Sugar Bowl check, and deposits on season tickets for the 1940 season, paid off the stadium in full and retired a $30,000 loan from the school.

Forgive us if we repeat ourselves, but some stories are worth repeating. The Athletic Council tore up his existing contract and gave him a new one for five years at an annual salary of $10,000. All other members of the staff, including the trainer and equipment man and secretaries, were given bonuses equal to ten percent of their salaries.

Something wonderful had happened to a good person and a deserving team and a school whose spirit could not be denied. The players celebrated that night in the French Quarter, and left New Orleans the next morning not much worse off than it had been before they came.

On the train bound for College Station, Dog Dawson walked through one of the cars waving a newspaper and pointing to a headline: "Hey," he shouted, "it says here we're the national champions. Did you know that?"

Tommie Vaughn, the center and team leader, known as Noise, looked up and said, "Hell, no. National champions? What is that, exactly?"

Howard Shelton

Chapter 8

Q. & A.—True Blue
WITH HOWARD SHELTON

They were known as cannon fodder, scout teams, scrubs. At A&M, they were the Blue Boys and Shelton was one of the leaders. Never a star, he took his role seriously, and years later became the president of the '39 alumni club and the team historian; his memory was still crisp, up to the last months before Howard passed away in the spring of 2006.

Q. How hard were the economic times?
A. Everybody was in the same boat. No one was down because they were poor, had holes in the knees of their pants, and so forth. There was just no money among anybody."

Q. How was the campus life at Texas A&M?
A. I had been there the year before I actually started going to school. I had visited a guy who lived in the dormitory. There were project houses south of Kyle Field. In fact, the project house Number 11 was located where the Texas A&M Foundation building is today. We lived in two of those houses, not too far from the stadium. Not just the football team, but basketball and baseball and a few track athletes, lived in the project houses.

From there, we walked to the campus and to class. There were no buses. I don't know how long the athletic department occupied those project houses, but we lived there the first two years and then we moved in the fall of 1939 into the new south campus. It was brand new. We occupied the Number. 12 dormitory. A lot of us stayed with our military units. My classmates were juniors at that time. I was first sergeant of K infantry. (Charles) Henke and Marshall (Robnett) lived in my dorm. John and Jack Kimbrough were over in E infantry.

Tommie Vaughn, (Jim) Thomason and some others lived over in Dorm 12, which was the athletic dorm at that time, even though all of us were in the military. Tommie became our Battalion Commander; and I was company commander. Thomason was a lieutenant colonel on the infantry staff. There were others who lived out with their companies.

Q. What exactly did being in the military mean?

A. That meant that you had a class and you had a lab in military. That was part of your course. That also entailed going to camp between your junior and senior year. The year after we were national champions, we went to camp in San Antonio and went on maneuvers in New Mexico for half of the summer. We got paid, not much, but that really helped in our senior year. You had to work in the summer to have any money during the school year.

Q. What were some of your summer jobs?

A. I was on a survey crew. The head of the highway department in Hillsboro was a Longhorn, but he hired me anyhow. I hurt my knee in spring practice my freshman year and I was redshirted. Due to the fact that I had a government scholarship, I had to work. So I tutored the freshmen—"Jitterbug" Henderson and that crowd. In fact, I lived down there with them.

Jitterbug was just a great guy, a fun guy. I was a sophomore and he was a freshman. He would always do things to me that would require I get the board (the paddle) after him. He just loved that. He would involve his friends, so that I would have to take the board to them. They would pull pranks, trivial things. And I would literally have to whip them with a board.

Anyway, on Fish Day that year, they all came to my room and got me, stripped me down to my underwear and left me out on the lonely road and I had to walk back. That's the day the freshmen do anything they want. It was an honor to me that they thought enough of me to do that.

Q. A&M and College Station must have been vastly different looking
   places back then?

A. Oh yeah, it was. We had resident halls right on the street. That's
   now the Joe Routt and John Kimbrough Boulevards. The coach
   lived on that street, and so did the dean. When you left the stadium to go to class or to the dorm, you'd go right in front of their
   homes. I would not say that it was a desolate atmosphere. It was
   a typical residential, college layout. But there was nothing to do.
   We didn't have money to eat at a restaurant.

   We were glad to get what was on the training table, when we
   were in football season. When we weren't, we ate with our companies. At the training table, you had unlimited supply of milk and
   other items. You wouldn't have that if you were out with the companies. You wouldn't have a different menu necessarily, you'd just
   have more quantities.

Q. What did you do for fun?

A. The most fun we ever had were the dances on the weekends during
   the fall. Like the T-club dance. When we were seniors, I was president of the T-club, which was open to anyone who had a letter in
   a major sport. The sole purpose to be in it was to attend the T-club
   dance.

   I don't remember how we financed them, but we'd have Wayne
   King or Tommy Dorsey or someone like that on a Friday night.
   Only the T-club members and their dates could attend. Then on
   Saturday night, you'd have a Corps dance. The same orchestra
   would play for both.

Q. Where did the girls come from?

A. The girls were friends from our hometowns—Hillsboro in my case
   —or wherever. We usually vacated a dormitory for the girls to stay
   in. Or residents in Bryan would have a room. My girl, I brought
   her down from Hillsboro. She'd come down on the bus and I'd take
   her over to this residence. That's where she stayed for the weekend.
   She'd get on the bus on Sunday afternoon and go back home.

   That was the most fun that we had. For more routine fun, there
   was a hamburger and beer joint on Wellborn Road called Hard

Liquors. If you had any money, you'd go down there in the off season and drink a beer. It was walking distance from campus. On the west exit that now goes to the airport, University Drive, we had a night club out there. They'd have a band on Saturday night. You'd go out there if you had any money at all, with a date or without a date, and this place was decorated with pictures of athletes all over the wall. It's gone now.

Q. Any good stories from those T-club dances or nights out?

A. I remember one Mother's Day we had a dance that Saturday night and I had a date down from Hillsboro. It might have been a T-club dance. We danced all night long. When I headed back to my room, my mother was sitting on the bus bench in front of my dormitory. She had ridden down on the bus for Mother's Day and was just waiting for me.

Q. How much was it to go grab a beer?

A. Hardly anything. Maybe twenty-five cents. But we didn't' do a lot of that. Generally, our activities were limited to school and sports. We had about 7,500 students on campus, and most of us were pretty close to broke.

Q. Were you at all reluctant about going to Texas A&M because of the lack of women?

A. No, I had no choice in the matter. That was the only scholarship I had. It was that or none. There was no reluctance about that. I was glad to have it. Besides, I really fit in more at A&M. My closest friend was a year ahead of me at A&M and he had a car. His daddy farmed all the land just east of downtown Hillsboro that is now a big outlet shopping center. We double dated in a Chevrolet his daddy bought him, a one-seater. It had a rumble seat in the back, but you were sitting outside. So in the winter, four of us would all be in one seat. In the summer, we'd be in the rumble seat.

Q. How did you get from Hillsboro to campus?

A. You hitchhiked. You had no problem in Hillsboro. In 10 minutes, you'd be in a car going to Waco. When you got to Waco, they'd let you out where Highway 6 goes to Bryan. There would always be a long line, a crowd of people there. They were all Aggies. There would always be a crowd there. Tommie Vaughn and Jim Thomason had an old Model T Ford. No one else had any cars. So, you highwayed it. That's where the Gig 'Em sign came from. Thumbs up. You'd actually stand out there and a car would come along and you'd give them a thumb. Sure enough, they'd pull up. Maybe the car would be full, and they'd say, 'I'm sorry, we got full up.' But there was a different attitude about highwaying then. But then it was a means of transportation. I never rode the bus. And you met a lot of nice people. You'd wear your uniform. Seniors wore their boots. Everyone was very polite, because you knew your next ride or the next ride your classmate was trying to get depended on the way you treated the people that picked you up.

Q. Back in those days, before limited scholarships, there were plenty of players on the team, right?

A. Yeah, we had a ton of scholarships when we were freshmen. And there were two kinds of scholarships. One came with $5 a month and one without. The ones without it were athletic scholarships, but they were funded from a different source. I don't know what that was. We didn't care. But for those guys that got the $5 a month, it was pretty good. Everybody was trying to make the team. We knew if we didn't do well enough, we might have to go home. The coaches could cut you. They cut a bunch of guys.

Q. What did you think about Homer Norton?

A. Smart guy. He was ahead of his time in football smarts. He was not a very sociable fellow. I got to know him a lot better after graduation, going back to reunions, than I did as a player. Homer was a little bit distant and maybe that was good. He was not real close with many players. We had a much better relationship with the assistant coaches, like Marty Karow, (John) "Dough" Rollins, "Uncle" Bill James. They took a personal interest in you. We didn't have that feeling with Homer. Some of the stars might have, but the general run-of-the-mill player did not.

Q. Is it true that you would usually sell your tickets for spending money?)

A. Yes, they gave us two tickets to each game. My roommate would come by and we'd still be in the dressing room, and I'd give my tickets out the window and he'd go sell them for me. Then he would give me the money. It was usually about $3 or $4. It wasn't much, but every bit helped.

Q. During the '39 and '40 seasons, how big were your crowds?

A. People were everywhere. Every game we played in 1940, when we were champions, we sold out. At the Texas game, they were just hanging from the rafters.

When I was with this bank in Houston, I traveled to West Texas and New Mexico and Colorado and called on other banks that had deposits with us, because of the oil relationships. I was in the Colorado Springs National Bank in 1958 and I met this elderly gentleman, who was the chairman of the board asked me what my background was. I told him I went to Texas A&M.

He said I had a memorable day at A&M back in '39. I said that was the year I played football. He said he and a friend were in route to Houston on Thanksgiving Day and decided to stop by and see the A&M-Texas game? They went down there with no tickets and had to pay, I forget how much, but it was a lot of money then. He said it was a heck of ballgame and A&M beat Texas, 20-0. I said that was our championship game. He asked if I played in that game?

I said yeah, not a hell of a lot, but we all enjoyed the win. They put a picture of the game ball on our stationery. It said, *"The ball that won it all."*

Q. Did the Sugar Bowl game count toward the national championship?

A. The bowl game counted, but you didn't have the publicity regarding the national championship then that you have now. You weren't vying for it necessarily. Our goal was to win every game we played, one game at a time. I've heard Homer say it time and time and time again: one game at a time. When we beat Texas, we knew we had won the Southwest Conference and then we would go to a bowl game.

The Sugar Bowl was the game. It was really not highlighted that the winner of that game would be the national champions. I didn't know we were national champions until the next day on the train back to College Station. Somebody came down in the train and said, "Y'all know we're national champions?" I said, "Really, are we?" It was not a big deal. The big deal was that we won every game.

Q. What were the circumstances leading up to the game?

A. We practiced before the Christmas vacation. I think we were only home Christmas Eve and Christmas Day. Well, it had rained and we practiced on Kyle Field and really dug it up, and when we got back from Christmas the field was so bad, Homer said we were going to go to Gulfport, Mississippi.

So, we all got in on the train and went to Gulfport for at least a week before the game. That may have saved us because we had a great practice down there. It was a great facility, green grass, isolated. I think that was really a great help in preparing us for the game. On the day of the game, we dressed, got on the buses and drove to New Orleans, to Tulane Stadium. We got off the bus and went into the stadium and played the game and won.

After the game, we were unloaded at a downtown hotel. We went up to the desk clerk and got the keys. We had been paired two people to a room. As we got on the elevator, two at a time, there was an attendant, a waiter on the elevator, and they opened up a bottle of champagne and gave it to us and we took it to our room. Everybody got a bottle of champagne. A lot of us hadn't had a lot to drink in our lifetime before that day, so it was something of an adventure.

Q. Was it a great celebration afterward?

A. Oh, yeah. We painted the town maroon that night. We had dinner, we had the champagne and dressed and met down in the lobby and got on the bus again and went to Antoine's for dinner. It was an eight-course dinner. We couldn't wait for them to get through with that dinner so we could get out on the town. We had a hell of a time in New Orleans that night. We celebrated throughout the French Quarter, Canal Street. We got on a train and went back the next day to College Station and went back to school.

Q. After winning the national title in '39, was there even more pressure on you guys in '40?

A. No question about that. I remember the SMU game in Dallas at Ownby Stadium. It rained, but they still had to put up temporary bleachers at the south end of the stadium for all the people who wanted to see that game. Those bleachers fell and injured a lot of people. Anyway, we went into halftime of that game and it was 0-0. You go in the locker room and sit down real quiet. Coach Homer came in with his entourage and got real quiet and he says, "Texas A&M nothing, SMU nothing. What are you going to do about it?" His entourage left. That's all he said. I think the first person who got up was either John Kimbrough or Jim Thomason. Then the other got up, then Tommie said something. I think somebody else said something, too.

We knocked that door down to get out. We beat them (19-7). Homer was great at that sort of thing. Against Texas the year before, it was also 0-0 at the half. We had practiced the hideout play. So Homer said, "OK, it's time to try the hideout play." We did that as we received the kickoff.

Q. As good as the Texas win must have felt in '39, the loss to Texas in '40 must have been hard to take?

A. We had the pressure on us going into that game in '40. I think we lost that game almost from the first play. We knew on the sidelines that we were going to lose. It was just a weird feeling that it wasn't going to be our day.

Q. What happened after the 1940 loss to Texas?

A. We had a meeting of the team. Homer said that we had been invited to play in the Cotton Bowl. Some of the players got up and said they had been invited to play in the North-South All-Star game, and that game was for money. Back then, the All-Star game was a pro-deal against pro teams. So, we told Homer that we just thought it would be best to let the guys who had been invited to do that and make that money.

Besides, we didn't want to play in the Cotton Bowl. There was a vote, and the vote carried not to play. But the next day, Derace Moser got up before the team and said, "Look, we appreciate the feelings you seniors have and your reasons for not wanting to play, but we have another year. It would help our team for next year if we could play in the Cotton Bowl and win. Jim Sterling got up, too. Someone said, "Under what conditions would we play in the Cotton Bowl?"

Back then you get a little gold football locket for winning the bowl game. That's all we got the year before. (My wife) Nan wears it on her arm today as part of her bracelet. Anyway, instead of the two tickets like we normally got, every member of the team, fifty some odd players, gets $50 worth of tickets to the Cotton Bowl, which was a lot of money back then.

So, that's how the discussion went. We decided to tell the coaches that we would play in the Cotton Bowl against Fordham if we got those stipulations. They said, "OK, that's a deal." So then they had the two cages there for tickets in that old athletic office. You went to one cage and got your tickets, and went to the other cage and got your money. We got our $50. The guys who had been invited to the All-Star game were going to get paid a couple hundred dollars, but they agreed to play in the Cotton Bowl.

Q. You guys traveled by train, right? How were those long trips?

A. They were nice. We played in 1940 at UCLA and in 1939 at Santa Clara. You'd leave after practice on Tuesday. The Corps would all be down there to see you off on the train. The train would go from there to Houston to El Paso. We'd get off the train the next after-noon and work out. We'd work out and get back on the train and then we'd stop up in the mountains someplace.

That would be Thursday, and we'd work out somewhere up in the mountains and then the next day, we'd get on into San Diego or Los Angeles. We went to San Diego in '39 and LA in '40. The '39 trip, I was not a member of the traveling squad to go to San

Diego. So my friend Bubba Reeves, who was the guard, he and I played on the Blue Boy team, went to Coach Norton and he gave up his spot for me. He said, "Coach, I can't go to San Diego because my grades are not very good. I need to stay here and study. Why don't you send Howard instead? You might need a backup center." Norton said, "Bubba, I'd like to take you. But whatever you say." And he scratched out Bubba's name on the bulletin board and wrote in mine.

Q. What was the Blue Boy team?

A. The Blue Boys were the scout team and we wore blue jerseys. Anyway, Bubba made the traveling squad in '39 and I did not. It was a really classy thing for him to do. We beat Santa Clara in that game (7-3), and we stayed an extra day. The next day, we went to the World's Fair. For a bunch of boys from Hillsboro and Brownwood and other places without any money, that was a hell of an experience. I borrowed a suit from my roommate, who was not an athlete. I didn't own one. We wore suits to the fair. We toured the fair the next day and headed back.

Q. Playing on the Blue Boys must have given you a chance to come face-to-face with John Kimbrough plenty of times?

A. Oh yeah, no question about it. We played against him all week. I was a linebacker and I'm sure I tackled John Kimbrough more than any human being. John understood that the shortest distance between two points is a straight line. If you were on that straight line in his way, you were going to get hit pretty hard. He was always leaning forward, never backwards.

Q. That old cliché about being in the trenches with the guys took on new meaning as war became imminent. Did all of you go into World War II?)

A. Most of us. I was very fortunate in that I graduated Number 2 in the military. I was assigned to Camp Walters, as was Charlie Henke, and Joe Routt was there, the All-American in 1936-37. I turned down a regular army commission. I had graduated with honors in electrical engineering, and I was looking forward to a career in that field. I had a commitment to General Electric to work in New York.

About another week or so, I got a call from the colonel's office again and he sent me to see Gen. Rhineheart, our commanding officer. The bottom line, he hired me as his aide de camp for about three years. He was a Major General and we traveled all over. He sent me to the officer training school in Fort Benning Georgia, then we went overseas. He was in charge of the 8th corps in England, preparing for the invasion of Europe. In the spring of 1944, I got a call from the General and he says, "Howard, let's go down to London tomorrow. We need to see Gen. Eisenhower." So we got a driver and went to Allied headquarters. This was in late March of '44. The invasion was in June. We went into Omar Bradley's office first. In a little bit, a full Colonel came in and said, Gen. Eisenhower is ready to see you."

With that, Gen. Bradley said, "Howard, you just stay in here with me." I was a major at the time. So I didn't get in and see Eisenhower, but I did stay with Bradley. He and I had a personal visit while the General was next door. Stayed in there about 30 minutes and came back and said, "Howard, we're going back to the states." Rhineheart did not have combat experience at that time. Eisenhower insisted that all of his corps commanders had to have been in combat either in Italy or in Africa. Eisenhower said, "No reflection on you, Gen. Rhineheart, but you can go back to the states and pick up a division and bring it back over here."

To make a long story short we flew back to the States, and picked up 69th division from Camp Shelby, Mississippi. By train we went to the port in New Jersey and shipped out in time to make the Battle of the Bulge.

Q. You lost some teammates during the war, didn't you?

A. We lost Herbie Smith, a little bitty guy, who blocked the extra point against Tulane to win the championship. He was killed when his training plane went down. Derace Moser, a great ball player, was also killed in a training flight. Cotton Williams won a Silver Star and Purple Heart, but died in France in 1944 with the D-Day invasion forces.

Q. During your days at A&M, were you worried about what was happening around the world?

A. Not really. We thought about it, but you didn't worry a lot about it. We were aware of all that was going on. Actually, when we were inducted in the June of 1941, six months before Pearl Harbor, we really felt like we were going into the service for just one year. When Kimbrough signed with the football Yankees, I doubt that he thought he would go into the military.

I recall so well, December 7, 1941, in Camp Walters. This major, who had a car, was living in the barracks. He said, "Howard, this is Sunday, let's go into Fort Worth for lunch today." I was making big money then, twenty-one dollars a month. We were driving along, had the radio on. Then we heard about Pearl Harbor. He turned to me and said. "Lieutenant, welcome to a long stay." Sure enough, it turned out to be five years."

The original Reveille, 1931-1944

Coach Norton speaks with John Kimbrough (39)
Marshall Robnett, and Jack Kimbrough (40)

Chapter 9

PULP FICTION

IN A MORE ROMANTIC TIME, a more innocent time, people really did believe in Frank Merriwell—and the players who embodied his spirit and sportsmanship: among them John Kimbrough, Tom Harmon, Nile Kinnick, Bill Dudley, Banks McFadden and others of a certain era.

Merriwell was once a part of our language, our vision of the way things ought to be. He was Frank Merriwell of Yale and there was no point at which he could sanction the words, "I quit." The sports arena was then, and is today, one of the dwindling few places where the impossible still happens. It teaches us to hope. A sample of the prose common to that period makes the point:

"Something is up. Hello! Merriwell is getting out of his sweater. I believe Putnam is going to send him out."

You imagine entire crowds driven bananas by the mere act of Merriwell removing his sweater.

He was to become the fictional godfather to an entire generation of sports heroes. They populated magazines printed on pulp paper that sold for a dime, and fed the national craving for feel-good stories in a time of desperate needs.

They had names like *Thrilling Football* and *Sports Action* and *Star Sports*. They carried stories entitled, "Tide of Battle," and "Smashing Through," and "Touchdown Kid."

It was a different era, even for pulp magazines. Their advertising columns offered everything from false teeth to German Lugers to cures for prostate trouble.

The action drawings that illustrated the stories somehow always featured heroic poses, halfbacks leaping over people or stiff-arming them—and smiling.

These were the 1930's, a golden age of moonlighting, when a writer like John R. Tunis or William Campbell Gault could pick up a penny a word creating such gems as *Block That Girl*. You could support a family on twelve dollars a week back in 1939, when pulp fiction was in its zenith.

Paper shortages of World War II halted publication for most, and the rest were driven out by the postwar paperback boom and a new national obsession, television. Nevertheless, a good many gridiron thrills were preserved in those yellowing pages, and the stories inspired the young athletes of another day.

The Roaring Twenties had been dubbed The Golden Age of Sport, and it spawned an interesting trend: sportswriters who honed their craft in the name of literature. Ring Lardner, Damon Runyon, Heywood Broun, Paul Gallico, and Ernest Hemingway had made the leap: from the perspiring arts to writing books and screenplays.

There was ample precedent. Winston Churchill had covered cricket during the Boer War. *The New York Times'* John Kieran was a sportswriter, but much more. When students at Yale protested that a sports reporter had been invited to give their commencement address, he delivered his speech in Latin.

Oddly, neither elegance nor stirring, rah-rah description had reached into the sports pages of the Southwest Conference. This may be viewed as a reflection of the seriousness with which Texans took their football than an indictment of Texas sports journalism.

But the coverage of the superb Aggie teams of 1939 and 1940 make the point. Removed from the metropolitan centers of Dallas and Houston, the Aggies labored in relative privacy. The accounts of their victories were for the most part bare bones; locker room sidebars or mid-week features infrequent, if not ignored.

The grandfathers of today's student bodies might recognize the by-lines in the chapters just ahead: Felix McKnight, in Dallas; Bruce Layer and Lloyd Gregory, in Houston; Jinx Tucker, in Waco; and Harold Ratliff, then a young hustler with the Associated Press who would become the dean of Southwest Conference writers in the 1950's and '60s.

Jinx Tucker had a following among fans and other writers, but his biting humor seldom surfaced in his game stories. Once, when the underwater explorer Jacques Cousteau prepared for a dive some 1,500 fathoms below the sea, Jinx confided to his readers: "When he gets there, we hope he will say hello to the Waco Tigers," referring to the local baseball team, then running last in the Big State League.

Ratliff became notorious for his constant baiting of college and pro coaches. Once, he asked Tom Landry, eventually revered as the architect of the Dallas Cowboys, what he considered the ideal "field position"—a phrase then in fashion.

The facial expressions of writers huddled nearby warned Landry to be wary, a courtesy he didn't really require. "Harold," he said, "I am personally attracted to my opponents' one-yard line."

But early deadlines and primitive methods of transmission made it hard to be creative when reporting Saturday's games. Most writers followed the same ritual. They filed for their first editions what was called the "running," a play-by-play narrative each reporter kept, since this service was not yet available on any reliable basis.

Until trained stat crews brought an accuracy and detail to the press box that eased the burden, this scene was repeated throughout the game. One writer would nudge another in the ribs with an elbow and ask, "Did you see what happened on that last play?"

Much of the information that appeared in the next day's papers was inconsistent and incomplete, but few readers expected much more. In some cases, the reporter would knock out a lead paragraph and then tack on their running—the entire play-by-play of the game.

Routinely, the second or third paragraph of many a story would consist of the sentence:

"The Aggies won the coin toss and elected to receive."

The pity of all this was the fact that the noble and gifted teams of the Thirties missed entirely the decades of wonderful writing that began to bloom in the Fifties.

The brilliant Blackie Sherrod headed a remarkable staff on the *Fort Worth Star-Telegram*, with such talents as Dan Jenkins, Bud Shrake, and Gary Cartwright. Tex Maule was a towering presence on the *Dallas Morning News*, and later a star *at Sports Illustrated*. Jack Gallagher, Tom Davison, and Clark Nealon provided a choice of styles for the *Houston Post*. Dave Campbell had succeeded Tucker in Waco, and along with Orville Henry in Little Rock and Lou Maysel in Austin wrote the kind of stories that were virtual scouting reports for coaches.

Still, the 1939 National Champions hardly missed the publicity. They didn't really expect it; didn't know for a long while how much they deserved it.

But in the pages that follow, you can reflect on the irony of coaches unafraid to open up, while the writers played it straight.

Chapter 10

GAME BY GAME—1939

Bill Conatser

Texas Aggies Smother
Oklahoma A&M, 32-0, in Opener

Derace Moser Sparks Offense of Norton Eleven

By Austin Bealmear

OKLAHOMA CITY, Sept. 23—(AP)—Texas A&M's towering Cadets tuned up for the title chase in the Southwest conference here by taking the football forces of Oklahoma A&M college apart, 32 to 0, in the season's opener on the sun baked turf of Taft stadium.

Six thousand sweltering fans watch the Texans run over a badly outclassed Missouri Valley conference club, making its first appearance under Head Coach Jim Lookabaugh in plus 90-degree heat.

Norton Experiments

Coach Homer Norton left his regulars in the game long enough to two quick scoring thrusts in the opening periods, then spent the rest of the afternoon experimenting with various combinations, each of which clicked almost as effectively as the first.

In unleashing enough power to carry them a long way in the high class Southwest loop this year, the Texans unwrapped a 180-pound sophomore, Derace Moser, who ran the halfback post once claimed by the great Dick Todd and earned the title of ace of the Cadet offense in his first college game.

Midway in the first period Moser uncorked a 39-yard run, which took him to the 15-yard line and set the stage for the first touchdown. John Kimbrough, 220-pound fullback, smashed over from two yards away, four plays later. Marshall Robnett missed the kick for point.

60-yard Run for Moser

The Oklahomans punted soon after the next kickoff and Moser took the ball on his own 40, scampered to the sideline and outran the entire Cowboy team to cross the goal line without being touched. Robnett's kick again was wide.

The Texans penetrated to the 11-yard line early in the second period, and Bill Dawson tried a field goal from the 18, but it was short.

After a punt exchange, the Texans engineered a 68-yard march, which ended with Marion Pugh smashing over from the 18-yard line for the third counter. Bill Conatser's 35-yard gallop and shorter gains by Pugh and Marland Jeffrey featured the drive, all on the ground. Dawson kicked the extra point.

Conatser Scores

After a scoreless third quarter, in which the Oklahomans succeeded in holding the Texas reserves pretty well in check, the Cadets opened the final period with a behind-the-line pass which was good for 29 yards and a touchdown, but the play was called back because of a penalty.

As if to avenge the loss of the ball to the Cowboys, Conatser gathered the next Cowboy punt in midfield and raced through the entire Oklahoma team behind splendid blocking for 50 yards and the fourth touchdown. Bill Audish kicked the extra point.

At that point Norton returned his original combination to the game and the regulars went to work with Moser, John Kimbrough and Cotton Price ripping off one sizable gain after another.

They started on their own 18 and drove to the Oklahoma 43 before a fumble cost them the ball. On the first play the Cowboys tried after recovering the fumble, Moser intercepted Jack Wurtz's long pass at his own 45, and zig-zagged 23 yards to the Oklahoma 32.

Here the Texans took to the air, Price passing to Jim Thomason for 17 and Moser tossing to price for 11 more. Thomason then carried the ball three times and split the Cowboy line on the third attempt from the two-yard line for the final tally. Dawson's kick for extra point was wide.

"Dog" Dawson

Kimbrough Supplies Power
As Aggies Defeat Centenary

Big Fullback Scores Twice in 14-0 Victory

By Felix R. McKnight

COLLEGE STATION, Sept. 30—(AP)—Jarrin' John Kimbrough twice blew down the bandaged Centenary Gents today, the Texas Aggies salting down a 14-0 triumph that buried, decisively, a seven-year jinx before 10,000 homefolk.

Outclassed, offensively, a Centenary team that surged only to the Cadet 40-yard line, twice folded before Kimbrough's destructive power driving and staved off other threats only on sheer stubbornness.

The massive Aggie line passed out yardage on the dole basis, permitting only 52 yards by ground and 11 by air. Meanwhile, a gang of Cadets that finally numbered 33 before the slaying was over, totaled 261 yards on combined running and passing.

Gents Line Fights Hard

Crippled even before start of the game, the Gents, encased in leg bandages and shoulder harnesses, suffered several more hurts, but never did its big line, led by Loyd Hearne, give the Aggies easy going.

One more Aggie touchdown, a magnificent 64-yard punt return by Bill Conatser down the sidelines, was nullified when officials recalled the play on an offside penalty. Big Bill Dawson's attempted field goal from the 13-yard line late in the second period drifted wide of the bar.

Stubborn Centenary, which until today hadn't been licked by the Cadets since 1931, was unable to move itself but was a worrisome bunch on the defense throughout the first period, twice repelling Aggie drives before Kimbrough put across his first touchdown on a strange amble wide of his left tackle.

Walemon (Cotton) Price set up the scoring play with a 10-yard pass Jim Thomason speared and carried 24 more to the Centenary 16.

Outrun Secondary

Kimbrough started over left tackle, found the door closed and then swung out around end to outrun the Gents secondary over the play on an offside penalty. Big Bill Dawson's attempted field goal from the 13-yard line late in the second period drifted wide of the bar.

Second stringers poured into the game and started punching through the Gents line on Bill Conatser's spinners and Marion Pugh's accurate passes to Duncan and White to travel from their own 28 to the Centenary 33 before the aerial raid was dissolved. First stringers re-entered the game and Sophomore Derace Moser grabbed Weenie Bynum's long punt and hurried 35 yards down the sidelines to the Centenary 37.

Moser, a great runner, first downed on a tackle thrust to the 27 and Price passed to Moser down on the 12, the slippery soph picking up seven more to the five, but Dawson's attempted field goal ended that drive.

One long drive, starting at their own 44 yard line after Center Odell Herman intercepted one of Bynum's numerous passes, produced the second Aggie score.

Price shot a 16-yard pass to Kimbrough on the Centenary 45 and then ran twice himself to make it a first down at the 34. Kimbrough and Jim Thomason started jarring the line and Price suddenly broke away for 12 yards to the five. Kimbrough's knees were bumping his chin when he plowed over the Centenary line, standing up, for a touchdown on his first blast. Price again delivered the extra point.

Two giant tackles, Ernie Pannell and Joe Boyd, broke up most of the Centenary playhouses, but it was Bill Buchanan, a first-year end, who stormed in with the second string and immediately became the bottom man on most of the tackles.

For Centenary's game but shattered forces, Bynum carried the load. The little fellow, himself favoring a bad leg, handled the ball on almost every Gent offensive effort.

Marion "Dookie" Pugh

Aggies Score in Last Period
to Defeat Santa Clara, 7-3

Pugh's 19-yard Pass to Thomason Nets Touchdown

By Bruce Layer, Post Sports Editor

SAN FRANCISCO, Oct. 6—The Duke of Paducah was pitching strikes in the chilled breeze that whipped over Seals stadium Friday night and pitched the Texas Aggies to a 7 to 3 victory over Santa Clara in an intersectional grid struggle that attracted a crowd of 12,000 fans.

The Duke, in case you don't know, is Marion Pugh, a big junior back from Fort Worth, and his performance was exceptionally gratifying to the few Aggie supporters here for the game.

Earlier in the evening, the Duke had looked bad when he entered the contest, but he whipped perfect aerials late in the fourth period to enable the Farmers to overhaul a 3 point Bronco lead.

Moser Takes First Pass

His first pass was to Derace Moser and went out into the flat. Moser fought his way to the 19-yard line, running down the sideline. On the very next play Pugh reversed the play, passed to Jim Thomason, a blocking back, and Thomason scampered over the goal line. He was in the clear all of the way.

For almost three quarters the game was one of those hard, head-knocking affairs with little offensive action. Then suddenly, just before the gun sounded to end the third period, Santa Clara took advantage of a break and Jim Johnson booted a 32-yard field goal to give the Broncs a 3 to 0 lead. Californians settled back to watch the Broncos protect that meager margin.

But they failed to reckon with what to expect from a trailing Southwest conference club.

The first Aggie drive was halted and Moser got off a long punt, and the quarter ended. Then as the fourth period opened Clark punted to the Aggie 29 and that is where the Aggie offense started clicking. In seven plays Thomason was over the goal line and the Aggies had a ball game.

Pugh passed to Smith for six and Jarring John Kimbrough rammed his way to the 40-yard stripe, Pugh passed to Buchanan for a first on the Bronco 49. The next pass was incomplete. Pugh passed to Moser for 5 and then the flat pass followed. The next strike went to Thomason.

After that the Aggies played heads up defensive ball. The pass defense they offered gave Santa Clara no chance and the yardage gained through the line mercly wasted up the precious remaining minutes.

Broncs Well Checked

Santa Clara's scoring opportunity came when Conatser fumbled on his own 15-yard stripe and Santa Clara was moving on when an intentionally grounded pass by McCarthy brought a 15-yard penalty and forced Johnson to try a field from his 32. He made the most of the chance and booted a perfect goal from placement.

A. & M.'s stout defensive play featured, Santa Clara was held to four first downs and gained 74 yards from scrimmage and 26 through the air.

The Aggies had nine first downs from 126 yards on running plays and 62 through the air.

Featuring the defense were Ernest Pannell, bruising tackle; Herbie Smith and Bill Buchanan, a couple of swell looking ends; Tommy Vaughn, aggressive center, Joe Boyd and Marshall Robnett.

Kimbrough and Moser were the chief ground gainers with big John showing tremendous power against the staunch Santa Clara line.

John Schiechl, an All-American center, was another Aldrich against the Aggies. He figured in about 70 percent of the plays and was the main reason the Bronco defense was double tough. Anahu, an end and Stubler, a tackle also played steady ball. Johnson was the one threat that Buck Shaw offered against Coach Homer Norton's crew, but aside from his field goal he could do little damage.

Weather is Cool

A crisp northwester, driving away clouds that gathered early in the evening, dropped the mercury to the high 40's as the teams took the field for the usual pre-game warmup.

Seals stadium, home of the San Francisco baseball club, supplied the game site and the field, running from the third base line out to deep right field, appeared to be in fine condition despite a rain Thursday night.

The skinned infield, from one goal line to near midfield, gave sound footing and the grass part of the field, although damp, promised no trouble for passers or receivers.

Fans, bundled in overcoats and blankets, were slow in coming, and the pre-game press box guess was 15,000 for Friday. Football under the arcs is new to Northern California and as a result grid followers here do not storm the turnstiles.

Santa Clara students, headed by the bands, occupied bleacher seats across the field from the regular stands. Some 300 Aggie exes, now living in California, were in the stands, and they flashed back to their days as twelfth man at Aggieland to whoop it up when the Farmers took the field.

Joe Boyd won the toss and chose to defend the south goal. Robnett kicked off to Johnson who was downed by Boyd on the Santa Clara 28.

First Period Dull

Running plays failed and an even kick exchange followed with Johnson punting for Santa Clara and Moser for the Aggies. On the next kick Johnson booted out of bounds on the Aggie 41-yard line, but the Santa Clara defense smothered three running plays and Conatser's kick was blocked by Anahu and covered by Roche on the Aggie 45.

Three running plays gained as many yards and Johnson punted out of bounds on the Aggie 23-yard line. Santa Clara was taking plenty of time in the huddle and wasting a lot of time after coming out of the huddle.

Officials seemed to okay the long delay between plays. Another exchange of punts gave the Aggies the ball on their own 37. Running plays failed and Conatser was roughed while punting, giving A. & M. first down on their own 40. It was the only first down of the period. Moser went through the line for seven yards, the first gain of the opening quarter, came as the period ended scoreless.

The second quarter opened with A. & M. drawing a 15-yard penalty when an ineligible man was down field on Pugh's incomplete pass. Conatser quick-kicked out on the Santa Clara 30.

Johnson's quick kick was blocked, but recovered by Santa Clara. Johnson then punted to Conatser who slipped and fell on his own 32-yard line. He went down on the skinned infield when he appeared to be on his way for a good return. Three running plays gained 8 yards and Conatser kicked to Peterson on his own six-yard line. He was downed on his 12-yard line. Santa Clara drew a 15-yard penalty, driving them back to their own 1-yard line.

Johnson kicked to Conatser on the Santa Clara 32 and he returned 5 yards. A shovel pass, Pugh to Conatser, followed by a lateral to Kimbrough lost 7 yards. Pugh regained 5 yards. Pugh was downed for no gain. Pugh's pass to Kimbrough was incomplete and the ball went over to Santa Clara on the Bronco 30.

Johnson kicked to Conatser who returned 20 yards to the Aggie 40 where he fumbled but Pannell covered for the Farmers. Again Santa Clara stopped the Aggie running game and Conatser got off a weak 17-yard punt on the Santa Clara 35-yard line.

Santa Clara's offense lost a yard in two tries and Johnson kicked to Conatser, who returned five yards to the Aggie 34. Moser passed to Buchanan for nine yards. Kimbrough ripped the Santa Clara line for a first down on the Santa Clara 48-yard line. Moser overshot Jeffrey with a pass and failed to gain on the next play. He was tackled hard and left the game with Spivey replacing him. Jeffrey passed to Herb Smith for eight yards.

Kimbrough raced around left end for a first down on the Santa Clara 28. Two passes failed and Dawson went in to try for a field goal, but the pass from Center was bad and the play smothered as the half ended. Score: A. & M. 0; Santa Clara 0.

Schiechl Shares Pass

A. & M. received and Conatser slipped off right tackle for eight yards, carrying the ball to the Aggie 44. Kimbrough smashed through for a first down on the Aggie 46. Conatser made seven yards at center. Jeffrey's pass was intercepted by Schiechl who was downed on Santa Clara's 48. Schiechl fumbled but the ball rolled out of bounds.

Johnson punted to Conatser who returned six yards to the Aggie 15. Conatser kicked to Johnson who was downed on the Santa Clara 48.

Aided by a five-yard offside penalty and Johnson's pass to Thom gave Santa Clara first down on the Aggie 31-yard line. It was the first time the Broncos made yardage.

Johnson gained a yard and then two passes failed before Johnson kicked across the field and out of bounds on the Aggie 13-yard line. Conatser punted to Peterson who returned 15 yards to the Aggie 45-yard line.

Santa Clara gained four yards in three tries and Johnson kicked to Conatser who returned 7 yards to the Aggie 17.

Conatser broke through for 7 yards but fumbled and Johnson recovered for Santa Clara on the Aggie 28-yard line. Johnson shot a pass to Bradfield for 13 yards and a first down on the Aggie 15.

Santa Clara Scores

Hanna hit right tackle for four yards. On a reverse Peterson made a yard. McCarthy fumbled, recovered and grounded the ball drawing a 15-yard penalty. Johnson dropped back to the 32-yard line and hit a perfect placement kick to give Santa Clara a 3 to 0 lead.

Peterson and Roche made it a first down on the Santa Clara 34 as the quarter opened. The attack bogged down and Clark punted to Moser who fumbled out of bounds on the Aggie 29.

Pugh passed to Smith for six yards. Kimbrough made it first down on the A. & M. 40. Pugh passed to Buchanan for a first down on the Santa Clara's 49. Pugh's next pass was incomplete. A shovel, Pugh to Moser, gained five yards. Pugh passed to Moser in the flat and the sophomore back bought his way to the Santa Clara 19-yard line. Pugh passed to Thomason for the touchdown. Dog Dawson went in and kicked a perfect placement. Score: Texas A. & M. 7; Santa Clara 3.

Dawson kicked to Peterson on the goal line and he ran it back to Santa Clara's 23-yard line. John Kimbrough intercepted Peterson's pass on the Santa Clara 33-yard line.

Three plays failed and Moser, back to punt, received a low pass from center, fumbled, and Santa Clara took the ball on its own 42-yard line.

Roche hit the line twice for a first down on the Aggie 47. Two passes failed. Roche hit the line for six yards. Roche broke through for a first down, but fumbled and Conatser covered on the Aggie 32-yard line.

John Kimbrough

Texas A. and M.
Jolts Villanova

By Staff Writer, *Philadelphia Inquirer*

TYLER, Tex., Oct. 14—Villanova crowded all of the poor football it didn't play last year and the year before into 30 minutes of gridiron action here this afternoon against Texas A. and M. and lost to the Aggies, 33-7. It was Villanova's first defeat since 1936 and the most humiliating reversal that the Wildcats have suffered for many years.

A crowd of 15,000 spectators saw the hard-hitting Aggies cross Villanova's goal line five times in the first half, twice in the first period and three times in the second period. Texas placement kickers harvested three out of a possible five extra points.

After the rest period, Villanova came out and played the sort of football that carried them through two undefeated seasons. Coach Clipper Smith's second and third stringers not only held the Texans scoreless in the last half, but put over a touchdown themselves on the second play of the fourth quarter.

Behot Intercepts

The period opened with the ball in Villanova's possession on the Aggies' 21, which followed Joe Behot's interception of Marion Pugh's forward late in the third quarter. Behot then rifled a pass to Romanowski, which enabled the latter to advance the ball to Texas A. and M.'s 13.

Then followed the most brilliant play Villanova engineered during the entire game—there were not many of them.

It started with Behot shooting a sharp toss to Murray, who was hit hard on the Aggie 6. But as he was going down, Murray adroitly tossed a lateral to Stem, who went over the goal line standing up. Behot then converted for the extra point bring the Wildcats' total to seven.

Thereafter, neither team was in scoring position, practically all of the night, and they did all things wrong. As a result, the Texans scored in various ways—on forwards, by rushing the ball and one touchdown, the fourth, culminated from a 75-yard run back of a punt by Conatser, a remarkable ball carrier in an open field.

When it is recorded that such a team of decisive tacklers as Villanova failed utterly to do more than make Conatser hesitate, as his swaying pipe hips and change of pace left the Wildcats flat-footed, the reader gets an idea of just how elusive this young Texan is.

However, Conatser scored only one of the five touchdowns spun by Texas A. and M. in the first half. What of the other four?

The Aggies jumped a somewhat overconfident Villanova team right at the start, breaking into the scoring column four minutes after the opening whistle. Quick work. Too quick for Villanova.

Start at Midfield

The Texans secured possession at midfield following a punt. Overhead and on the ground the Aggies immediately started on the march, and on their 13th play sent Johnny Kimbrough crashing over for a touchdown from the two-yard line.

That was that, a 50-yard march into pay-off territory. The Aggies scored their next, the second, on one heroic overhead pass.

A penalty for unnecessary roughness gave Texas the ball on Villanova's 48. With no hesitation, Pugh flung a long forward into the arms of Moser, who was a very busy ball player all afternoon, and, after making the catch on the Wildcats' 19, Moser resumed his journey over Villanova's goal line, unmolested.

Nothing more happened, nothing more could happen, during the first 15 minutes. But after the teams had changed terrain, the Villanova rout continued.

Kimbrough Scores

Getting possession on the Main Liners 35, following an exchange of punts, Pugh threw a forward to Smith that brought the play to

Villanova's 15, from which point the Aggies took the leather over in four smashing plays, Kimbrough making his second touchdown of the afternoon.

It was only two plays later that the Aggies again crossed the 'Cats goal line on a long forward pass that caught the Villanova backfield flat-footed. But the ball was called back due to the fact that a Texan had become a bit too destructive for no reason at all, and the Aggies not only lost a touchdown, but suffered a 15-yard penalty as extra punishment.

The 75-yard touchdown run of Conatser has already been described. The fifth and last trip Texas made across Villanova's goal line was directly due to a fumble by McMahon, who let the ball slip away from him when hit hard by two tacklers. This miscue gave Texas possession on the 16 and in two cracks outside tackle, a third stringer by the name of Spivey took the leather over the line. That was the end of Texas' scoring, there wasn't any more—but it was enough.

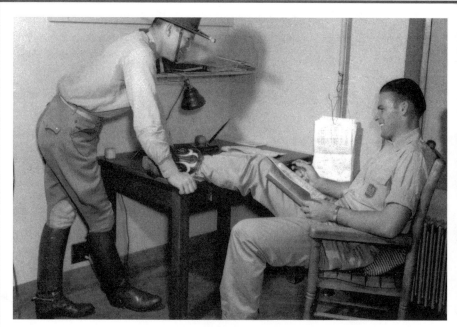

John Kimbrough (seated)

[And, now, the Texas version:]

Texas Aggies Annihilate
Villanova by 33-7 Score

By Harold V. Ratliff

TYLER, Oct. 14—(AP)—Bald Homer Norton, the gridiron master of Aggieland, turned loose a Texas hurricane here that flattened the forces of Villanova college like pancakes, burying the hitherto unbeaten Wild Cats under a 33-7 score.

Norton's greatest Texas A. & M. team blew tempestuous fury to pile up all its points in the first half, then with second and third stringers doing most of the work coasted the remainder of the way.

A crowd of 14,000 witnessed the game, played as a climaxing feature of the annual Rose festival. The tilt was a rough-and-tumble affair with several of the opposing players threatening to take pokes at each other.

The Aggies scored early in the first quarter with Big John Kimbrough who played less than a third of the game, smashing over from the two-yard line. Bill Dawson missed the goal.

The Texans had another touchdown within two minutes, Marion Pugh pitching a 31-yard pass to Derace Moser who ran 18 yards untouched for the counter. Marshall Robnett missed the goal.

A sensational punt return by Moser that carried to the Villanova 26 set the stage for the next Aggie score. Pugh passed to Herbert Smith for 10 yards, Moser circled end for seven and Kimbrough started over tackle then cut out around end for the touchdown. Robnett kicked the goal.

The next two A. & M. touchdowns were made in rapid order. After a 15-yard penalty had nullified a 35-yard touchdown pass from Marland Jeffrey to James Thomason, Bill Conatser took a punt on the

A. & M. 30 and raced through the Villanova team for the counter. Bill Audish kicked the goal.

A fumble led to the final Aggie touchdown. Leon Rahn recovered a fumble on the Villanova 10-yard line. Marshall Spivey made two, Audish three, Spivey cracked the line for the counter. Audish kicked goal.

The Wildcats came back fighting to get their touchdown early in the fourth period. Joe Behot flipped a pass to Bill Romanowski who lateraled to Paul Stenn and the latter ran 13 yards for the score. Behot kicked the goal.

While A. & M. had ruled a slight favorite to win the game, the margin of superiority astounded the noisy crowd—all partisan. Other Aggies played bruising, crashing football with Kimbrough, Moser and Pugh as the mainsprings of one of the most devastating offensives ever shown in the annual festival game here.

Leading the line was the play of the ponderous Marshall Robnett who seems to have taken up where all-American Joe Routt left off.

Villanova had come here with one of the finest records in collegiate football—19 victories in 22 games and the other three ties. But Villanova never had a chance against the driving, smashing attack of the Aggies.

The Wildcats put up a much stiffer battle in the last half with Bill Howlett's fine punting finally gaining enough in the exchanges to drive deep into Aggie territory, where Andy Chisick, who turned in a fine game at center for the Wildcats, intercepted one of Pugh's passes on the Aggie 26. Here Villanova got its passing attack to working for one score.

The Aggies made seven first downs to four and rolled up 208 yards on the ground and in the air to 74 for Villanova. The Aggie aerial offensive got as much territory as its running game. In fact, this was one of the most versatile teams ever to come out of the Southwest conference.

Kimbrough Powers Aggies to 20-6
Triumph over Horned Frogs

Farmers Fight Back After TCU Scores First

By Bruce Layer, Post Sports Editor

FORT WORTH, Oct. 21—Doc Psychology, Old Man Hex, and tradition were on the Horned Frogs' side here this midsummer afternoon, but Jarrin' John Kimbrough, the greatest fullback in America, wore the maroon and white of Texas A. & M., and he whipped all the added weight on T. C. U.'s side as the Aggies scored a 20 to 6 triumph over the 1938 Southwest Conference champions.

It was a sweet victory for A. & M.—the first scored on T. C. U. turf in 20 years—and keeps the Nortonmen as one of the major undefeated and untied teams in the nation.

For almost 30 minutes it appeared that the decade-old tradition would hold good. T. C. U. struck in lightning fashion in the first three minutes. A break gave the Horned Frogs an opening and before the crowd of 28,000 had finished filing into the stadium, Rusty Coward had whipped a 30-yard pass to Earle Clark for a touchdown and the Frogs were on their way.

Then in an inspired fashion the Frogs fought the Aggies to a standstill, but the jarrin' from John proved too much and in the fading minute of the first half the big fullback took a flat pass from Cotton Price and drove over the goal line to knot the score at 6 all.

In the set-up for the scoring play big Kimbrough, he weighs 210 pounds and runs with the drive of a freight engine, had smashed the line for 7 yards to carry the ball to the 3. There the Aggies called time and drew a five-yard penalty. The pass followed.

All Aggies in Last Half

After the half it was the Aggies all the way. The defensive play of the Maroon and White line smothered running plays and the passing failed to click as the Cadets rushed the passer and covered would-be receivers.

It was Kimbrough who set up the touchdown that broke the deadlock. Moser intercepted Cowart's pass on the Aggie 13 and tossed the ball over to Kimbrough. Jarrin' John headed for the sidelines, cut down field and returned 26 yards to the Aggie 39 before he was stopped.

Marion Pugh, the Duke who came home to show the folks a thing or two, broke off tackle to the Frog 44. From there Kimbrough raced right end for a first down on the Frog 13.

Kimbrough hit the line for a yard and then Derace Moser, high stepping soph, raced right end for the score. Audish added a needless point.

Conatser's Sprint

The other touchdown was supplied by Bill Conatser. He intercepted Cowart's pass on the Aggie 8 and raced the distance. He was afforded brilliant downfield blocking featuring Jim Thomason and Kimbrough, and when in the clear out-ran Kring.

During the first half the Aggies looked ragged in spots, but the tremendous power of a great machine was not to be denied.

Once under way, the Farmers' ground game rolled up the staggering total of 212 yards to a mere 46 for the Frogs. The Toads attempted 22 passes, completed 12 for 60 yards, and half that total came on the touchdown play. The Cadets passed 15 times, clicked five for 81 yards. The total yards showed the Aggies with 293 to 106 for the Frogs. The first downs were A. & M. 13 and T. C. U. 3, one of which came on a penalty.

Kimbrough Stopped But Once

Kimbrough carried the ball 23 times during the game for a total of 84 yards and was stopped once for at two-yard loss. He had an average of 3.56 yards per try. Besides his offensive work his blocking was vicious and his defensive play flawless.

Marshall Robnett, Joe Boyd, Herbie Smith, Charles Henke and Ernest Pannell were the defensive giants for the Aggies. They were all over the place with Robnett the pacesetter for the linemen. Jimmy Thomason, blocking back, turned in a fine job backing up the line.

Connie Sparks, Frog fullback, was stopped cold offensively, but played his heart out on defense. His work was outstanding. Don Looney was another to play a whale of a game for the Frogs. He was in many a play while in the game and was the man who dropped Kimbrough for the loss, a feat few will equal.

Offensively there was little from the Frogs. Clark, who usually runs the reverses, was injured early and missed most of the game.

He was in there long enough to slip down field for the big pass. Herring picked up a little yardage on reverses, but once the Aggie defense got set, that attack was halted. The Frogs broke out a spread, but like other formations failed to worry the Cadets.

Cotton Price, who kicked a point after touchdown here two years ago to give the Aggies a tie, returned to the Aggie lineup and was acting captain for the day. The pass he tossed to Kimbrough was a honey, as he was rushed and managed to get the ball away as three Frogs smothered him.

The defeat was the second straight for T. C. U. in league competition and it was the Aggies first appearance in championship play. They will tackle Baylor, another undefeated team, in conference play, next Saturday.

Frogs Score Quickly

Texas Christian cashed the first break of the game to score in 3 ½ minutes of play. The Frogs received, and three running plays netted 8 yards, advancing the ball to the Frog 27 where Sparks punted to Moser who fumbled and Cook recovered for T. C. U. on the Aggie 28.

Herring lost two yards on a reverse. The Aggie forwards smothered a passing play. On third down Cowart shot a long pass to Earle Clark who took the ball a couple of yard short of the goal line and stepped over. He slipped in back of Vaughn to take the pass. Boyd broke through to block Horner's placement and T. C. U. led, 6 to 0.

The Aggies received and Moser ran the ball back from his six to the 37. With Moser and Kimbrough alternating as ball carriers the Aggies advanced to the T. C. U. 34, where the drive bogged and Moser punted over the line on fourth down.

As the second quarter opened, Herring failed to gain on a reverse and Cowart overshot Herring with a pass. Sparks punted to Jeffrey and he returned 16 yards to the Aggie 32, but the Aggies were guilty of clipping and the ball was moved back to the A. & M. 12-yard stripe.

Conatser punted to Cowart in midfield and he fumbled, with Pugh covering for A. & M. on the Aggie 47.

T.C.U.'s Clark ended this threat when he intercepted Pugh's pass, intended for White, on his own 23-yard line and returned to the Frog 27.

An Aggie Surprise

Conatser made a nice 27-yard return of Sparks' kick, getting back to the T. C. U. 42, but another clipping penalty took the Aggies back to their own 43.

Big John Kimbrough faded back and shot a long pass to Conatser for a 30-yard gain and first down on the Frog 25. Kimbrough made two yards at left tackle, but Conatser lost it on the next running play. Pugh passed to Conatser for four yards. Pugh's pass over the goal line to Conatser was batted down by Cowart and the ball went to the Frogs on their own 20.

Two running plays failed and Sparks' punt was grounded on the Aggie 46.

Kimbrough made four and Pugh passed to Buchanan for a first down on the T.C.U. 44. Kimbrough faded back to pass and then raced right end for a first down on the Frog 32. On fourth and four, Price passed to Smith for a first down on the Frog 10.

An incomplete pass, a Kimbrough smash and a penalty, the Aggies faced third down from the eight. Price passed to Kimbrough in the flat and Big John was met by Cowart a yard from the goal, Kimbrough ran over the little Frog back. Moser chipped in with a fine block on Clark. Audish stubbed the try for point and the score was T. C. U. 6; A. & M 6, with less than a minute left in the first half.

Clark Injured

Clark took the kickoff at his own three and returned to the Frog 20. He was hit hard by Robnett, who had booted the ball, and Clark was aided off the field. He appeared to have a knee injury. Spud Taylor replaced him. T. C. U. was offside on a running play and that pushed them back to the 15-yard stripe. The half ended with the score tied.

TCU was late in reporting for the second half and drew a 15-yard penalty. Robnett kicked off from the Frog 45-yard stripe, as Coach Dutch Meyer raced on the field to protest the penalty. The officials changed the decision and Coach Homer Norton came on the field to give them an argument.

It was finally decided that the Aggies would kick off from their own 40. Robnett's kick went out of bounds on the 10, the ball cutting out at right angle after hitting the grid, and T. C. U. took the ball on its own 35.

Clark attempted to return to the lineup, but was limping badly and left the game after a couple of plays. He took a short pass from Cowart for four yards, the only gain of the series, and then retired. Sparks punted out of bounds on the Aggie 21-yard line.

Three running plays gained seven yards and Moser got off a very poor punt that went out of bounds on the Aggie 46. On a triple reverse, Cowart fumbled and Pannell covered for A. & M. on the Frog 49.

Pugh passed to Moser for a first down on the Frog 39. Kimbrough smashed right tackle for seven yards. Kimbrough made two and one-half yards. He failed to gain on his next try. His next smash at the line was good for a first down on the Frog 27.

Horner Snares pass

Horner intercepted a flat pass from Pugh and raced back to the Aggie 25 before Robnett overhauled him and pulled him down. It was a 41-yard return.

The Frogs tried a forward lateral, Sparks to Looney to Coward, but Looney's toss to Cowart was wide and Robnett covered for A. & M. Moser fumbled and Looney covered on the Aggie 26. Herring was tossed for 12-yard loss, but the Aggies were offside and that gave T. C. U. five and the ball on the A. & M. 21. On a reverse Sparks made four yards. Sparks fumbled going into the line and there was a scramble for the ball with Shook covering for T. C. U. The play was called back and T. C. U. drew a five-yard offside penalty. Cowart's pass to Looney was wide. Moser intercepted Cowart's pass, shot a lateral to Kimbrough and Jarrin' John raced it back to the Aggie 39. It was a 26-yard return.

Price broke through tackle for a first down on the Frog 44. Big John Kimbrough raced right end for 31 yards before being forced out of bounds to advance the ball to the Frog 13-yard line.

Moser Tallies

Kimbrough picked up a yard. Moser raced right end for 12 yards and a touchdown. Audish hit a perfect placement for the extra point and the Aggies led, 13 to 6. Fifteen seconds remained in the quarter as Robnett kicked to Spud Taylor, who returned from his six to the Frog 33 as the gun sounded. Score: Texas A. & M. 13; T.C.U. 6.

Another interception accounted for the final Aggie points and this one covered almost the length of the field.

Conatser picked off Cowart's pass intended for Brumbaugh and, behind perfect downfield blocking, he raced 92 yards for the touchdown. He ran for the sidelines, gave his teammates a chance to clear the way and then won his footrace with Kring in the final ten yards.

Dog Dawson added the extra point on a bank shot.. The ball hit a Frog player and bounced over. Score Texas A. & M. 20; T.C.U. 6.

Undefeated Farmers Trounce Baptists
For Sixth Consecutive Victory

By Lloyd Gregory, Post Staff Correspondent

COLLEGE STATION, Oct. 28—On the door of the equipment store-room in the Texas Aggie gymnasium, there hangs a challenging sign: "SO MANY BEGINNERS, SO FEW FINISHERS."
Sergeant Jim Carroll, gray-haired equipment storekeeper, who used to be a sergeant in the regular army, placed the sign there.
Coach Homer Norton's magnificent Texas Aggie grid machine, probably the greatest in the history of the school, took "Sarge" Carroll's hint here this beautiful Saturday afternoon in smashing the Baylor Bears, 20 to 0, before 21,000 customers.

Smith Steals Ball

The Aggies started fast enough, scoring a touchdown in the first minute, when "Little Herb" Smith, 173-pound end for San Angelo, "stole" the ball from "Big Jack" Wilson and raced 29 yards for a touchdown. Wilson was back to pass. A couple of husky Aggie linemen had hold of Wilson's legs when Smith grabbed the ball from the Baylor back.
Except for that one break, Morley Jennings' Bears held their own in the first half, the big green and gold line smearing "Big Jawn" Kimbrough, mighty fullback. The score at the half was A. & M. 7; Baylor 0.
But the last half belonged to the Maroon and White Cadets. The Aggie blockers went to work with a will. And as the Baylor defense concentrated on stopping the bull-like rushes of Kimbrough inside

tackles, Derace Moser, classy sophomore from Stephenville, skipped merrily around the Baylor ends.

Aggies Have Everything

The Aggies showed just about everything you'd expect of a classy football team:

They netted 240 yards from scrimmage, compared with 44 for the opposition. Poor punting in recent years had plagued Norton's teams; but Saturday the Aggies averaged close to 43 yards on their boots. Moser once pulled the Aggies out of a hole with a 70-yard quick-kick.

Charles Henke, 204-pound guard from Kerrville, and Marshall Robnett, 205-pound guard from Klondike, blocked well, and had much to do with the success of their team's running attack.

Joe Boyd, 210-pound tackle from Dallas; and Ernest Pannell, 207-pound tackle from Waco, looked good on defense. Defensive laurels for the day, however, went to the Aggie ends, Herb Smith and Bill Buchanan.

Dough Rollins, Aggie end coach, insists Smith, pound for pound, is the finest end in the country, and he may be right.

Baylor's pet play was to run the speedy, 200-pound Jack Wilson wide around the left side of the Aggie line. Smith would dive into the blockers, stripping the interference, and leaving Wilson an easy mark for the hard-tackling Jim Thomason, who was backing up the left side of the line.

Tommie Vaughn, 185-pound center from Brownwood, also looked good in backing up the line.

Kimbrough Not Only Gun

Operating from a single or double wingback, the Aggies were smooth and polished. It was difficult for the defense to figure just where the Aggies would strike.

They have the Southwest conference's best line smasher in "Big Jawn" Kimbrough; but he is by no means their only big gun. This Moser is a whirlwind at carrying the mail. "Cotton" Price also looked good carrying the ball.

Jim Thomason, 200-pound back from Brownwood, is as valuable a man as the Aggies can offer. He is a crushing blocker, and tackles savagely.

Marion Pugh is one of the league's best forward passers.

Patterson Sorely Missed

The game demonstrated how sorely the Bears miss Billy Patterson, their marvelous triple-theater of last year. When their running attack was smeared, the Bears were through, completing only two passes.

Although his legs and shoulders were in bad shape, Robert Nelson, 210-pound Baylor center from Bryan, was the outstanding defensive player for the Green and Gold, backing up the line with teeth-rattling tackles.

Jack Wilson also looked good on defense; but had a net yardage gain of only half a yard a try. Wilson is big, fast and powerful, and a truly great prospect.

The Aggies kicked off to start the game, and Wilson returned 25 to his own 34.

Wilson smashed center for two, carrying to the Baylor 36. On second down, Wilson fell back as if to pass. The Aggie forwards charged through viciously. Herb Smith, Aggie end, "stole" the ball and ran 29 yards for a touchdown.

Price kicked goal, and the Aggies led, 7 to 0, in the first minute.

Shortly thereafter Witt sparked a promising Baylor drive. He returned a punt 15 to the Aggie 45. Wilson gained four around the Aggie left end. Merka hit center for a yard. On a reverse around the Aggie right end, Witt gained 10, carrying to the Aggie 30.

After Herb Smith had stripped the interference, Thomason threw Wilson for a five-yard loss in a try at that Aggie left end. Thomason grabbed the powerful Wilson around the neck.

Kimbrough Snares Pass

Witt made seven through the middle, carrying to the Aggie 28. On the next play, Witt raced the Aggie right end for eight, carrying to the Aggie 20.

Kimbrough caught Wilson's forward pass in the Aggie end zone for an automatic touchback. The ball was brought out to the Aggie 20, and Moser pulled the Cadets out of a hole with a magnificent quick kick that Sterling killed on the Baylor 10—a kick good for 70 yards.

Midway of the second period, Baylor threatened again. Wilson brought back an Aggie punt 15 yards to the Aggie 36, gained six on a cutback, then passed to Grumbles for a first down at the Aggie 17. After Wilson lost two, Grumbles gained five on a quick opener outside the Aggie right tackle.

The Bears were executing their plays well, but Wilson's pass to Grumbles in the end zone was broken up by Herman, Aggie center. A pass to Witt in the flat was good for only one yard, and the ball went over to the Aggies on their own 13.

Aggies Halted Near Goal

With three minutes of the first half left, the Aggies just missed counting.

Moser intercepted a Baylor pass on the Baylor 35. He brought it back two, and, as he was tackled, lateraled to Kimbrough, who brought it back three more, the ball being killed on the Baylor 35.

Kimbrough passed to Buchanan for 13 yards, taking it to the Baylor 22. Pugh then swung into action with accurate short passes.

Pugh passed to Spivey for five. He then shot a low pass over the middle to Buchanan, who was downed on the Baylor eight for a first down. Pugh passed to Herb Smith for a three-yard gain, carrying to the five. Pugh's pass to Kimbrough was incomplete.

By now the Bears were looking for the pass, and Wilson intercepted on the Baylor two. Baylor kicked out, and the first half ended, with the Aggies leading 7 to 0.

Baylor received the second half kickoff and returned to its 30. Grumbles fumbled diving into the line, and Thomason recovered on the Baylor 32.

Big John Kimbrough, who had done little damage in the first half, on a reverse inside the Baylor right tackle gained nine yards, carrying to the Baylor 23. Price went inside the Baylor left tackle for six more to the 17.

On a reverse, Moser showed speed and elusiveness in racing wide the Baylor right end, taking the pigskin to the Baylor four-yard line.

Price smashed through center to within one foot of pay dirt, before Kimbrough slashed the Baylor left guard for the touchdown. Price kicked goal, and the Aggie led 14 to 0.

The Aggies scored their third touchdown early in the last period. Moser raced the Baylor right end for 36 yards, carrying to the Baylor 36. Jeffrey gained six inside right tackle. On the next play, the Aggies were penalized five yards for backfield in motion, but Pugh's pass to Buchanan gave the Aggies a first down on the Baylor 10.

Moser Tallies Again

Moser raced the Baylor left end for eight, carrying to the Baylor two-yard line. Kimbrough was piled up at center for no gain.

While Baylor was worrying about Kimbrough, who faked a smash into the center of the line, Moser took the ball on a reverse, and went wide around Baylor right end for the score.

Marshall Robnett failed to convert, and the final score was: Texas A. & M. 20; Baylor 0.

Cotton Price (punting) and Leon Rahn

WINNING 7

Aggies Display Power
To Burn In 27-0 Win

FAYETTEVILLE, Ark., Nov. 4.—(AP)—Repealing the embargo on touchdowns in Bailey stadium, the Texas A. & M. Aggies hurdled another obstacle in their quest for the Southwest conference championship by triumphing over the University of Arkansas Razorbacks before 11,000 homecoming fans Saturday, 27-0.

The Aggies notched their seventh straight victory, three of them in league play, in rather easy fashion, considering the fact that the Razorbacks held the edge in most of the statistics. Coach Homer Norton's Maroon and White raiders, however, had power to burn when they needed it. Driving to the Porkers' 20 midway in the opening quarter, only to lose the ball on a pass interception, the Aggies pulled a 60-yard touchdown aerial from Quarterback Marlin Jeffrey, a substitute, to End Herb Smith, just before the period ended. Substitute Bill Audish was rushed in to placekick the extra point.

Early in the second period, Guard Marshall Robnett, who played a stellar defensive game, intercepted a pass from Arkansas' star halfback, Ray Eakin, and raced 30 yards before flipping a lateral to Fullback John Kimbrough, who was hauled down after 23 yards on the Porkers' seven. Substitute Bill Conatser, a halfback, raced around end on the first play for the second score.

Audish, playing guard before moving back to the backfield, late in the last half, again added the extra point by placement.

The Aggies, sensing that the defense of the Arkansas team was weakening, drove 46 yards for the second touchdown of the period, with an 18-yard forward-lateral; sub quarterback Jeffrey to substitute End Bill Buchanan to Tackle Joe Boyd, pulling the trick. Bill Dawson, substitute end, booted the extra point from placement.

Porkers Blow Chance

Arkansas blew three scoring chances in the third period while holding the Aggies in check. Three power passes, Eakin to End Maurice Britt, Halfback Walter Hamberg and Quarterback Ralph Atwood, a substitute, netted 68 yards, but Conatser intercepted an Arkansas aerial on his own 17 and Halfback Derace Moser punted out of danger. A forward pass, Eakin to Britt, on the A. & M. three was ruled complete by interference, but the Aggies displayed stiff defense to take over after four downs on their own five. Moser kicked short, one of the few poor kicks he and Conatser got off, to the Aggies, 33 and Eakin shot an aerial to End Howard Hickey for 17 yards but the attack ended 16 yards short of pay dirt.

The Aggies staged an 84-yard touchdown march in the fourth quarter after the last Arkansas scoring chance fizzled. Halfback James Thomason raced 16 yards off tackle and on the next play Conatser worked his way behind the Porker defense and grabbed a 46-yard scoring aerial from Moser. Audish missed the placement try for extra point.

A 50-yard quick kick by Eakin sent the Aggies off stride later in the period and a series of successful short passes and several Aggie penalties piled up yards but no touchdowns for the Porkers.

Kimbrough is Star

Coach Fred Thomsen of the Porkers probably felt better over the defeat than any of the others suffered this season. The Aggies swarmed all over Arkansas at the right moment and centered on Eakin, who was a marked man. There was no more field goal to feel badly about as in the Baylor and Rice losses here last season. Neither were there any long last-minute runs such as against Texas and Villanova this year. The Porkers were really beaten.

Kimbrough didn't take part in the Aggie scoring, but he starred with Jeffrey, Moser and Conatser in the backfield. Boyd was second to M. Robnett in outstanding defensive work in the Aggie line.

Quarterback Floyd Lyon and Eakin paced the early Arkansas ground attack and Atwood came in for some gains later in the conflict but these runs along with the completed passes were in the middle of the field.

Arkansas made 21 first downs to the Aggies' nine. A. & M. gained only seven more yards from scrimmage, 89 to 82. The Razorbacks ran up 238 yards on 13 completed passes against the Aggies' 174 on six.

Even in the first period Arkansas drove to the Aggies' 18 from their own 35, but failed to push the ball any farther. Twice the Porkers needed a yard, but stabs at the line failed to make the required distance.

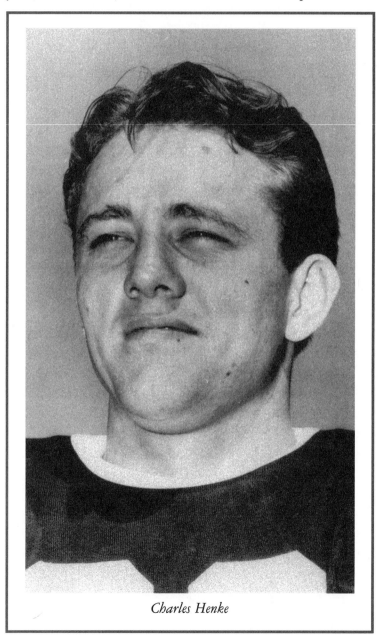

Charles Henke

WINNING 8

Mighty Texas Aggie Eleven
Turns Back Stubborn Mustangs

Close Play Near End Almost Gets Tie for Mustangs

By Jinx Tucker
Tribune-Herald Sports Editor

KYLE FIELD, COLLEGE STATION, Nov. 11—Behind the flying, churning heels of powerful 210-pound John Kimbrough, a mighty Texas Aggie team rode to victory this afternoon over the S. M. U. Mustangs of Dallas by a score of 6 to 2.

Under sullen, dripping clouds that varied in color as the game progressed from gray to black, this mighty son from the plains of west Texas took charge when the crucial moment came, and as each churning step caused moisture to spring from the wet turf, more came from the eyes of the rabid Southern Methodist fans.

Thirty thousand fans, drenched to the skin, sat in rapt amazement at times and with maniacal enthusiasm at other times as they saw two of the finest teams in this country tear into each other with all the fury that their youthful, sinewy muscles could muster—with courage and energy that laughed at the elements, and as they did so they made it the greatest football game waged under adverse circumstances that this country has ever seen.

It was perhaps the largest crowd that ever saw a football game at College Station despite the fact that the weather was the worst for a game that this section had known since 1936, and if it was not the largest crowd that ever saw a game here, it was certainly the most enthusiastic.

Greatest Team Yet

And as we write these lines the Farmer alumnus of the early nineties is lifting his glass to his son and alumnus of the younger generation, saying, "here is mud in your eye," as he toasts the greatest Texas A. and M. football team in the long gridiron history of the state institution. He toasts Homer Norton, the coach the wolves were after a short year ago as the man who has given Texas A. and M. the most devastating and most destructive football team in 50 years of the game.

When Official Ab Curtis in the gathering darkness raised his hands to indicate the stormy game was at an end, a little maroon flag waved higher over historic Kyle Field than any has waved in five decades. For out of the muck and undefeated for the first time on this late November date since 1919—an Aggie team that for the week becomes the toast of the nation and flies close to the top in national ranking.

The prestige of the Southwest Conference, a prestige that grows in the minds of nationally famous critics each year, is saved once more, for Texas A. and M., over a terrific grind on this Armistice Day night is one of the three major undefeated and untied elevens of the country. Also of the three, the Aggies have played by far the hardest schedule.

Keeps Old Tradition

This Aggie team, which won this torrid battle of the day as a high wind and rain drenched the field, had the fight to uphold the Fighting Aggie tradition of old. It had the courage of those heroes of the past such as the lamented Charley DeWare and Johnny Garitty, around whom football legends are known. It had the power of a West Indies tornado and the defense of a granite wall.

It was meeting a team which had ready for the occasion every weapon known to the game—a team equipped with unyielding defensive forts, and every gun known to modern gridiron warfare. It had trained men who knew how to use these weapons to every advantage.

And this battling Aggie team saw nearly every break known to the game go against it. Out in the mud and rain this afternoon, if the Aggies had been given the breaks from Dame Fortune that the team got against Baylor, the score would have been the same as it was against Baylor, but one break after another went against the Farmers.

Once Bruce Conatser, unluckiest of all gridsters of this conference, but a great one all the way, punted a quick kick 74 yards all the way to the four-yard line. There it was killed, rocking the Mustangs back on their heels, in a hole that they might not have managed to escape. But the ball was brought back and the Aggies penalized five. The penalty cost the Aggies not only the chance to get the ball back deep in SMU territory but put the Aggies in a hole for really it was a loss of over 40 yards.

Long Run Nullified

Again in the third quarter Conatser broke away on a beautiful run, racing all the way to the three-yard line for a first down and what looked like a certain touchdown, but again the ball was brought back and the Aggies penalized. This was just two in a long series of bad breaks that the Aggies got, but the Farmers did get one break. That one came in the closing minutes of the first half. A punt had sailed out on the Pony 10. With the quarter about over and the Mustangs playing against the wind, the boys in blue did what looked like the wise thing. They decided to hold it while the minute hand of the big clock ticked the game away.

Only about two minutes remained. They had a good chance to kill most of that time, but the strategy backfired. On the first play the brilliant Preston Johnson fumbled. An Aggie pounced on the ball.

Now is when Jarring John Kimbrough jarred SMU right out of the Southwest conference championship picture. The big clock was still ticking the half away, as Jarring John got the ball. Like a bolt from the dark blue clouds he crashed into that mighty, powerful Mustang wall. It had to yield and it did yield for seven precious yards. Once more the powerful son of west Texas took the ball. He hurled himself into the middle.

The blue tide rose from the drenched turf to meet the assault. It hit Jim at the line of scrimmage but he rolled through to the one. The clock said a bit more than 30 seconds to play when the signal was called for the next play. Again SMU was set for a desperate lunge by Kimbrough. The backs had moved to the line, daring A. and M. to pass, hoping it would take that chance, but Kimbrough faked as if he were going into the line, but instead he whirled around right end.

The Aggies helped with the fake and there was none to run interference for Jarring John. Only one SMU player caught on. He lunged at Kimbrough on the five, but literally slid off the pounding legs of Kimbrough who whirled on across for victory midst the wildest scene that this historic field has even known.

Power No Myth

Nationally famous announcers told the world through the air that the power of A. and M. was no myth, that it had what it took to go when it had the chance. The telegraph instruments clicked to the world that despite the rain and mud, greatest of all football equalizers, the Aggie power was in command and that the Farmers had scored. They knew when they sent the line of A. and M. 6, SMU 0, that the game was over. They knew that the SMU team could not stage a comeback and smash over the stubborn, unyielding Aggie defense for a score.

But that Mustang team, inspired for the occasion, playing demonic, desperate, daring football came close in that last quarter. SMU had had the wind in the first quarter and with that wind, had played on even terms with the Aggies, but had fallen far behind when the Aggies had the wind. Into the third quarter whirled the stormy game with the rain ceasing for a while, but the ball still wet from the slippery turf.

Again the Aggies had the wind in the third quarter and were in complete charge, with the fighting SMU team repulsing one drive after another, only to get right back in the deep hole. How the Mustangs got out of that quarter without being scored upon, is still a miracle. Their superb fight was one cause.

Ground Game Bottled

Heart-rending breaks against the Aggies was another reason, but the fact remains that the Mustangs did start that last period with the wind at their backs and only six points behind. For half of the period the battle surged near the center of the field, but that marvelous toe of

Preston Johnson kept pushing the Aggies back. Still the SMU ground game had no more chance against the Aggie defense than a grammar school team would have against the Waco Tigers. Never during the second half did SMU gain as much as four yards running. Never did it come close to getting a first down, so seeing the ground game hopelessly shackled, the dying SMU team grabbed at the last straw.

The Mustangs went to the air and all of a sudden the Aggie team, instead of playing smart football began playing very dumb football. The fight was still there and the sensational crushing fight won despite the mistakes. The most dramatic mistake of them all came when the clock said less than five minutes to play when it was absolutely imperative that A.&M. get the ball away from SMU. It did, for Moser, who had played a grand game in the first quarter, intercepted an aerial.

Instead of holding to the ball for dear life he tried to lateral it when there was no chance to get anywhere with the lateral, and the lateral became a forward, so the Aggies were penalized back to their five. There Conatser got back to punt, SMU set up a 10-man line, rushed in and blocked the punt. It could have been disastrous to the Aggie cause, for it was anybody's ball just inside the end zone. Conatser dove for it and so did an SMU player, but Conatser got it and it was a safety, two points for the Mustangs.

Ponies Thunder Back

When the Aggies kicked the Mustangs thundered back, but that drive was stopped on the 40 or near that mark by a pass interception by Kimbrough, but after intercepting and running a few yards he fumbled, with the Ponies recovering for a first down that they would not have had had the pass been completed.

But the courageous Aggies dug their cleats in the ground. The break did not dampen their enthusiasm but did add to that of SMU's. They took the ball away from the Mustangs and made a first down that seemed to clinch the game. There were only 30 seconds left to play when Conatser punted, but again SMU opened up with a desperate passing attack with Junior Clements passing magnificently with the wet ball. An SMU player dropped a short one. Had he held it enough time might have been consumed for the game to be over.

Then the Aggies quit rushing Clements, drifting back to knock down long ones that might go for a touchdown, but in doing so they let Clements have more time to throw long ones and that mistake could also have been costly. Three more times did SMU pass and the last one with one second to play was across the goal, but knocked down and the hysterical fans who had not swooned in their seats rushed to the field. Others remained trying to recover their composure, realizing for the first time just how wet they were. They had forgotten their discomfort while enjoying the thrill of the stormy game.

Will Be a Saga

It will be a game that you will hear told and retold down through the years—the greatest wet weather game in the history of man. And the two heroes were Jarring Jim Kimbrough of the Aggies and Preston Johnson, a sophomore back of Southern Methodist, who bids fair to become one of the greatest gridsters in the history of SMU, a boy who can kick with the brilliance of the greatest punters of southwestern history, and a boy who can do everything else asked of a fine back.

But it was the boys in the line who took the punishment in the grueling battle, and the line that Bill James has given Texas A. and M. met the test—the most severe test an Aggie line has ever known, for as great as was the SMU line this afternoon, the unyielding Aggie line was greater.

It had rained in College Station all night just as it had in Waco. It rained all morning and as the crowd filed into the stands it was still raining. It stopped when the cover was removed from the field, but the clouds were heavy, threatening to start leaking again at any moment. Despite all of the rain, there were 25,000 on hand when the two teams trotted on the field. The Aggie team, as it went on the field was given the greatest ovation of any A. and M. team that we have seen on this historic field.

The gridiron was in about the same shape as Muny stadium was Friday night, which should explain very well to the Waco fans the condition of the field. The Ponies got the first break of the mud battle, winning the toss as the fans now numbering about 28,000 continued to pour in.

Jeffrey at Quarterback

Norton decided to start the heavy Jeffrey at quarterback. The Ponies defended the north goal and received. The ball was brought back by Johnson to the 23, but the Aggies were off side. Thus the Ponies also got the second break, and then the ball was put in play on the 33. Dawson kicked off against the wind in great style both times and went out of the game. Bearden went off tackle for three.

On third down, Johnson kicked 64 yards across the goal, and it went to the three-yard line before it hit the ground. Kimbrough gained four on the Aggies' first play at right tackle. Moser with dazzling speed in the mud and great elusiveness ran for a first down on the 33. He went around left end. Kimbrough tried to run wide and lost four yards at right end. Kimbrough then smashed through for five, and on third down, Moser kicked nicely out of bounds on the Pony 25. Johnson got through for seven at right tackle. He failed at the other side, and then Johnson made it a first down.

Bearden smashed right through center for six. The game had progressed eight minutes and the jerseys were not muddy, so the field evidently was not as soft as it looked, thanks to the cover. Johnson on third down ran wide at right end for a first down on the Pony 47. Now the Aggies stopped the Mustangs for three plays and Johnson kicked out of bounds on the 15. Moser faked a punt and ran wide at right end for a gain of almost five. He had to use speed altogether, however, as SMU was not fooled on the play. With one to go for a first down, Kimbrough ploughed for eight.

Another Great Boot

The Aggies kicked on third down and it sailed 43 yards. Johnson was brought down on the Pony 32. The Aggies were penalized five after the Mustangs failed on two plays. With the quarter almost over Johnson kicked 62 yards across the goal line. Moser gained five and then on the next play SMU was offside, so it was a first down on the 30. Thomason broke through and gained 15 to the 45 as the quarter closed. It was about an even quarter though the Mustangs had had the advantage of the wind.

SMU had been playing a five-man line all during the first quarter. Three plays by Kimbrough gained only six, so Conatser kicked across the goal line, and it was the Pony's ball on their 20. The Aggies were also playing a five-man line. SMU was forced to punt and Johnson booted it 50 yards. Conatser brought it back to his 45. Kimbrough failed and as Conatser plowed for three, Sanders of SMU was hurt. It now started raining for the first time during the game.

Fumble Costs Cadets

Thomason drove to within inches of a first down. The pass back from center to Conatser was bad and he fumbled losing eight and SMU took the ball on downs on the Aggie 45. It was the first fumble of the game, and a tough break for the Aggies as it deprived them of a great opportunity to put SMU in a hole, and instead the Aggies got in a good spot to be placed in a hole.

Clements, the Pony passer, went into the game. Clements passed to Johnson for three. Clements then deliberately grounded the ball to keep from losing 20, but he threw it before he was tackled, so there was no penalty. Johnson kicked out on the Aggie 25. Conatser faked a punt and ran for five yards around right end with remarkable interference. Conatser made a magnificent quick-kick to the Pony four, but the Aggies got another terrible break as the ball was brought back and the Farmers penalized 15 yards for holding. The kick was for 71 yards and gave the Aggies their best chance of the day. Conatser then stood on his five and kicked, with the Ponies getting it on their 47, so the penalty cost the Farmers 43 yards. Conatser is the hard-luck boy of the conference. Ninety per cent of his sensational plays this season—and he has made many—have been nullified by penalties.

Kimbrough Gets Score

Johnson kicked out of bounds on the Aggie 14. The rain was peppering down, but the fans refused to leave their seats. Conatser got off a long spiral of 59 yards and the Ponies got the ball on their 33. The Aggies had not tossed a pass as yet, and SMU did not start passing until it began raining. Clements broke through for eight, the Mustangs' first appreciable gain of the period. Johnson lost, and then Clements gained five but fumbled, and Kimbrough recovered on the 50. Conatser ran wide at right for three. On third down Conatser kicked out on the nine. Johnson tried to run, fumbled, and Vaughn recovered for the Aggies on the SMU 10. Kimbrough crashed through the left side for six to the four. He then plowed for another gain to the one. With the clock saying 35 seconds to play, Kimbrough took the ball and tore around end without interference. He fooled all SMU players save one, and that one had a clear shot at him on the five, but missed him, causing him only to stumble a bit, and then he broke right on across, creating one of the wildest scenes in Aggie history. Audish kicked wide, and it was 6 to 0.

Dawson went in and kicked off for the Aggies. The ball was put in play on the 17. One play later the half ended. It was a half which saw the Mustangs get all the breaks until the last four minutes. Then the Farmers got two, and the second break gave the Farmers their score. Down in pay territory, in the slop and mud where the going is tough when conditions are ideal, the Aggies had their greatest punch of the day. There they became a machine of destruction, which refused to stop short of a touchdown.

To start the second half, the Aggies had the wind, and Dawson made a long kick to the goal line, but Brown brought it back to the 24. Johnson got off a marvelous kick against the wind to the Aggie 32. Conatser made a quick-kick back, but it did not sail over the safety man's head, and the ball was in play on the 29. Johnson was hurt on the next play and was taken from the game. Bearden's kick went out on the Aggie 40. The first pass of the game for the Aggies was blocked with a man loose in the flat. Conatser made a poor kick out of bounds, the first poor one of the game, and the Mustangs took it on the Pony 35.

Pugh went in for Jeffrey of the Aggies. A little boy named Brown tried to run against the rugged Aggie defense and lost three yards on two plays. Bearden was rushed on his punt and booted poorly out of bounds on the Pony 40. SMU was missing the punting of Johnson very much. Pugh smashed through for seven. Kimbrough dove for a first down on the 30. Conatser got only two, and Pugh got three more. Pugh got two more, and with two to go on fourth down, Kimbrough failed to make the first down by inches, so the ball went to SMU on the 20. Bearden had to kick, and it was high but short, falling dead on the Pony 49.

Moser Bottled Up

Moser went in for the Aggies but could not go, so on fourth down with two to go, Moser kicked out on the 16. The Ponies lost four on two plays and then Bearden kicked out on the 50, but the Aggies were penalized for roughing the kicker, giving the Ponies a first down, a fine break, for the quarter was nearly over. They had a chance to hold the ball until they could kick with the wind. SMU fumbled and an Aggie player dived at it but missed, and SMU recovered. One more play failed, but that was all right for SMU, as the quarter closed and SMU go the chance to kick with the wind. The Aggies had kept the Mustangs in a hole during the quarter but had not offered a real scoring threat.

Johnson, however, was not back in for SMU and Clement's kick with the wind was poor, going out on the SMU 30, a great break for the Aggies. Pugh crashed into the Pony line for five. Conatser with great interference went around right end for 14 yards. He fumbled, but got a break as it went out of bounds. The ball was on the 11. Pugh drove through for two, and the Aggie stands were in an uproar again, at least more of an uproar.

Field Goal Fails

Conatser ran wide at left end, was almost knocked off his feet three times but plowed on to the three-yard line. Again, the Aggies got a tough break for the Aggie backfield was in motion and the Aggies were sent back to the 14 when they had a touchdown in their grasp. Conatser ran wide at the same spot but got only three. Conatser put it back in front of the goal post and Dawson went in to try for a field goal from the 20. The kick was poor and short and SMU got the ball on the 20.

SMU was penalized five on the next play. Johnson went back in for the Mustangs. Three plays failed to gain and Johnson kicked low to the Aggie 42. Conatser made a quick kick to the Pony 25. Clements lost five at right end. Johnson had to punt and it was a great kick with Conatser being downed on his 31. With the wind the Mustangs were slowly pushing the Aggies back but the quarter was exactly one-half over. Now the Aggies were penalized 15 back to their 23 for holding. Conatser kicked on first down to the Pony 42.

Moser went in for Pugh, and it was growing darker, the clouds lower. It had not rained since early in the second period. Clements passed to Mullenweg for a first down on the Aggie 42 and he came close to breaking loose as an Aggie tried to get the ball from his hand. Now a long pass was batted in the air four times first by an Aggie player, then by SMU. Moser finally got it and after running around for a while made a mistake of trying to lateral. It was caught, but it was a forward instead of a lateral and the Aggies were penalized 15 back to their six-yard line.

There Conatser's kick was blocked and an SMU player dived at the ball, but Conatser recovered for a safety. Audish went into make the free kick from the 20. Moser's lateral had come dangerously close to costing the Aggies the game.

Mustangs Fill Air

Audish kicked and SMU brought it back to the Aggie 45. Both stands were now in a frenzy. The clock said a bit less than five minutes to play and SMU was passing on every down. Kimbrough intercepted the second pass but fumbled and SMU recovered on the Aggie 40. It was also a first down for SMU.

A pass from Clements to Goss gained three. Kimbrough intercepted a long one on the 15. Thomason went through the middle for seven. Kimbrough stopped at the line, ploughed on for two. Kimbrough tore on with all his great power, and it was a first down, also a most important first down for only two minutes remained.

The Ponies got it back about the middle of the field and in the last 30 seconds had the Aggie fans with their hearts in their mouths, as they started a flurry of passes, one being completed on the 20. The last dying, desperate thrust of SMU with one minute to go was an incomplete pass at the goal line in a corner of the field.

Joe Boyd

Farmers Mix Passes
With Ground Attack

Rice Held to Eight Yards!
Texas Alone Bars A. & M. From Undefeated Season

By William T. Rives
Associated Press Sports Writer

HOUSTON. Nov. 18—Its offensive ticking like a watch, Texas A&M pasted the punchless Rice Owls Saturday with an almost unbelievable offensive that rolled up a 19-0 conquest.

Big John Kimbrough, the demon fullback, and a couple of other backfield gems, Bill Conatser and Derace Moser, sped behind superb interference to bury a crippled Rice eleven that could rack up only eight yards net.

The Aggies' furious charge brought them 339 yards as Rice was completely baffled by a versatile attack that disproved any claims the A&M band could gain only on the ground.

Twenty times the Farmers passed and 10 times the ball struck against a receiver. The passing yardage total—181—exceeded the ground values, although none could say Jarrin' John Kimbrough failed to do his usual stint. The big fellow gathered 92 yards in 17 tries for a 5.4 average.

One Game to Go!

The win left the bowl-bound Aggies with but one game to play— the always unpredictable fracas with the Texas Longhorns, the age-old rival, on Nov. 30.

On the showing Saturday, none but the brave would give Texas a chance.

Olie Cordill, a grand back, did his level best to keep the Owls in the game. His spiral punts and broken-field efforts kept the Aggies on edge throughout. The three-touchdown margin did not represent a fraction of the difference between the two teams.

The Aggies started the fireworks early, with Kimbrough plunging over for the first score in the opening quarter. The drive started on the Rice 42. Kimbrough's plunging and a short shovel pass carried to the 31.

Then Moser scampered to the seven in a couple of essays from a spread formation, which the Aggies introduced for the first time this season.

Kimbrough pounded over in two plunges. Audish missed the extra point try.

19-Yard Pass Clincher

In the second, A. & M. drove 65 yards to its tally, as Walemon (Cotton) Price, always a thorn in the Owls' side with his passing, hit mostly short aerials to Moser and the ends, Bill Buchanan and Harold Cowley. Mixed in the assault was a tricky lateral with Kimbrough on the tail end.

The clinching pass on the drive was the 19-yarder to Cowley, Price converted to make the score 13-0.

Rice held in the third, but a dazzling run by Conatser scored early in the fourth. This time the Aggies drove 79 yards. Kimbrough bruised his way through the sagging Rice line for three first downs to the Owls' 34.

After a two-yard gain, Price shot a short one to Conatser in the right flat. He cut toward the sidelines, reversed his field through a mass of tacklers, shook off four other tacklers in the clear, cut back again, and breezed over.

The 25,000 fans, who braved threatening weather, roared with admiration.

Rice's only chance came in the second period, when Billy Heard, burly tackle, recovered Marland Jeffrey's fumble on the Aggie 24. Bob

Brumley passed to Cordill on the 15, but penalties hurt and Billy Cline finally was smothered back on the A. & M. 37, as he vainly tried to run.

Rice, playing without its passing expert, Ernie Lain, held off one deep thrust with great defensive play. Kimbrough was stopped cold along the three-yard line in the second period.

Rice		Texas A. & M.
1	First Downs	14
12	Yards Gained Rushing	158
29	Yards Gained Passing	181
4-18	Passes Completed	10-20
2	Passes Intercepted	1
37	Punts, Average Yardage	35
80	Penalties, yards	55

Bill Jeffrey

Aggies Splash To
20-0 Victory Over Texas

38,336 See Climax of First Perfect Season for A & M Since '19

By Bruce Layer
Post Sports Editor

KYLE FIELD, COLLEGE STATION, Nov. 30—Showing the fight of a real champion, Coach Homer Norton's Texas Aggies came back in the second half to pass and splash their way to a 20 to 0 victory over the University of Texas here Thanksgiving Day, climaxing an undefeated and untied season.

It was the first perfect year for an Aggie team since 1919, when Dana X. Bible, Texas coach, was over on the other side of the field.

A rain-soaked crowd of 38,336 saw an inspired Texas line battle the Aggies to a standstill for the first half and saw the nation's number one team muff its one scoring chance. There were many in the packed horseshoe who feared the clinching of a conference championship a week early had played the Aggies false.

They did not reckon with the Aggie passing attack and when Cotton Price started whipping overheads with a slippery ball the Longhorns were whipped. A play as old as this historic old field rocked the Longhorns back on their heels as the second half opened and they never recovered.

It was the old hideout play. One that has been used time and time again and one that the Aggies called on in San Francisco four years ago to rout a team that led 14-0 at halftime.

Bama Smith Hides Out

Bama Smith, a reserve back who had played but little football for the Aggies this season, stuck close to the muddy sidelines. He took Price's pass and fought his way to the Texas 26 before Gilly Davis pulled him down. The delay was short-lived, as the Aggies plowed to the 16 before another pass from Price found Jim Sterling over the goal line and the scoreless deadlock was broken. After that there was no stopping the Aggies. They rushed and passed and the greatest line in the business bottled the Longhorn attack.

A few minutes later the Aggies passed their way into position for a second touchdown and then a break set up the third. The Longhorns, punting from deep in their own territory, were guilty of a foul while the ball was in the air and A. & M. took charge on the Texas 14.

Three plays later Big John Kimbrough, All-America fullback, plunged over for the touchdown that gave him the conference scoring championship. The big back played 59 ½ minutes of the game, but was forced to call time twice. He suffered a leg injury in the third period, but stuck it out until just before the final gun sounded.

The play of Marshall Robnett, a guard who rates plenty of all-America consideration, featured the stout Aggie defense. For 60 minutes he smeared the Longhorn play. He was down field, through the line and all over the place and his performance sparked the forwards to an exhibition that held Texas to a net gain of 24 yards for the afternoon.

Right on his heels was Tommie Vaughn, a mud-spattered center; Jimmy Thomason, line backer; Ernest Pannell, Joe Boyd, Charlie Henke, Herbie Smith and Leon Rahn, a reserve guard who turned up with many a tackle.

The Texas line headed by Park Myers, Ted Dawson, Derwood Peneto and Don Weedon, played the finest game of the season. The Longhorn forwards had leaked badly in the other conference tilts, but Thursday they were hard to block out and for half the game had the Aggies worried.

Moser, Conatser and Kimbrough were the ground gainers for the Aggies with Conatser coming through with another topnotch game. Price's passing with a wet ball was exceptionally good.

Gilly Davis Texas Star

For Texas it was Gilly Davis all of the way. He was the "little man" of the day, overshadowing Jackie Crain's performance. Davis' punting kept the Aggies at a distance through the first half and he played his heart out. It was Davis who supplied the spark that upset the Aggies at Austin last year.

The first break of the game came late in the opening period. Conatser had quick-kicked from his own 14 to Crain on the Texas 30. He returned three yards and on the next play Pannell knifed through and crashed Crain. The Texas ball carrier fumbled and Vaughn pounced on the ball on the Texas 33.

Conatser slipped around right end, reversed his field and carried to the Texas 21. It was a beautiful run. Kimbrough picked up three yards and Pugh passed to Smith for six more. Kimbrough smashed the line for a first down on the 10-yard line.

Conatser then raced right end, carrying the ball to the three-yard line, but the timer had called the quarter over before the play started and it was carried back to the 10.

On the first play of the second quarter a bad pass from center cost the Aggies five yards. Two more running plays failed and then a pass over the goal was incomplete with the ball going to Texas on its own 20 (under the rules of that era).

Davis' Great Punt

That was really the only scoring threat of the period. Texas was in another deep hole later, but Davis got off a 58-yard punt to pull them out of trouble. An Aggie punt rolled out on the 19 and, as Crain lost two yards the Longhorns were holding and the penalty drove them back to their two-yard stripe.

Davis stepped back to the goal posts and calmly booted the ball out of bounds on the Aggie 40.

Later, the Longhorns clicked on a pass, Davis to Crain, for four yards to account for the only Texas first down of the half.

That set the stage for a whirlwind finish. The Aggies received at the start of the third period and 'Bama Smith "camped out." Price got off a long pass, but the fleet Smith had to back up to take it and that is the only reason it wasn't good for a touchdown. Davis pulled him down on the 26.

Aggies Score on Pass

Kimbrough went off left tackle for six yards. Thomason picked up a yard and Conatser cut through for a first down on the Texas 16. Kimbrough was downed for a four-yard loss, Red Goodwin making the tackle. Conatser made four yards at left end and then Price passed to Sterling in the end zone for the score. Audish added the extra point.

After an exchange of punts the Aggies took the ball on their own 45-yard line and another touchdown drive started.

Kimbrough went off tackle for eight yards and suffered a "charley horse" in his leg but stayed in the game. Price then passed to Herbie Smith who fought his way to the Texas four. On the first play Conatser knifed off right tackle for the touchdown. Frank Wood missed the try for point and it was 13 to 0 A. & M.

Penalty Sets Up Aggie Score

After about four minutes of the final quarter, Conatser punted out of bounds on the Texas 14-yard line. A short pass failed and Davis got off a good kick, the ball being grounded on the Aggie 40. But it went for naught as Texas committed a foul while the ball was in the air and it was called back, going to the Aggies at that point of foul on the 15-yard line.

Conatser raced right end for seven yards. Then, he ran back to the other side of the field, being stopped a yard short of the goal. Kimbrough went over. Audish added the point from placement.

Texas had its one scoring opportunity just before the end of the contest. Crain punted to Conatser who was downed on the Aggie 14. His return punt was partially blocked and Davis took the ball on the Aggie 35.

Crain raced right end for first down on the Aggie 15. Puett lost 10 yards on a bad pass from center. On the next play Buchanan intercepted Davis' pass on the 15 and ran it back to the Aggie 22.

The Farmers ran three plays and punted. Texas ran one play before the gun sounded.

Aggies Have Big Edge

Texas A. & M. had nine first downs against three for the Longhorns and the Aggies rolled up a net gain of 204 yards from rushing and passing. Passing accounted for 117 yards.

Crain carried the ball four times for a total gain of 24 yards. Davis handled the pigskin 11 times and picked up 36 yards but was trapped for 15 yards in losses.

Conatser toted the leather 15 times for 53 yards and Kimbrough carried 17 times for 42 yards but his losses were 14 yards, cutting into the big star's average.

The all-victorious season marks the fourth time Homer Norton-coached elevens finished without defeat. He had three unbeaten teams at Centenary, but two were tied. His 1927 club marched through to 10 straight wins. Norton has served as head coach at Texas A. & M. for six years and has been a head coach for the past 19 seasons.

"Bama" Smith

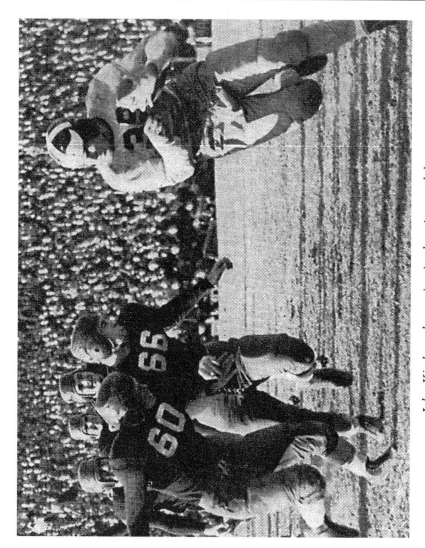

John Kimbrough running in the tying touchdown

Aggies Wouldn't Have Won
Without John Kimbrough

By Thad Holt
Atlanta Constitution

NEW ORLEANS, Jan. 1, 1940—A former Tulane freshman named John Kimbrough today dazzled a record Southern and Sugar Bowl crowd of 73,000 with one of the greatest exhibitions of carrying the football ever witnessed on a Dixie gridiron, leading the unbeaten and untied Texas Aggies into a powerful claim for the national championship over the Tulane Green Wave which fell in a bruising struggle, 14-13.

No story of the hundreds written about this sixth annual Sugar Bowl classic, scarcely no paragraph, will fail to feature the blazing achievements of the big supercharger from Haskell, Tex., who today drew praise from friend and foe as one of the truly great running backs of American football history.

Without this 210-pound deer and dynamo the resourceful Aggies from the Southwest would have been unable to come through against a clumsy but ferocious Wave, which was good enough to wipe out the Texans' 7-0 half-time lead and thunder into the front by 13-7 with only 11 minutes to go.

Offer Rejected

Kimbrough attended Tulane for seven weeks. He demanded a seven-year medical course as his price for playing football. His offer rejected, Kimbrough, now a junior, enrolled at Texas A. & M. Today a great many Greenie supporters would have given the magnificent stadium here and tossed in New Orleans' share of the Mississippi river just to have Jarrin' Jawn on their side.

Kimbrough scored both touchdowns for the Aggies. They gave him the ball when the going was toughest and when a yard or so meant the difference in a breakdown and a touchdown drive. He carried the ball 26 times for 152 yards. Once he was stopped for a five-yard loss. His net average was 5.7 yards per try. He played 60 minutes against fierce tackling and at the finish he was leading another mad charge, which the final gun halted near the Wave goal. He ran the ends like a halfback, handling his 210 pounds with the grace and adeptness of a broken-field runner. Going into the line he was unstoppable, often taking with him three or four burly tacklers as he tore along.

This was the greatest of the Sugar Bowl games. The best team won, but before that final gun there was enough football drama to thrill, dismay, and finally exhaust a magnificent gathering of sports followers from all over the United States and many points in Canada.

One Drive Halted

The Aggies scored midway of the first quarter after the desperately fighting Greenies had stopped a previous Texas drive on the one-foot line.

Stanley Nyhan kicked to the Aggies, who took the ball at the Wave 32. Kimbrough's rushes carried to the 18 and when John Mandich, Tulane center, roughed Derace Moser on an end run the Southeastern Conference eleven was penalized 15 yards to the three-yard stripe. It was a demoralizing, destructive play and Kimbrough needed only one mighty plunge to roar across the goal line. Price placekicked the extra point and the Texas folks went berserk. They were soon to learn Tulane was not beaten.

Seventy-two thousand wild-eyed football fans got their money's worth here Monday when Texas A. and M's national champions, led by the greatest piece of football flesh this writer ever saw, Jarrin' John Kimbrough, nosed out Tulane's mighty Green Wave, 14-13. Years from now, when the sun sets on this magnificent Sugar Bowl, the ghost of that great Texas Aggie fullback will come back and still flit over those chalk lines and challenge any hopeful who dares to excel his performance here today.

The man is too much football player for any team to stop. He runs the ends like a halfback, hits the line like a modern tank and does everything expected on defense. A 60-minute performer, a tireless, relentless worker, he was the difference in the ball game here that set a new high in Southern attendance.

With Price and Kimbrough leading the way early, the Aggies scored in the first quarter. They moved to Tulane's 18 and received a penalty that put the ball on the Greenie five. It was a matter of no time before Kimbrough plowed over. Thomason converted.

Aggies Lead at Half

The half ended with the Aggies leading, 7-0, and Tulane within jumping distance of a touchdown as Butler, Cassibry and Hays began to click in the second quarter.

In the third quarter, Robert "Jitterbug" Kellogg electrified the colorful crowd by taking Conatser's quick kick on his 25 and scampering 75 hard-earned yards to get the Greenies even. Thibaut aided the extra point and the New Orleans fans went wild.

Inspired by Kellogg's great run, the big Wave moved goal-ward again in the fourth quarter. Cassibry, Hays and Butler, on short reverses inside tackle, placed the ball on the two-yard stripe. Butler went over and the Tulane partisans went wild. Thibaut's attempted conversion was blocked by several Aggie linemen. Tulane led, 13-7.

But not for long as Kimbrough, Price, Smith, Sterling, Conatser and company immediately went to work. They passed, ran the ends and hit the middle after taking the fourth-quarter kickoff. Then Price faded, faked to Sterling but tossed to Smith. Kimbrough, running near his mate, took a lateral from Smith and went from the Greenies' 16 across standing up after brushing several tacklers aside.

With the coolness of a big leaguer under fire, Thomason added the extra point. The Aggies led, 14-13. They were on their way to another marker when the game ended, having taken the ball to Tulane's five. Kimbrough was doing the "taking."

It was truly a battle between two of the nation's outstanding elevens. Offensive maneuvers clearly overshadowed defensive strengths. But with Kimbrough on the offense and Kimbrough on the defense, the Aggies earned the right be called the best team in the United States.

Jarrin' John makes them just that

Southern football fans never before saw such a riot of color as that presented by the thousands of hats, coats, uniforms and college ribbons and flags of the thousands in the stands.

In the South end of the stadium, A. and M.'s student body, mainly comprised of cadets, stood during the entire game—most of them at "attention."

A stiff breeze from the north kept hundreds of flags, representing many of the states and colleges, fully unfurled, adding to the color of this greatest gridiron classic the South has ever seen.

Representing the agricultural crop which gave the Sugar Bowl its name, giant stalks of sugar cane wave majestically over the throngs of excited fans, who, in addition to witnessing the most elaborate pageantry ever staged on a Dixie gridiron got their money's worth so far as the hard-fought game was concerned.

Texans Impressive

Consistent with the size of their state, the Texas folks in New Orleans staged every feature in which they participated in a gigantic and impressive manner. After numerous downtown demonstrations in which the big-hatted and high-booted men from the Lone Star State did themselves proud. Thundering cannon fire (it must have been a one-pound artillery piece smuggled in by some Texas ranger or cowboy, who make no secret of the fact they carry big and potent firearms) heralded the appearance of the Aggie gridders on the field. Then, as the whistle blew Kimbrough and Company took the spotlight to overcome the powerful Tulane Green Wave.

Most impressive of the Southwesterner's stunts was that staged by the 200-piece Aggie band—as snappy a military band as this correspondent's ever saw. First, the musicians wrote "Sugar Bowl" in massive letters, then drew a complete map of the state of Texas on the gridiron. With 73,000 spectators standing bareheaded, the band played the A. and M. alma mater, in slow tempo, accompanied by soft, rhythmic yells from the Aggie cheering section.

The game was so completely sold out that at 1 o'clock—15 minutes before game time—it was announced over the loudspeaker system that 73,000 persons had passed through the turnstiles. With its seating capacity at 70,000, naturally the Sugar Bowl was crowded to the sidelines.

Not to be outdone by such a thing as the South's greatest gridiron classic, Louisiana politicians—you know they have them in droves down this way—made themselves conspicuous with skywriting airplanes during the game. The name of at least one candidate in the bitter governor's race—Noe—who like several of his opponents has gone about the Teche country raking the old Long faction up and down the spine—was written in white smoke far above the stadium.

Kicking the winning extra point

Texas A&M 14—Tulane 13. How sweet it was! January 1, 1940

WINNING THEM ALL

Texas Aggies Are
National Grid Champs

By Doyle Beard
Houston Chronicle

NEW ORLEANS, Jan. 1—Ladies and gentlemen, I give you the
national football champions, those rip-roaring, Fighting Aggies from
Texas Agricultural and Mechanical College, who closed out an undefeated and untied season with a 14-to-13 victory over Tulane's mighty
Green Wave in the Sugar Bowl grid classic.

It was a sensational game—a thriller from start to finish with more
than 70,000 fans kept in a furor. The Aggies won like champions, getting up from the floor to come from behind and win in the closing minutes of the hard-fought battle. After "Jitterbug" Bob Kellogg, Tulane's
classy little speedster, and Monette Butler, a hard-driving back, had
sparked the Wave to the lead, the Aggies proved definitely that they
had what it takes when the going gets rough by smashing their way to
the front again.

Jarrin' John Kimbrough, the Aggies' All-America fullback, proved
his class, turning in one of the greatest performances ever seen on the
New Orleans gridiron.

It wasn't all Kimbrough by any means, though. The rest of the
Aggies played bang-up games, but Big John was by far the best back
on the field today, if not of all time.

The junior fullback from Haskell rushed for 159 yards in twenty-
five carries and scored both touchdowns, the second a 25-yard bull rush
to tie the score. His backfield mate, Cotton Price, kicked the conversion for the winning point.

Chapter 11

TIME OUT:
A Tale of Two Seasons

THE TEXAS AGGIES HAD NO POWERFUL REASON to think that 1939 would be their breakout year. They were, after all, coming off a four-win season and the coaches thought if anything wonderful awaited them it would happen in 1940.

That was when their celebrated roundup of the state's most desirable players would pay off like a gum ball machine—that would be Tomorrow's Team, made up of mostly seniors.

But the Aggies surprised everyone by running the table, winning eleven in a row and turning back Tulane to seize the National Championship a year early. And how fateful was it, back in 1937, when the equipment manager handed a fullback named John Kimbrough jersey Number 39?

Gee, too bad they didn't think to upgrade him to Number 40 a year later.

But in the minds of those players, the coaches and many of their fans, the months all ran together—one team, two seasons, one heart. The goal was to win back to back championships, a feat not easily done, not since the years when the pollsters didn't look much beyond the Ivy League.

So why not the Aggies? They had lost only a handful of players from the '39 team, notably Joe Boyd, their All-America tackle, Cotton Price, their fair-haired passer, and heroic little Herbie Smith.

Twenty-three lettermen had returned, including fifteen seniors, meaning a starter at nearly every position. At the top of the pyramid was Kimbrough, who had ranked fourth in the Heisman Trophy voting in 1939, when the award went to Nile Kinnick of Iowa.

Did any team have a back more feared than Jarrin' Jawn? Tom Harmon, of Michigan? Close. But *Time Magazine* had called Harmon the best high school player in the country his senior year, so think of how much ground Kimbrough had made up.

The teams that trailed the Aggies in the 1939 final standings were Tennessee, Southern Cal, Cornell, Tulane, Missouri, UCLA, Duke, Iowa and Duquesne. Are you kidding us? Cornell? Duquesne?

None of the teams were loaded with veterans the way A&M was. What team could equal such talent as Jim Thomason, Bill Conatser, Derace Moser, Marion Pugh, Marshall Robnett, Ernie Pannell, Big Dog Dawson?

Winning them all, again, wasn't an obsession with the Aggies, or Coach Homer Norton, but they had to love their chances. The Southwest Conference had produced three national champions in the Thirties, SMU in 1935, TCU in 1938 and the Aggies in 1939. The hotter the fire, the stronger the steel.

So the Cadets reported for fall practice in 1940 with an unbeaten streak that would reach nineteen games, and another national title a win away, and an invitation to the Rose Bowl resting in the coat pocket of Coach Homer Norton.

This was their dream, to follow their star, no matter how far. The words and music for Camelot had not been written yet, of course, but what the Aggies wanted was not one, but two bright, shining moments.

In truth, those who played on both squads saw this as a seamless time, a season twenty games long. In their age of innocence, they had not realized they were competing for a national championship until it was theirs. Now, to repeat, to win in back-to-back seasons, would validate them as one of college football's legendary teams.

How close they would come. What a ride it would be—and what an awful, tumbling fall would end it on an improbable day in Austin.

Celebrating in New Orleans

Chapter 12

GAME BY GAME—1940
ᕯᕯᕯ

Cotton Price

Powerful Texas Aggies Open Title Defense
by Turning Back Texas A. & I. 26 to 0

COLLEGE STATION, Texas, Sept. 28—(AP)—Coach Homer Norton's pat hand in the Southwest Conference race gave observers a glimpse of what they can expect of the Texas Aggies this year, when the Maroon and White rolled over the Texas A. and I. Javelinas on Kyle Field here today, 26 to 0.

The Aggies well-oiled machine was substituted in waves, 41 players seeing action during the game, which saw two touchdowns roll across in the first period, one in the second, and one in the fourth.

Norton unveiled briefly an attack appearing more baffling than that of last year.

It includes all of the tried and trusted formations so successful last year, plus liberal doses of spinner, reverse, and fakes. After the first two markers were chalked up the Aggies went the balance of the way under wraps, but their defense was airtight, even with fourth stringers in the lineup.

Jarring John Kimbrough, the Haskell juggernaut, still has his bone crushing power, and he has added a vicious stiff-arm, an adept hip-switch and accurate passing arm. He didn't kick any today, but that is a possibility for later in the season. Norton's great blocker, Jim Thomason, also performed brilliantly in his usual role. He caught a touchdown pass for good measure in addition to paralyzing would-be tacklers and ball carriers. Norton also uncovered another brilliant blocker in John Abbott, junior from Corpus Christi, who left little to be desired a the spot made so potent the last two years by Thomason.

Ernest Pannell, senior tackle and all-conference performer last year gave notice that he still is able to be up and about. His tackling was accurate and his blocking was all that could be desired. Marshall

Robnett played his usual spectacular game at guard for the Aggies. For the Javelinas, Clarkson at center was outstanding on defense and Rucker, a converted guard, acquitted himself with distinction at quarterback, his first game at that post since high school at McAllen.

Ags Get Their Kicks

The Javelinas were able to reach the Aggie 42 yard line on one occasion and they made only two first downs to 11 for the Aggies.

The dearth of kickers around Aggieland for years definitely is now an abundance for Moser, Conatser and Jeffrey all exhibited rare toe technique on the five occasions when it was necessary to punt. The kicking average of this trio was 34.8 yards, one of Conatser's going out on the one yard line, Jeffrey's stopping dead on the three and Moser's going over barely by inches when he booted a short one from the 35.

Not a single Aggie was injured

Marion Pugh at quarter and Marshall Spivey at left halfback gave promise of being consistent ground gainers this year to supplement the efforts of Kimbrough, Moser, Conatser, and Marland Jeffrey, the Aggies' very dependable swing-man in the backfield.

Norton was able to sub freely and his team apparently emerged from the game in good health.

Kimbrough carried 10 times, gained 50 yards; Pugh carried 12, gained 42, and passed 13 times, connected with nine that gained a total of 113 yards. Spivey attempted two passes and both were completed for 34 yards total. Jeffrey, Bando, and Kimbrough also passed.

WINNING 13

Aggies Maul Tulsa
In Runaway 41-6

Conference Champs Dedicate New
Stadium at Santone Before 20,000

SAN ANTONIO, Texas, Oct. 5—(INS)—Twenty thousand spectators in San Antonio's new Alamo stadium saw Texas A. and M. crush Tulsa University today, 41-6, in another long step toward their goal of a second consecutive national championship.

The Golden Hurricane fought off the Aggies' superior forces valiantly, but had no reserves to stem the ruthless onrush of power. A.&M. counted in every period, scoring the first time they had possession of the ball.

The first touchdown came after Derace Moser, Marion Pugh, and John Kimbrough had worked the ball from their own 38 to the Tulsa 13. Moser swept untouched around end, with perfect interference, for the score. In the second quarter Kimbrough intercepted Keithley's pass on the Tulsa 28 and smashed his way to the four-yard line. Two plays later he exploded through the middle of the line for a touchdown.

Their Passes Click

Two more passes counted six points each in the third period, one from Pugh to Elvis (Boots) Simmons for 21 yards and the other from Pugh to Bill Henderson for 55. Jeffrey plunged over from the three-yard line in the final quarter and Earl Smith closed the Aggie scoring with a pass interception and 70-yard dash. Pugh kicked three conversions and passed to Simmons for the fourth.

Tulsa's only tally came when Moore plunged over from the one-yard line after a downfield march midway in the last period.

The Texans got 108 yards on the ground to Tulsa's 88, but amassed 200 by the aerial route to the Oklahoman's 115.

An Aggie fumble in midfield set up the Hurricane score. Calvin Purdin uncorked a rainbow pass to Malcom Strow, who ran to the Aggie four. Lester Moore slashed through tackle for the tally on the third attempt.

John Abbott

Aggies Salvage Glory for Southwest; Win is 14th Straight for Texas Eleven

John Kimbrough Generates First-Period Scoring Drive
But Excessive Heat Slows Down Offense of Teams

By Robert Myers

LOS ANGELES, Oct. 12—(AP)—The big maroon touchdown machine of Texas A. and M. ran into a heat wave and a band of fired-up Bruins of UCLA today, but managed to achieve a 7 to 0 victory.

The Aggie eleven from the Southwest conference, ringing up its fourteenth consecutive victory and its third straight of the 1940 grid campaign, showed a powerful defensive squad to the 60,000 sweltering fans—the temperature was in the 90's at kickoff—but couldn't keep its scoring spark ignited to roll up a big score.

In the end A. and M. had four backs who outgained the Pacific Coast conference team, and doubled the first down count, but the only score of the day came in the first quarter.

Aggies Roll

Big John Kimbrough, the Cadets' All-American fullback of 1939, intercepted a pass a few minutes after the kickoff, and the Maroon eleven began to roll. It rolled 44 yards in eight plays, with Kimbrough cracking the Bruin line for five, six and reserve back, Bill Conatser, lending a hand with more such smashes until the ball was on the nine-yard line. Here Kimbrough hit the left side of the Bruin line, cut over and charged on across the line standing up for a touchdown. Dookie Pugh kicked the extra point.

U.C.L.A. couldn't work up much of an offensive. Its ace ball carrier, Jackie Robinson, went out of commission and out of the game in the second period, and didn't come back.

Messrs. Kimbrough and his mates, meanwhile, roamed up and down the field, eating up yards in huge chunks, but fate and fumbles stepped in no less than four times to thwart a score. Twice fumbles interrupted sustained marches, and twice alert Bruin ball hawks reached into the air to snare Aggie passes.

Twice the Bruins penetrated deep into A.&M. territory, once on a pass good for 47 yards from Leo Cantor to Halfback Ray Bartlett. The threat ended on the Texas eight, however, when charging Cadet tacklers smothered the Bruin offense.

The defeat was the Bruins' third this season.

Robinson Bottled Up

A superior and greater number of backs and harder-charging linemen spelled the difference between the Aggies and Bruins. Robinson was hamstrung. He figured in one pass, catching it and lateraling to Bartlett for 10 yards. A moment later he had the wind knocked out of him and was removed from the game.

Kimbrough in the early stages lived up to all expectations, although he looked ragged at the very start. Toward the end the heat told on all the Aggies and while Kimbrough played the full 60 minutes he couldn't generate much power in the closing plays. Marland Jeffrey came into the game at the halfback spot in the final quarter and ripped off gains of 14, 7, 14 and 1 yards, and passed to Simmons for seven to reach the Bruin 29-yard line. Cantor was the best runner for the Uclans, snagging Jeffrey's pass to end the threat.

Robinson gained nine yards. Kimbrough got 74 yards in 19 attempts. He failed to gain five times, mostly in the last quarter.

On the scoring drive from the Bruin 44, Conatser got three off tackle, Kimbrough got six and two before Conatser added nine. Pugh threw an incomplete pass, but Kimbrough came back for five yards and a first down on the 18. Conatser skirted left end for nine before running out of bounds. From there Kimbrough crashed through his right tackle, slanted to the right and went on over.

An early check disclosed no Aggies injured.

Champs Do All Their Scoring In Second Quarter When They Make 3 Touchdown Passes

By Vin Burke
Beaumont Enterprise

COLLEGE STATION—Oct. 19—The champion Texas Aggies sailed serenely over the first hurdle in their race for another Southwest title (and whatever New Year's booking that honor might bring) by handing the Texas Christians a 21-7 pasting here this afternoon before 22,000 fans. The Aggies are aiming at Pasadena and from the way things were happening in the second period today they may get into the Rose Bowl on a pass.

Concentrating all their scoring in that quarter, they fired over three touchdowns through the airways after the sophomore Horned Frogs threw up an unexpectedly stout defense against the Farmer running attack. Nor was the home club at all hot during the second half, although it didn't have to be.

The Christians also scored on a pass—in the third quarter—and although their offense was never a threat to their more illustrious opponents they did slow down the Aggie running game and big John Kimbrough to a noticeable degree.

Midway in the first quarter the champs put together two first downs, moving to the Frog 28, but there the march stalled and a punt was ordered. On the final play of the period Jim Thomason lugged the ball to the Frog 34 for a gain of eight yards, and after the teams had changed direction the Aggies with two to go and second down pulled a fast one.

Looking for another ground play the Frogs were caught napping when Marion Pugh faded back and heaved the ball to Elvis Simmons, the sophomore end from Somerville, who made the catch on the 13 and drove over for the score; carrying a Frog along with him. Pugh's kick was good, as were the succeeding two conversions by this stalwart.

Second Touchdown

In just the twinkling of an eye Pugh had intercepted a Frog pass to set up the second touchdown. It came when Kimbrough, after trying a running pitch in the direction he was moving, started another play the same way only to suddenly whirl about and throw a cross-fire to Thomason, waiting patiently in the opposite flat, Jim stepping gingerly across for an over-all gain of 19 yards.

Not satisfied, the Cadets were moving a moment later to their third score. Derace Moser returned a punt to the T.C.U. 40, Pugh ran it to the 24 after failing to locate a receiver, and Kimbrough fumbled and lost 11 yards. This in-and-out procedure ended on the next play, however, when Pugh whipped the ball straight over the line to Thomason, who shook loose from three tacklers and charged across the goal line.

At this point, the Aggies made the umpire the goat by sending in a stream of substitutes, right down to Beaumont's own Butch Bando. On the last play of the quarter, Bando trotted onto the field in time to take the pass from center, neatly sidestepped two chargers and unwind a left handed heave far down the field—into the arms of a Christian.

Coach Homer Norton was more sparing with his subs in the second half and although his big shots were in there most of the time they were to see the Fort Worth boys really playing the better ball.

The third quarter was almost over when little Dean Bagley made a long throw down the middle. Tommie Vaughn managed to tip the ball into the air just enough for Ronnie Braumbaugh to take it well back of the Aggie secondary and lope down the field for the score, the entire play being good for 47 yards. Phil Roach booted the extra point.

Marshall is Battered

A.&M.'s great guard, Marshall Robnett, took a bad beating during this part of the game, twice being all but out but refusing to give way to a substitute. After his first time out he staggered to his feet in an obvious daze but instinct allowed him to break through the Christian line a play or two later and throw the ball carrier for a substantial loss.

Thomas emerged from the role of blocker to claim leading honors for the day both as a running back and a pass receiver. Pugh's passing and running and Robnett's vicious play in the line also stood out.

The Frogs managed to stop 220-pound Kimbrough quite frequently, and all the other Aggie ball carriers whenever a drive was impending. But the versatile champions merely turned to the air, and had that course failed, probably would have tunneled under.

Jim Thomason (47)

WINNING 16

Texas Aggies Batter Baylor Bears Into Submission After Bitter Struggle, 14 to 7

By Felix R. McKnight

WACO, Texas, October, 26—(AP)—The bulging Texas A. and M. snowball gathered in gallant, geared-up Baylor today 14-7, tumbling to its sixteenth straight triumph in one of the stoutest tests of the long string.

Hobbled at critical moments by the famed Baylor line, the Cadets drew deeply on their power, experience and passing game to build a two-touchdown lead that withstood Baylor's last-minute surge.

Battered, weary, the screams of 20,000 fans beating their ears the last 20 minutes, the Aggies were glad to leave Municipal stadium and a Baylor team that had been pointing for them since the playing date was announced months ago.

True, the Aggies outgained and outscored the Baylors, but they had to fire All-American John Kimbrough, big Jim Thomason, Marion Pugh's aerial darts and their great line for 60 minutes to get on the winning side. The Aggies swept to 263 yards on a slightly slippery field, 155 of it from running. Baylor rolled up 145 yards.

Baylor Line Tough

The first down margin went to the big Red touchdown machine, 14 to six, and many times they lost scoring opportunities on their own errors and Baylor's valiant stands, but still they had to scramble to stifle Baylor in the last period.

Only one minute remained when the Aggies finally got the situation under control again. Then, on Kimbrough's battering forays outside the tackles, they were sweeping ahead on the Baylor 13-yard line as the game ended.

Nine minutes remained when Baylor, never able to get off a sustained offensive drive, suddenly cut loose. Jim Witt, a grand ball carrier and leader, sprinted back 40 yard from the goal line with an Aggie kickoff. Then he started passing to Sophomore Jack Russell and Milton Crain, finally getting the ball down to the Aggie 29.

Tiny Dwight Parks took over the chunking there and lofted a 15-yarder that Witt bagged at the 14 and took it across for a touchdown. Bob Nelson kicked the point.

Great Kicking

Great kicking by Derace Moser and Bill Conatser in the dying minutes kept Baylor deep in its own lot, but they pitched a thrill with every pass that had Aggies running all over the field batting them down.

The Aggies drove to the Baylor 5, 13, 14 and 22-yard lines on different occasions. But always there was magnificent opposition—that Baylor line and a fine linebacker in Milton Merka—to throw them back.

The defending national champs were denied a scoring chance in the first five minutes of the game, when Jim Thomason's power spurt on deep reverses and Marion Pugh's passing and running carried them from their 33 to the Baylor 14. But the Cadets came pounding back at the period's end to get past the grand Baylor line.

Dwight Parks' meek kick-back that sailed out on the Baylor 40 started proceedings. Kimbrough and Conatser, jabbing the tackles and skirting the ends, took turns about upsetting the Bruins. Just as Baylor's line girded down on their four for some of Kimbrough's bull rushing, Conatser tailed out around left end for the score, untouched. Pugh kicked the point.

Bears Threaten

Twice Baylor threatened just before the half. Milton Merka broke through on a sneak play over center, and rambled 37 yards down the sidelines before Kimbrough blocked him out of bounds on the 28. But

Parks was smothered on passing attempts, tackled for big losses as the Aggies finally took over on their own 48.

Parks started connecting with passes to Witt that gained 22 and 11 yards in a drive that started from the Baylor 32. It ended in futility on the last play before the half when Odell Herman, Aggie center, intercepted on his own five and dashed 23 yards before being smashed out of bounds.

The second Aggie score came deep in the third period after Baylor had turned them back from the five-yard line on Moser's fumble. Back on the Baylor 45, where Witt's kick settled, Reserve Back Marland Jeffrey spun a 15-yard pass that Sophomore Bill Henderson, a gangling, six-foot, six-inch end, grabbed and took across on a beautiful sprint. Jake Webster kicked the point.

Listening to the Aggies on the radio

WINNING 17

Arkansas Razorbacks are 17th Straight Victim of Texas Aggie Might, 17 to 0

By Felix R. McKnight

COLLEGE STATION, Texas, Nov. 2.—(AP)—Giant John Alec Kimbrough hurtled like a vagrant meteor through Arkansas today to shepherd the Texas Aggies to their seventeenth consecutive triumph, 17-0.

The laughing, 222-pound, All-America fullback, shook a touchdown out of the mountainous Razorbacks midway of the first period with some of his old-fashioned line plowing and then riddled their two boldest aerial attempts with stunning interceptions and runbacks of 47 and 38 yards.

But behind Jarrin' Jawn today was a vicious Aggie line that manufactured break after break with jolting tackles that caused Arkansas to commit five fumbles—all recovered by the Cadets—at quite crucial moments.

Fumble Turns Tide

Time and again, just as a sort of grimly determined Arkansas team seemed to be making knots with a surprising ground game, Aggie linemen bolted through to divorce a runner from the ball and choke off a threat.

The Aggies won handily by their late surge, but for the first time since the Arkansas game a year ago they were outgained. The towering Porkers gained 226 yards—151 by passing—to the Aggies' total of 185 yards.

It was definitely a ball game for the first two periods. Arkansas took bad breaks on the chin and came back for more. But their inability to hold to the ball finally cost them dearly.

On Arkansas' second scrimmage play of the game the Aggies flushed a great break when Tackle Chip Routt's vicious block of little Walt Hamberg's attempted quick kick gave Ernie Pannell a chance to recover on the Arkansas 12.

There the Porkers put on a grand defensive show, taking over the ball after Kimbrough's two runs and two passes failed to score.

Marion Pugh

'Forget About Rose Bowl—We Play Rice Next Week,' Says Homer Norton After Victory Over SMU Mustangs

By Harold V. Ratliff

DALLAS, Texas, Nov. 9—(AP)—Coaches Homer Norton of Texas A. and M., and Matty Bell of Southern Methodist University, bitter rivals on the football field, clasped hands today after their teams had fought all over the gridiron and said "You're the best."

Norton declared the S. M. U. team that his Aggies beat today, 19-7, was the finest eleven the Cadets had met "to date."

Bell praised the Aggies as a better team than the one that smashed to an undefeated season and Sugar Bowl laurels last season.

Norton brushed aside the question: "How about the Rose Bowl?" with "we're not talking about bowl games now. Our next opponent is Rice."

A person partial to contrasts would have gloried in a visit to the dressing rooms of the two squads. In the Aggie room, down under the big shell of Ownby stadium, all was confusion and laughter.

Norton, a 12-inch cigar—one of the show kind—clamped between his teeth, was really letting himself go. He posed for a photographer with his arm around Big John Kimbrough the All-American fullback, and Bill Conatser, the boy who broke S. M. U.'s heart today.

"You can say John Kimbrough is the greatest fullback of all time," Norton roared. "My all-time All-American backfield would be Kimbrough, Nagurski, Grange and Thorpe."

In the S. M. U. dressing room the boys said little, but they did not express great disappointment, all agreeing that the Aggie team was the best they ever had met.

"A. and M. has a truly great team," said Bell. "We got some breaks against us. The worst one when Ray Mallouf's pass was batted down into a fumble and A. and M. recovered deep in our territory. But I'm not taking anything away from A. and M. It was a great team."

"This is the first time I've ever turned loose," Norton grinned as he pushed the giant cigar to a 45-degree angle. You know, we coaches have never done this before, but we have been saving up for this occasion."

Marion Pugh, the pass-pitching Aggie quarterback, came out of a shower dripping wet and put soap all over the writer.

"They had a good team," he said. Then he turned to Norton: "Coach, I love you," he bellowed.

Norton praised Pugh, Kimbrough, Robnett and Conatser and added loudly: "And don't forget Tommie Vaughn—he's the best defensive center in America."

Then, another afterthought: "Preston Johnson of S. M. U. is a great player. They have everything."

Johnny Clement, S. M. U. backfield star who was injured in the second quarter, said he didn't know what happened the rest of the game. "They were a great ball club—what I remember of them," he said.

Ray Mallouf said the A.&M. team was better than any he had ever played against.

Morshall Robnett

30,000 Watch Cadets
Win 19th in Row

Bill Henderson Is Hero of Farmer Victory

By Bruce Layer
Post Sports Editor

COLLEGE STATION, Nov. 16—The greatest collection of football players in the history of Texas A. & M. College flashed over Kyle Field Saturday afternoon for the first time to gain a 25 to 0 victory over Rice Institute.

For 22 members of Coach Homer Norton's great machine it was the final home appearance, and they closed out their careers for the twelfth man in a blaze of glory that left little doubt about the Aggies being the Number 1 football team of the nation.

When a stout Rice line threatened to shackle the Aggie ground game the Cadets moved into the air and passed their way to two touchdowns in the first seven minutes of the second period.

Clinch Tie for Title

Two other overhead scoring drives came later on, but it was merely adding to the margin, for once the Aggies were out in front the Owls could do nothing until the final period when the invaders started driving.

The crowd of 30,000 saw the Owls move deep into Aggie territory in the closing minutes, but Cadet forwards dug in on the 11-yard line and for the third straight year Rice suffered a shutout.

Saturday's victory was the nineteenth in a row for the Aggies and it assured the mighty men of Aggieland no less than a tie for the championship won last year.

Henderson Great Catcher

Rice and S. M. U. are the only teams with a chance to share the title and the Aggies can eliminate that possibility on Nov. 28 when they meet the University of Texas Longhorns at Austin in a belated Thanksgiving Day encounter.

From out of the game that was for all of the chips, Bill (Jitterbug) Henderson, a gangling kid from the Heights in Houston, stepped out as the hero. His pass catching was sensational. Eight straight times he snared overheads and he set up the first touchdown with one of the catches, scored the third and set up the fourth.

The big boy was taking them over the center, off to the sides and all over the place and there was little the Owl defense could do about the towering wingman.

A. & M. figured to whip the Owls on wide stuff and passes and that was just what happened. The Aggie yardage came around the ends and on cutbacks from running plays and through the air on well directed passes by Marion Pugh and Marland Jeffrey.

Jarrin' John Kimbrough, All-American fullback, had another good day. Last week it was his work through the line against S. M. U. and today he was going wide, and going like a runaway locomotive.

Bob Brumley, one of the most improved ball players in the conference, was right on Big Jawn's heels for offensive honors. It was Brumley's ball toting on spinners and handling on reverse that kept the Owls in the ball park, and backing that line he was a tower of strength.

Owls Best in First?

Through the opening period Rice played the Aggies to a standstill and held the upper hand in yardage. But that was before A. & M. elected to whip out its most dangerous weapon.

The first Aggie drive started on A. & M.'s 26 shortly before the close of the period. They had advanced to their own 44 and, on fourth down with a yard to go, the Aggies gambled and won. Kimbrough smashed through for a first down. As gambles go, this one was not exactly a bet-the-farm wager.

At that point Henderson took charge. He grabbed a pass from Jeffrey on the Rice 34 and raced 14 more yards to the 20. He took another two yards and then Jim Sterling, whose play this season has matched the name, sneaked into the end zone to snag Jeffrey's pass for a touchdown.

Three minutes later the Aggies got the ball on their 43 and Pugh passed to Henderson for a first down on the Owl 39. Moser took the next aerial and ran to the five. From there Moser circled end for the touchdown.

About three minutes before the half Pugh whipped a 14-yard pass to Henderson and he stepped over the goal line for touchdown Number 3.

In the last three minutes of the third period, the Aggies took the ball on the Owl 41. Pugh passed to Sterling to the 20 and a pass to Henderson was good for a first on the Rice four. Kimbrough raced right end for the touchdown. Pugh failed on the try for point and the score was Texas A.&M. 25, Rice 0.

In the fourth quarter, a 15-yard penalty moved the Owls to within 16 yards of the Aggie goal, but Rice was unable to convert the threat and four plays later they had gained three feet and the ball went back to A.&M .

In the last two minutes the Owls drove back to the 11, where Brumley's fourth down spinner lacked inches of making a first down and the Cadets held the pigskin until the gun sounded.

LOSING ONE

Fighting Longhorns
Tumble Mighty Aggies, 7-0

45,000 Watch Layden Score in First Minute

By Charles Burton
Dallas Morning News

AUSTIN, Nov. 28—It happened: the Texas Aggies, one of the greatest football machines the Southwest Conference has ever seen, came to the end of the road here Thursday as a daring, fighting University of Texas eleven struck in the first minute for a 7-0 triumph before 45,000 persons in Memorial Stadium.

Texas' brilliant triumph was cleancut and decisive. There was nothing flukish about it. The Longhorns, led by brilliant Pete Layden, a dynamite triple-threater, simply outplayed and outfought an Aggie team that Coach D. X. Bible's inspired players wouldn't allow to get going.

The Aggies have never won a game on Memorial Stadium turf. Wednesday night, the Longhorns vowed they would protect this tradition. And Thursday, fifty-eight seconds after the opening whistle, the Longhorns had scored a touchdown that kept their promise.

The Aggies won the toss, and Jim Thomason pointed to the south goal, taking a slight wind to their backs. Dog Dawson went in for Bill Buchanan at end to kick off for the Aggies, and his kick sailed out of bounds just short of the goal line. Texas put the ball in play at its own 35-yard line.

Four plays later, the Longhorns scored. Layden's opening aerial shot settled into the arms of tricky-stepping Jack Crain and he was spilled on the Aggie 32. Layden, whose pitching was perfect Thursday, tossed again and hit End Preston Flanagan, but he dropped the ball.

Layden then fired at Noble Doss, who caught the ball in the right hand corner of the field. He swerved sharply toward the sideline as he took the ball over his shoulder and apparently couldn't recover his sense of direction entirely, for he skidded out of bounds three inches short of the goal line. He could have stepped over the double stripe just as easily had he been able to regain his balance a moment earlier.

But that made no difference, for on the next play Layden ankled up to the Aggie right tackle position and simply stepped mincingly behind his forwards as they pushed the whole left side of the Aggie line back far enough for Pete to score.

Crain Kicks Extra Point

Crain, always as cool as the top shelf in the refrigerator, place-kicked the extra point in his usual effortless manner.

And, that, for all practical purposes, was the ball game. The Cadets fought back, but Texas fought back even harder.

Both teams threatened to tally in the second period, Crain intercepting a pass and giving the Longhorns a chance from the Aggie 34. The Steers traveled right on down to the 10-yard line, but Layden failed to handle a snap from center and Buchanan recovered the ball for the Aggies.

Given a start by a 15-yard penalty, the Aggies surged down to the Texas nine, with Jarrin' Jawn Kimbrough bowling his way for most of the distance. There, the attack was bogged down by Texas' battling defense and Kimbrough's pass was intercepted in the end zone by Doss, ending the drive.

Texas wasn't hanging on desperately in the second half, either, the Longhorns carrying the battle to the Cadets at every opportunity, once reaching the College Station team's 24-yard line.

Game Studded with Stars

Crain, who called the signals for the Longhorns, played one of his best games. Layden was sensational, but give the whole, inspired Texas team credit for playing a great game, for it did.

On the other side of the line, the steady, dependable Kimbrough, Wild Bill Conatser, Chip Routt and Marshall Robinett, the Cadets' All-American guard, deserve special credit. If any other Cadet didn't stand out, don't blame the Aggies—credit the Longhorns. The way the Steers fought Thursday at every turn would have taken the luster off the play of most any football player.

Victory would have given the Cadets their second national title in a row, and second Southwest Conference title, but defeat left them in danger of being tied by Rice or Southern Methodist, if either of those teams wins its remaining games. Victory, too, probably would have sent Coach Homer Norton's team marching to the Rose Bowl. But defeat left that matter in doubt.

However, the Cadets won nineteen straight games before they were upset, and that is a conference that is likely to stay on the boards for a long while.

Each team Thursday made 11 first downs. The Cadets marched for 155 yards on the ground, where Texas rushed for 150. Kimbrough picked 101 yards, in 20 carries, running fiercely as the tailback in a spread formation.

But in the air, the Longhorns were superior, with 97 yards to 51, and picking off five passes, three by sub quarterback Marland Jeffrey. A.&M. had as many interceptions as it had completions.

Pugh Plays Very Little

The Cadets played without the services of their top passer, Marion Pugh. A bad Charley horse allowed him to play for only a few downs here and there. He might have made the difference between defeat and victory, but that is doubtful for the Texas pass defense, usually weak, was close to being airtight Thursday, allowing only five of eighteen tosses to connect.

Anyway, the Aggies wouldn't want Pugh's absence to be construed as an alibi, for they were beaten squarely and fairly and quite decisively. It was just their tough luck to have to take that last step toward the Rose Bowl on the turf of Memorial Stadium.

And in retrospect…

One is tempted to take issue with the accounts of the game by Charles Burton, sports editor of the *Dallas Morning News*, and others.

To describe the Texas victory as "decisive" seems a touch of overkill. With five of their passes picked off, the wonder is that the Aggies lost by only a touchdown.

And far too little was made of the absence of Marion Pugh, who led the Southwest Conference in passing in 1939, sharing time with Cotton Price. Nor are we at all sure that the Aggies would be too proud to blame the loss, at least in part, on Pugh's injury.

Another puzzlement was the lack of a reference, in any story of the game, to the fact that the Aggies moved up and down the field from the spread formation, then went back to the single wing once they were near or inside the Texas ten, as they were twice.

And it would be unthinkable today that no writer would ask Homer Norton why his incomparable fullback, John Kimbrough, never carried the ball when the Aggies were on the cusp of scoring.

"I wondered about that myself," said Norton, years later, in response to a question from Kern Tips, for so many years the voice of Southwest Conference football.

This may be a mystery that few ever knew about, or those who were there forgot long ago. But it turned out that the Aggies, needing one more win to run their streak to twenty and repeat as national champions, changed their strategy for Texas. This was prompted by Pugh's leg injury and Norton's respect for D. X. Bible and his two fine runners, Crain and Layden.

Homer moved Kimbrough to tailback and Thomason to fullback. Near the goal line, expecting to key on Jarrin' Jawn, the Aggies gave the ball to Thomason and Bill Conatser, with Kimbrough used as a passer, a decoy or a blocking back.

And when he led the interference, so many Texas linemen moved with him that the Aggie ball carrier couldn't get through the traffic.

To add insult to injury, the headline in the Dallas paper referred to the "Fighting Longhorns." The Aggies thought they had a copyright on that adjective or, at least, shared it with Notre Dame.

Here is another perspective on the game, a sidebar by Felix McKnight, then with the Associated Press, later the editor of the News:

Jinx Holds; Longhorns
Upset Aggies, 7-0

Chances Are Slim, But Texas Aggies May Yet Receive Rose Bowl Bid

Defeat Gives Farmers' Bowl Hopes Big Jar
Texas Gridsters Protect Home Field

By Felix McKnight

AUSTIN, Nov. 29—(AP)—Numbed, driven into silence by defeat, the once invincible Texas Aggies weren't certain today whether they would just call it quits for the 1940 season or play in a New Year's Day post-season game.

The one foot they had in the Rose Bowl was jarred from it's mooring yesterday by a gallant University of Texas team that simply gave them a country licking, 7-0, before the largest throng in all Southwest college football history—45,000.

The Cotton Bowl classic in Dallas is probably theirs for the taking, despite their defeat. The Texas Aggies still are a great football team, one that had won nineteen successive game before Texas reared up and preserved a 18-year-old jinx that has kept the Aggies from winning in Austin since 1922.

Won't Talk of Bowl Tilt

The Aggies wanted no part of bowl talk today, but Coach Homer Norton said that after a holiday the players would gather on the campus down at College Station Tuesday and "think it all out."

The Aggies still haven't given up the idea of playing in a bowl game, as was evidenced by the fact that they still planned to scout

Tennessee and Fordham in Saturday games. There was considerable talk of a Fordham-Aggie game in the Dallas Cotton Bowl.

Norton emphasized, however, that it was entirely up to the players themselves as to whether they would play a post-season game. The matter was not mentioned after yesterday's defeat.

The Aggie team that stood on the threshold of football immortality—on the verge of clinching an undisputed Southwest Conference title for the second straight year – was just another football team yesterday before the Texas onslaught. The distinction of being the first team in all history to play in the Sugar and Rose Bowl on successive years had been within their grasp, and now was gone in a minute.

Texas Was Better Team

True, their quarterback and spark, Marion Pugh, was out of the game with an injured leg, but the Aggies weren't as good as Texas University—for the day.

It took just 57 seconds—the first 57 seconds of the game—to prove it.

In that brief span Peter John Layden, a magnificent player, and Texas, struck like lightning to win the game. Layden shot 34 and 33 yard passes to Cowboy Jack Crain and Noble Doss to move to the one-foot line and then plunged over himself for the game's only touchdown. Crain converted—and that was the game.

The Aggies came back on one drive, a truly marvelous effort by their All-America fullback, John Alec Kimbrough, but it just wasn't in the books.

Kimbrough simply overpowered the Texas line for sixty-three yards on nine bull-like carries to blast down to the Texas nine deep in the second period, but there the Aggies halted. Kimbrough, a tired boy, tried a bit of strategy and threw one of his infrequent passes on fourth down, but it was intercepted in the end zone by Doss for a touchback. That was the drive that might have saved the day for the Maroon and White.

Texas drove down to the Aggie eight on another big assault started on Crain's interception of a pass, but fumbled and End Bill Buchanan recovered for the Aggies to start Kimbrough's big march.

Too much Layden and Crain was the answer. They shot through the vaunted Aggie line, they threw passes, intercepted them and chilled the Aggie aerial game.

"We just had enough spirit, enough hustle to get into the Aggie backfield," quoted Dana X. Bible after his sweetest victory. "But I would like to say a word for this boy Kimbrough, or better still, to tell you that my boys think he is great. Why, I saw him tackled right under my feet once, by our boy Layden."

"What did he say?"

"That's a swell tackle, Pete."

"He's a great player—a great boy."

Statistically, the Texans were only little better than the Aggies. But it really wasn't much of a contest. Texas won, all the way. The Aggies gained much ground on Kimbrough's jabs—101 of the 155 yards gained—but the touchdown business was never evident.

John Kimbrough (left) and fellow cadets

Chapter 13

THE WAR YEARS

ᴄᴀᴋᴏ

THE 1940 AGGIES MAY OR MAY NOT HAVE BEEN OVERCOME with sympathy for what happened to Texas a year later, but they surely could relate to how the Longhorns felt when their highest hopes were rocked.

You begin with the November 17, 1941 issue of *Life* magazine, which featured something never before seen on the cover of that distinguished publication: the University of Texas football team, ranked Number 1 in the nation.

Or was. Unhappily for Texas loyalists, lowly Baylor, coached by Frank Kimbrough, had tied the Longhorns, 7-7, at Waco in a game that still rates as one of the epic upsets of Southwest Conference lore. When *Life* hit the newsstands, Texas had fallen to Number 2 behind Minnesota. There were fourteen faces on the cover, eleven starters and three key reserves. Inside was an eight-page spread that depicted the players on the field and around the campus. The magazine cost ten cents and seemed to be well worth it.

There was more bitter news ahead for the Longhorns. TCU shocked them a week later, 14-7, and a season of golden promise had gone up in flames. No national title. No invitation to the Rose Bowl. Sound familiar?

In the *Austin American-Statesman*, Weldon Hart wrote: "When the gay young blades of Texas U., current vintage, are old and gray and come back to the Forty Acres as honored guests, they will still be trying to explain the inexplicable Texas Longhorns of 1941."

This had been trumpeted as the greatest team Texas had put on a football field, and some still consider it so today. No Longhorn ever had been named to an All-America team. Four from the '41 lineup would be honored: Pete Layden and Jack Crain, the gifted runners, and two rugged linemen, tackle Mal Kutner and guard Chad Daniels.

Texas regrouped to roll past A&M, then entertained Oregon, a team that had been projected earlier as a possible Rose Bowl foe. Once proved to be enough. With eight players scoring touchdowns, the Longhorns were not very kind to their web-footed friends, cruising by 71-7. The date was Saturday, December 6th, 1941.

If that one-sided win was not enough to make brooding Texas fans forget about the tie with Baylor and the loss to TCU, another event would in less than twenty-four hours. It was just over the horizon, in that obscure place called Pearl Harbor. Their world, everybody's world, would be turned upside down and not even a *Life* cover, or a national championship, would again seem quite so important.

If you don't remember the words, you may hum along: Diving out of the cover of a rising sun, Japanese planes bombed and sank American ships, strafed American troops, left our Pacific fleet a smoldering shambles and wrenched us into World War II. The date, as no one needs to be reminded, was December 7th, 1941.

The Aggies were still out west, preparing to beat Washington State in their final game before heading to the Cotton Bowl.

Within hours of the first bulletins from Hawaii, it was announced that the Rose Bowl might be canceled because of fears that the Japanese would soon be attacking California.

College football went to war, too. Within weeks, half the A&M players had exchanged their jerseys for military tailoring. Those with reserve commissions went almost directly overseas.

Most of the sixteen seniors at Texas were in the service by the end of the month. One of the faces on the *Life* cover, Chad Daniels, would crash and die on a training flight in February, 1943.

Football didn't shut down, but there was another and deadlier score-keeping going on in places whose names we had never heard and couldn't spell. Iwo Jima. Okinawa. The Aleutian Islands. Stalingrad. Anzio. Dunkirk. Everyone had to grow up, or so it seemed, overnight.

Baylor is believed to have been the only university in the country with two athletes who received the Congressional Medal of Honor. Jack Lummus earned his leading a Marine charge at Iwo Jima, and was still shouting orders as he lay dying, after a land mine blew off both of his legs. Lummus had lettered in three sports, was an all-conference outfielder in baseball and an end on the football team.

Jack (Killer) Kane commanded a low-altitude, long-range bombing raid on Hitler's oil refining complex in Ploesti, Rumania. It was a suicide mission. Of the 166 planes that took off, 73 failed to return. Five Medals of Honor were awarded to pilots, the most ever from a single military operation. Only Citizen Kane and one other lived to receive theirs.

A&M's casualties bear repeating: Two stars of the 1939 National Champions died in plane crashes, Herbie Smith and Derace Moser. Joe Routt, the two-time All-America tackle (in 1936 and '37), died a hero at the Battle of the Bulge. It was the news of Routt's death that reached Homer Norton by telegram just before he delivered a speech at the East-West Shrine game. When he read the wire aloud, those in the room, coaches and players and fans, wept with him for Joe and all the young men like him who would not return.

The Aggies had their own war movie, the cult favorite, *We've Never Been Licked.* World War Two was not a movie, but we were reminded again of the vitality of college football and sports at large. It would take more than a global conflict to knock out our preoccupation with our national pastimes.

You gain a sense of how strong this interest was by looking again at the predicament of Texas A&M, a military school where the cadets were put through a crash course to graduate them a year ahead of schedule. After the 1942 season, the Aggies lost virtually every experienced player and most of the coaching staff.

Worth retelling is the story of how Norton received a phone call from Colonel Earl (Red) Blaik, then the head coach at West Point. Blaik asked Homer to send him a list of his best players, explaining straight out that he could arrange to have them appointed to the U. S. Military Academy, or drafted and then transferred.

In fairness to his players, Norton obediently sent along a list that included DeWitt Coulter, Hank Foldberg, Goble Bryant, Milt Routt and Marion Flanagan. Blaik took them all, and a year or so later he added Charley Shira, Dan Foldberg and Bill Yeoman. Five of those Aggie conscripts went on to win All-America acclaim at Army.

The Twelfth Man was no longer a nice tradition for students; it now applied to the entire football team. Norton issued a call for walk-ons to fill out a squad that kept losing players every week. The 1943 team, known as the Kiddie Korps, with an average age of seventeen years and four months, posted a 7-2-1 record and went to the Orange Bowl, where they lost to Louisiana State, a team they had defeated, 28-13, early in the season at Baton Rouge.

Because of travel restrictions, Norton was unable to reserve pullman cars for his team, and the players slept sitting up for two nights on their way to Miami. Norton believed they left their game on the train. LSU edged them, 19-14, behind the running of Steve Van Buren.

But the losses that mattered were on the fields of Europe and the Far East, in the skies and on the oceans. Texas mourned the deaths of Ralph Geear, Shelby Buck, Glenn Morries and another starter from the 1941 team, Mike Sweeny, whose bomber crashed over Germany.

The large majority lived through it and returned to pick up the threads of the world they had left behind. Of course, old plans were torn up or altered and replaced by new ones. Tommie Vaughn, the center and co-captain of the '39 Aggies, wound up going through flight school with Pete Layden of Texas, and served with Ollie Cordill, of Rice. Tommie had wanted to be a rancher. Instead, he became a rich Houston car dealer.

A bomber pilot named Tom Landry returned to Texas to finish playing football and go on to a career in the NFL as a player and coach. Another pilot, Guy Lewis, enrolled at the University of Houston on a basketball scholarship and stayed 30 years, coaching the Cougars into the national rankings.

Rice welcomed back a couple of Marine officers, Weldon Humble, an All-American guard in 1946, and Buck Sloan, who had been the center and captain on Jess Neely's second Rice team.

Among the returning veterans were names that could fill a hall of fame: Jitterbug Henderson and Marion Settegast, of the Aggies; Buddy Gatewood, of Baylor; Stan Mauldin, Sr., of Texas; Ralph Ellsworth, who played at Texas and Annapolis; Rice's Dick Dwelle, who became a newspaper publisher in Athens, and TCU's great tackle, Derrell Palmer.

And, of course, the most famous duo of all, Bobby Layne and Doak Walker, who had been teammates at Highland Park in Dallas, came out of the Merchant Marines to go their separate ways in 1945. Layne went to Texas and Walker to SMU, and their teams faced each other their first Saturday at home, with both in the starting lineups. There was clearly a great deal of lost time to be recovered. Layne and his Longhorns won, 12-7, and Bobby and Doak went on to become two of the names that would be symbols of the sport.

In strange places, at the least predictable times, we learned of the enduring appeal and power of sports. There was a B-25 bomber flying out of England called "The Galloping Ghost," the nickname of Red Grange of Illinois. And the B-29 that dropped the atomic bomb on Nagasaki had no markings except for the numerals "77" painted on its side. William Laurence of the *New York Times* mentioned in his report of the bombing that this had been Red Grange's jersey number.

Football was in a category well apart from baseball, mainly because the college game was then supreme and the players were mostly 18, 19 and 20-year olds. The military academies, West Point and Annapolis, were enjoying their greatest seasons, and suddenly army and navy and air force bases were fielding teams that showed up in the national rankings.

Iowa Pre-Flight was ranked second in the country behind Notre Dame in 1943, with the Great Lakes Navy team, coached by Paul Brown, rated sixth. In 1944, Randolph Field was third, behind Army and Ohio State.

Art Donovan—called "Little Arthur" for family reasons—was the inheritor of a colorful family tradition. His grandfather Mike was the world middleweight boxing champion after service in the Civil War. His father, Big Arthur, was one of the most famous boxing referees of his time, the third man in the ring for 18 World heavyweight title fights, including the historic rematch when Joe Louis knocked out Max Schmeling.

Little Arthur served with the Marines in World War II aboard the aircraft carrier, the San Jacinto. His father volunteered, although he was then in his 60's, to work with USO sports tours, an assignment that brought him one day to a dirt road on an island called Guam. He turned to a companion, pointed, and said with some excitement, "That Marine coming down the road, I know him."

The Marine was his son, Little Arthur, now grown to a brute of a fellow at 255 pounds, casually bumping into his old man halfway across the world from their home in the Bronx.

Which brings us to Paul Brown, who treated football almost as seriously as he treated war. When he was coaching at the Great Lakes Naval Air Station, Brown once caught a glimpse of one of his players on a day off, taking a train to the next town. The player was smoking a cigarette. When he got back to the base, Brown cut him from the team. In less than a month, the player was among the Marines landing on the beach as the Marines recaptured Okinawa. After his return to civilian life, Brown was asked if cutting a player in the NFL was hard, he always replied, "No, not so hard." Yeah, it was one thing to get cut and have to look for a 9-to-5 job, but another to get cut and wind up on Okinawa.

The National Football League, struggling to survive, looked to its past, bringing back a number of retired veterans, including Bronko Nagurski, whose legend was close to Paul Bunyan proportions. He played tackle and fullback at the University of Minnesota and later with the Chicago Bears.

He was 35 with two bad knees, but still as strong as anyone in the league, when George Halas talked him into making a comeback in 1943. Halas was on his way to the Navy and turned the coaching duties over to Hunk Anderson, who intended to play Nagurski strictly at tackle as a concession to his aching knees.

In his first game against the Green Bay Packers, he sacked quarterback Frank Sinkwich twice, telling him after the second indignity, "Sonny, I'm too old to go after you. You'll have to come to me."

At the end of the season, the Bears were trailing the Chicago Cardinals in the Western Division final, when Nagurski put himself in the lineup at fullback. He carried seven times on one drive for a touchdown, cutting the lead to 27-24, then set up Sid Luckman's pass for the winning score.

In the championship game against the Redskins, Bronko bulled across to tie the game at 7-7, and the Bears went on to win in a romp. He retired once again to his home in Minnesota, and made a nice living as the owner of the gas station that did the most repeat business in the state.

When a visitor remarked that this must be a measure of Nagurski's fame and popularity, a native replied, "No, it's because when he screws your gas cap on, nobody else can get it off."

The war postponed, but didn't cure many of America's social problems. Jesse Owens, hero of the 1936 Olympics, came home as a captain in the army and couldn't find a job. To support his family he took part in a series of promotional stunts, such as racing a horse, until he found a niche in public relations.

But before and after the war, Owens was involved in a story that captures the humanity that is at the heart of great wars, and even sportsmanship, a word that from time to time falls out of fashion.

Late in his life, I interviewed Owens, the black track star who won four gold medals in the '36 Olympics in Berlin, infuriating Adolf Hitler and undermining the Nazi propaganda of a superior Aryan race.

When Owens was going for his fourth gold medal in his best event, the long jump, his chief rival was a German favorite named Luz Long. Owens fouled on his first two jumps by stepping across the takeoff line. He had one try left, or else he would be eliminated and Luz Long would be the sure winner.

But Long drew Owens aside, suggested he draw another line in the dirt, several inches inside the official one. Long laid his warm-up jacket next to the line as a marker for Owens. Jesse qualified easily and went on to win the finals, beating the German on his last leap. This wasn't the Super Race against the African Auxilliary, as the papers had billed it. These were two athletes in the fellowship of pain.

Owens and Long became friends, and toured Europe for some post Olympic meets. Owens was cheered everywhere, the greatest sports hero of the day. They corresponded after Jesse returned home, but a few months later Luz Long was in uniform, fighting on the Italian front. The letters stopped.

In 1951, Jesse Owens returned to Berlin for the first time since his Olympic triumph. For a little touch of sentimental pageantry, Owens put on his old Olympic track suit and jogged slowly around the stadium while 75,000 roared in recognition.

As he left his hotel that morning, a teenager had asked for his autograph. Owens signed the book, handed it back, then spun around. "That book," he said, "may I see it again?" He looked at a picture pasted on the inside page. "That's a picture of Luz Long," he said.

"My father, sir," said the boy. He told Jesse that his father had been killed in the war. Owens put his arm around the youngster's shoulder, and they walked off the field together, an Olympic champion and the son of a man who might have been his enemy, but became his friend.

Jim Thomason

APPENDIX

TEXAS A.&M.'s 1939 NATIONAL CHAMPIONS
Player Biographies

John A. Abbott, back, sophomore.

John was an outstanding back at Corpus Christi High School and was a blue chip prospect. Unfortunately, he arrived at a time of an over-abundance of other great backs. He did manage to get in some playing time on the Championship team, but not enough to letter that year. By the time the road block ahead of him had cleared, his time had run out and he never had a chance to become the star he might have been, but for others like Kimbrough and Thomason or Webster and Zapalac. He did win his "T."

His two sons, Jack and Mark, both attended Texas A&M, where Jack won two track letters in the hurdles and sprints, and won All-American honors as a member of the 440-yard relay team in 1969. He thus became the '39ers first "son" to win such an honor. His picture, with his teammates, now hangs on the All-America wall in the Lettermen's Lounge. Mark was a football prospect in 1969, but the transfer rules kept him off the field.

After serving in the army, John raised Brahman cattle and was part owner and operator of the Harlingen Gin Co., the Valley Grain and Elevator, and the Harlingen Compress. He served as a deacon in the First Baptist Church, on the boards of the Valley Baptist Hospital and the First National Bank of Harlingen, and a trustee of the Cotton Producers Institute.

William Audish, guard, senior

The All-State fullback out of Brenham High School earned his nickname, "Rock," when he became ineligible after a great freshman season—as in, "rocks in his head." He had a shot at being a starter at fullback as a sophomore, but by 1938, the traffic at that position was so crowded the coaches moved him to guard.

He became a great one. Arkansas feared him more than Big John because of his success on the guard-around trick play.

He received his bachelor degree in Sociology in 1940, and in 1941 married Jerry Ivie, of Arlington, Texas.

During World War II, Rock served in the U.S. Navy and was a Chief Petty Officer when he left the service in 1946, after collecting five service medals. His teammates say he should have won another for his marksmanship with the sling shot, a weapon he was most proficient with on the campus.

Rock and Bubba Reeves, the two smallest men on the squad, provided the comedy relief to keep the team loose. Their favorite foils were their roomies, Big Dog Dawson and Martin Ruby, the two largest men on the squad. Rock summed up the 1939 season on the bus back to the hotel from the Sugar Bowl victory. He kept shouting to the people in passing cars: "Texas Aggies, undefeated, untied and unaccustomed to the whole damn thing."

Gus Bates, Jr., guard, senior

An all-district guard at Fort Worth Central High School, Gus was a well regarded recruit at A&M, but fame and glory were destined to elude him. Just about the time he was ready to move up, injuries would throw him for a loss. In spring practice, in 1939, he looked great, but again an injury set him back. He did eventually play and got a letter.

He received his degree in Animal Husbandry in 1941, and spent a year as a cattle buyer before joining the service. While on duty, he captained the Fort Warren (Wyoming) Broncos, then transferred to the Veterinary Corps at Fort Omaha (Nebraska) for the duration.

He went into business for himself after the war, as an independent cattle buyer and broker; rancher, truck line and feed lot operator. He was returning to Fort Worth from a cattle-buying trip into Oklahoma when his car crashed and he was killed on June 22, 1960.

William Blessing, end, sophomore

An outstanding football and basketball performer at North Dallas High School, Bill arrived at A&M via the North Texas Agricultural College, in time to be eligible for the 1939 team. However, an appendectomy that fall put him out of action. He was back in 1940 and did get in some playing time and later received his "T."

Bill majored in architecture, but the war came along before he could complete the work for his degree. He served in the Air Corps until 1945, and was a first lieutenant at the time he left the service.

He made a career in real estate and construction, and helped develop several apartment complexes south of College Station.

One of his sons, William Scott, an Aggie grad, lettered in track and was a football squadman until a severe injury in the 1966 Rice game ended both sports careers.

Hugh F. Boyd, Jr., end, senior

An All-Junior College end at John Tarleton in 1937, Boyd had to sit out one year to gain eligibility in 1939. By that time the team was set, so Hugh spent much of that year as an end on the Blue Boys. He did log enough varsity playing time to letter.

He played his early football at Jacksboro High School and made All-District twice and won three letters each in basketball and track as well. He and Joe Boyd were not related.

In 1940 he received his degree in accounting and a commission as a second lieutenant in the infantry, but then transferred to the Air Force and rose to the rank of colonel.

He saw service in the European, China-Burma-India, and Asiatic Theatres and among other decorations received the Air Force Commendation Medal and the Legion of Merit. When hostilities ended, he remained in the service, which took him to Newfoundland, Germany and the Philippines. Later, he served as Director of Supply and Services at Randolph Field.

Joe Boyd, tackle, senior

Joe reached A&M via Crozier Tech High School, in Dallas, and Paris Junior College, where he lettered one year and then transferred. He won his first "T" in 1937; made the All-SWC team in 1938 and All-America in 1939, when also was a tri-captain with Herbie Smith and Cotton Price.

He received his bachelor's degree in Agricultural Administration in 1940, and went to work for Todd Drydock in Galveston. When he tried to enter military service he found that he had been frozen in a vital war industry.

It was while working at Todd that Joe received his call to the ministry. After the war ended, he entered the Southwestern Baptist Theological Seminary, in Fort Worth, received his Master's degree and began his fulfilling career as a Baptist evangelist. He has been engaged ever since in that calling, which has taken him to all corners of the United States and the world. He had held pastorates at times but never at the cost of leaving his great crusade to save souls.

In 1964 Joe was named to the Silver Anniversary All-America football team selected by *Sports Illustrated*, and in 1966 was inducted into the A&M Athletic Hall of Fame.

William Buchanan, end, sophmore

Buck had been an All-Junior College end at Weatherford, but Coaches Norton and Rollins felt he could benefit by being held out one year. Then a sub was needed for Jim Sterling in a tough game against Centenary, so Buck found himself in the thick of the 1939 season.. From then on he and Jim split playing time. At the end of the year, his ten receptions were second only to Herbie Smith's 17. In addition to his two football letters Buck also won a baseball letter in 1941.

In 1943 he received his degree in Physical Education and later added his Masters at the University of Colorado. When he graduated from A&M, he went on duty with the U.S. Navy and saw service in the Pacific. When he came out in 1946 he held the rank of lieutenant, junior grade.

Buck began his coaching-teaching career in Florida in 1947. After three years he moved to Alabama, where he retired from high school coaching in 1964 to devote full time to teaching and administration.

Roy Bucek, guard, junior

Coaches hunt for those big and fast linemen, so when Lil Dimmitt signed up Roy they certainly found one. At Schulenburg High School, he was an All-District guard and champion sprinter and hurdler for three years. At 205 pounds, he had to be fast as well as big.

At A&M he proved himself by backing up Marshall Robnett, and then won his track letter on the sprint relay team and in both hurdles. By the time he graduated, he was SWC Champion in the hurdles and high point Man in the conference track meet in 1942. That same year he became the Number 1 hurdler in the nation to win his All-American honors. and a place in the Aggie Hall of Fame.

After graduating in 1942, Roy did his fighting in Europe, where he was awarded the Purple heart and lost the sight of an eye.

Discharged as a first lieutenant, he came back to Texas A&M as an Assistant Dean of Men under Dough Rollins, but after two years opened his own business as the Oakridge Smokehouse in Schulenburg. He expanded into Dairy Marts and a string of Kountry Kitchen Restaurants, with one in College Station. In his hometown he was a councilman and mayor pro tem.

Willard Clark, end, sophomore

Another of those outstanding end prospects in 1939, who found a traffic jam at that position on the varsity and had to settle for a sub role. A highly touted graduate of Hull-Daisetta High School's powerful teams, he had to settle for a key job on the Blue Boys, the scout team who practiced against the varsity. There he portrayed the next opponent's top pass catcher. He and his teammates played a tough schedule for they took on the 1939 National Champions five days a week — the opponents only had to do it once a season.

In high school Willard won his letters in football and basketball; captained his 1937 football team; made All-District two years; All-South Texas one year; and was picked on the third All-State team once. At A&M, he won his Freshman numeral in both sports. but afterwards concentrated on football. Although he spent most of his career playing for the Blue Boys, he did eventually won his letter.

After graduation, he served in the European Theater, in the Infantry, and was discharged with the rank of Captain. His company was awarded the Presidential Unit Citation, and Willard won the Silver Star and the Purple Heart.

Bill Conatser, back, junior

A product of Denison High School, Bill was recruited with the 1937 blue chip crop of freshmen strictly as a punter, but he developed himself into a great broken field runner.

Against Villanova he returned a punt 72 yards without a single block, although 10 Wildcats had a clean shot at him. The next week he ran back an intercepted pass against TCU for 92 yards.

Conatser and Derace Moser formed an unbeatable duo at wingback, where they split playing time almost equally. When time consuming plays were needed it was Conatser who was called on to run the wide stuff to chew up the clock. That running speed also won him his three track letters.

He received a degree in Economics in 1941, and then went to work for Uncle Sam. When he got back to Denison in 1946 he was a Captain and had seen extensive service in the China-Burma-India Theatre.

With the development of Lake Texoma, Bill was one of the founders of the Yellow Jacket Boat Company. He sold his interest in 1951 to join the insurance firm his father had founded many years before.

William Dawson, end, junior

The Big Dog compiled a great record in football and basketball at Crocket High School and Lon Morris Junior College. At A&M, he won All-Conference honors in basketball and also three letters each in his two sports. His high spirits played no small part in the success of the 1939 team. He won him a berth on the West squad of the Army All-Stars and was a starting end, sending All-American Holt Rast to the bench. Dog also converted every field goal and extra point he attempted.

He earned a degree in Agriculture in 1942 and went into service as a second lieutenant. When he came back from Europe he had won a Silver Star, Bronze Star, the Belgium Croix de Guerre and wore the gold oak leaves of a major.

He then became a coach at A&M, but after five years lost out in the many coaching changes of that time. He started a new career with Great Southern Life Insurance Co. and became one of their top producers.

Henry "Bud" Force, back, junior

Bud enrolled in 1937 as a member of that bumper crop of blue chip recruits. At Orange High, he had been an All-District back in football and as a forward in basketball, lettering in each sport four times. At A&M, however, he played football only.

Like many others on the 1939 Aggie team Bud arrived when the backfield was all stacked at his position, wingback, behind Derace Moser and Bill Conatser. Since those two played practically full time, little was left for the understudies. Although he did not letter in 1939 he did get his "T" later.

In 1941 he received his degree in agriculture and returned to his home in Orange where he had lived all his life.

Bud did his World War II hitch in the U.S. Marines from 1943 until the Japanese surrender in 1945. Back from military duty, he became a land developer in Orange, but later expanded his operation out into Newton County.

Henry Hauser, tackle, junior

Henry turned out to be probably the most brilliant of the '39ers. He could boast of membership—although he wasn't the type to boast—in the National Academy of Sciences, and several societies involved in a field called Photographic Engineering, in which he won international renown.

As Colonel Hauser, he headed up an entire Army Photo Interpretation program for more than a quarter century. He attended 11 advanced military schools and was the author of 28 publications on military procedure. He also handled translations in Japanese, German, French, Italian and Hungarian.

An All-State blue chip center out of Tivy High School in Kerrville, Henry wound up as a tackle and won All-American honorable mention. He also was the SWC golf champion for three years. At 6-4 and 225, the big fellow from the Hill Country was nicknamed "Bear Tracks."

He received his degree in Marketing and Finance in 1941 and went on active duty at once as a second lieutenant. He was assigned to intelligence and while in the Pacific served on the staff of General Douglas MacArthur.

When he retired as a full Colonel, he held the Bronze Star, the Army Commendation Medal with Two Oak Leaf Clusters, the American Defense Medal and Philippine Liberation Medal with three Battle Stars, and the Reserve Officers Ribbon.

Bill "Jitterbug" Henderson, end, senior

Robert William Henderson was one of a kind. An All-State basketball player at Houston's John Reagan High School, the Bug was recruited for basketball only, but he had different ideas.

Before he was through he had won eleven varsity letters in five sports, was heavyweight boxing champion and handball singles king. He is the only Aggie ever to win four letters in one year and got two of those (track and baseball) in the same afternoon. He won his handball crown that night. In track he was a five-event man. He made All-American as a javelin thrower and got a second team All-American place in football. He was all-conference in basketball three straight years.

He received his degree in Sociology in 1943 and went to service immediately and was a Captain when discharged in 1946 after Philippine Liberation Service.

Upon discharge he joined American General Life Insurance Co., where he set a record of 98.3 percent for his renewals. In 1952 he was elected to Texas Legislature but resigned in 1954, having been diagnosed with Multiple Sclerosis, saying that he would not accept pay for work he could no longer perform. He passed away in Houston December 27, 1954.

Henderson Hall, the Texas Aggie athletic dormitory, is named in his honor. He also was one of the first five Aggie "greats" elected to the Athletic Hall of Fame in 1964.

Charles Edward Henke, guard, junior

A product of Kerrville's Tivy High School, Henke, known as "Mush," came to Aggieland after making the All-State team as a tackle in 1937. He won his first "T" as a tackle, but was moved to guard in 1939.

With All-America Marshall Robnett playing the opposite post, he was frequently referred to as "the other guard." Still, Charles left his mark on the All-Time Cotton Bowl team for his play against Fordham.

He received degree in Animal Husbandry in 1941, along with his commission as a second lieutenant, and went on active duty immediately. General Bob Neyland, the great Tennessee coach, drafted him to play for the Army All-Stars, who played the pro teams for the benefit of the Army Relief Fund. After the Summer of '42, Henke rejoined his outfit in time to be shipped over to Europe.

There he won the Bronze Star, the American Defense, American and European Theater Medals before being discharged as a first lieutenant.

He went back to Kerrville, where he joined Uncle Bill James in a partnership of a tractor, farm implement, and Jeep dealership and also did some ranching.

Odell "Butch" Herman, center, junior

Strange as it may seem now, Butch Herman, the All-State fullback at Abilene High School, was the prime blue chipper the Aggies were after and not another back on that same team named John Kimbrough.

Butch was headed for great things until the Baylor game of 1938, when he was injured. Bob Hall subbed in for him and when Hall was hurt there was no other healthy fullback but Kimbrough. John's play that day made a great center out of Herman who won his three letters playing that spot.

Herman had an uncanny knack for diagnosing plays, so that he always was in the wrong place at exactly the right time, like Ki Aldrich of TCU.

Butch received his degree in Marketing in 1941 and shortly thereafter he was on military duty. He had battled his way across Africa, Italy, and France before shipping out to the Pacific Theater of operations. He ended up as a Major with several decorations.

William Marland "Jeff" Jeffrey, back, sophomore

An All-State back at Thomas Jefferson High School in Port Arthur, Jeff was one of the prime prospects recruited in the 1937 dragnet. He was a versatile back playing all four positions, an important factor in Coach Norton's future plans. The 1939 setup called for Jeffrey and Marion Pugh to alternate at quarterback, since Cotton Price had suffered severe burns and was not counted upon to play.

Price made an astonishing recovery, so Jeff became a backup at all four posts as originally had been planned. He always had enough time to win his three football letters and added three more as a slugging out-fielder in baseball.

He received his degree in Business Administration in 1941 and also a commission in the army. He served five years, coming out as a captain and wearing several decorations. He was with the Jefferson Chemical as a junior accountant and purchasing agent at their Port Neches plant, before joining Gulf Supply Co. in their sales division.

He worked for Metropolitan Life Insurance for three years, before deciding that Gulf Oil was a better place to make his career. For diversion he officiated high school and college football games for 20 years as a member of the Southwest Football Officials Association.

Jack Kimbrough, end, junior

Jack was the third in a string of five Kimbrough brothers to attend Texas A&M. First came Ernest and then Bill, a football letterman, then Jack, to be followed by John and Wallace. Only Frank, who won fame as a coach at Hardin-Simmons and Baylor, got away.

Jack came out of Haskell High School, where he was an All-District end and also won three letters in track. He was captain of both his junior and senior football teams.

He won his freshman numeral at A&M in 1936, but an early injury in the 1937 season caused him to leave school. When he came back in 1938 he was still unable to go at full speed and did not get lettering time. He did, however, make his letters in 1939 and 1940. At A&M he passed up track.

Jack received his degree in Agronomy in 1941, along with his army commission, and then reported to Camp Walters, Texas. For his next assignment, of all places, he was back to the Texas A&M campus as a staff officer in the ROTC program, where he remained for the duration of the war. When he came out of the service he held the rank of major.

When Jack left the Army, he went to work in sales for Humble Oil & Refining Co. He moved up the ladder at Midland, Albuquerque, and Abilene, where he was the district manager when he passed away from a heart attack on February 24, 1965.

John Alec Kimbrough, back, junior

Big John probably did more to place Texas A&M in the National football picture than any other Aggie player before or since his time, and he did it as a bruising fullback on the 1939 National Champions.

Big he was not, for he weighed only 212 pounds stripped and the bruising came simply from his powerful knee action drive. No injury to any player ever was intentional. To John football was not a game he loved as some players did—to him it was only the means to an end. His goal was to obtain a college education for himself, and his crippled brother, Wallace, who turned out to be almost as valuable as John for as the team tutor he kept them eligible.

John had lettered at Haskell and Abilene High School and was on the list of the Wanted Forty boys in 1937. However, Tulane also wanted him, so when he graduated at mid-term he went to New Orleans. When he asked Coach Red Dawson for a job for Wallace they had a disagreement and John came back to A&M. He was given his scholarship and a job for Wallace was found in the mess hall.

Injuries kept him from winning his freshman numeral and up to the 1938 Baylor game he had been the fourth string fullback.

The rest, as they say, is history and an oft-told story.

He received his degree in Agricultural Administration in 1941, and then signed a personal services contract with a New York promoter. This led to several unwanted situations, such as endorsing a cigarette although he was a non-smoker. He also found himself signed to a professional football contract, which he certainly did not want. This led to the original contract being taken over by the Bing Crosby Enterprises. As part of the settlement, he did play the final game of the season in New York and then made two Class B movies, both westerns.

Called active to duty as an infantry officer, he transferred to the Air Force and was a captain after flying in the Pacific Theater until 1946. He then played three seasons for the Los Angeles Dons, but retired to begin ranching at Haskell, where he still lives. He was elected to Texas Legislature, but retired after one term.

In 1942 he married Barbara Golding, of Houston, and they had two children. His son, John, played his football at tackle for SMU.

Big John was the first Aggie to be elected to the National Football Hall of Fame. John Kimbrough passed away on May 9, 2006.

Derace "Mose" Moser, back, sophomore

After an outstanding career as a triple threat back and a trackman at Stephenville High School, Moser followed his brother, Ralph, to Aggieland. His Fish performance was so good that he became one of the two sophomores to make the starting team of what turned out to be the 1939 National Champions.

In 1940, and again in 1941, he was a standout when the Aggies repeated for the Southwest Conference championships, twice picked on the All-SWC team and as winner of the Houston Post Most Valuable Back for 1941. He just missed making the All-America team when Bill Dudley, of Virginia, overtook him as the nation's leader in total offense. Moser had to settle for second team honors.

As a sprinter, he won track letters each year.

When he graduated in 1942, he reported for duty as an officer in the artillery. However, he was drafted to play on the West football team. coached by Wallace Wade, for the benefit of the Army Relief Program. That team virtually was the 1939 Champions—of the starting team eight were Texas Aggies.

However, a transfer to the Air Force he had requested came through, so he left the team and reported in rank to the Pyote, Texas, Flight Training Center. After advance training at Brady, Texas, his next transfer was to the McDill Air Force Base, in Florida for the final flight training to become a bomber pilot. It was here that he was involved in a training flight when a collision took his life. He died on November 19, 1942.

Ernest "Ernie" Pannell, tackle, sophomore

Ernie was another of those top talents ferreted out by Lil Dimmitt, while he was playing at the State Orphans Home in Corsicana. At John Tarleton, where EW won two letters and made the All-Junior College team.

Lil convinced him to transfer to Texas A&M at midterm, thereby making him eligible for the freshman team and three years of varsity ball. He won his Fish numeral in 1937 and by the third game in 1938 he had moved in at left tackle. He made the All-SWC team in 1939-40 and earned honorable mention for All-America.

Ernie received his degree in Business Administration in 1941 and accepted a Navy commission as an ensign, going on active duty immediately. Before he finished he was a lieutenant, junior grade, commanding a PT boat in the New Guinea area and had been awarded the Silver Star, along with other decorations.

After his discharge, he signed with the Green Bay Packers and won a starting berth at tackle with them. He played three years and retired to enter the oil well servicing field in which he was engaged for several years.

By 1965, with family investments in good shape Ernie and Dorothy decided to retire and settled down at Rancho Contento, Guadalajara, Jalisco, Mexico.

Charles Walemon "Cotton" Price, tailback, senior

Cotton came to Texas A&M from New Castle High School, where he had won three letters each in football, basketball and track along with two more in tennis. At A&M he stuck to football, winning his letters in 1937-38-39 and was co-captain with Joe Boyd and Herbie Smith of the 1939 National Champions.

Coach Dough Rollins once said of Price that he had ice water in his veins in place of blood so cool and composed was he under severe pressure. He cited the time in the TCU game in Fort Worth of 1938 when, during a blinding rain storm, Cotton went in to try the extra point which meant a tie, 7-7. He made it and when he came off the field he told Dough, "You thought I couldn't make it didn't you? Well, I knew I could, so never worried about it." Then again there was the summer of 1939, when he was severely burned in a gasoline fire. It was thought that his playing days were over, but Price said he would make a comeback and did.

He ended his career in the Sugar Bowl by kicking the extra point which meant winning, 14-13 and then played ball control for the last nine minutes of that game so Tulane would have no chance to score.

In 1940, Price received his degree in Physical Education and shortly after that he was in the Navy serving in both Atlantic and Pacific Theatres. When he came out he played one year of professional football with the Detroit Lions and then two more with Miami in the new All-America Conference.

Upon retirement, he settled down in College Station, where he opened an insurance agency handling all forms of risk. After 12 years, he sold out and moved to Odessa where he had another large insurance agency with a branch located in Midland.

Marion "Dookie" Pugh, tailback, junior

An All-State quarterback at Fort Worth North Side High School, Dookie became the first to sign up for the 1937 Fish team, which was destined to become the 1939 National Champions. He won four freshman numerals and then added three varsity letters each in football and baseball. He was voted Most Valuable in football in 1940 and made All-SWC in baseball in 1941.

He got in one year of pro football with the New York Giants in 1941 and another in 1945, but jumped to the Miami Sea Hawks for his final year in 1946.

He received his degree in Sociology in 1942 and went into the service with the Tank Destroyers, making the rank of captain before his discharge in 1945. Before going to Europe he played for the West team of Army All-Stars, coached by Wallace Wade.

In combat, he won the Purple Heart three times, the Bronze Star twice, the Unit Citation three times in all.

When he quit pro football in 1946, Dookie came back to College Station to start his own construction company. By 1949 this had expanded into the Marion Pugh Lumber Co., and the Pugh Realty Co. He served eight years on the College Station City Council.

John "Bubba" Reeves, guard, sophomore

As the self-proclaimed captain of the Blue Boys, Bubba Reeves never was one to hide his light under a bushel basket. He probably still contends that had it not been for his Blue Boys the Aggies never would have won the 1939 National Championship. He probably is right, for they played the Champs five days a week and got them ready for the upcoming game.

It wasn't easy to make Captain Bubba's Blue Boy team, either. Once, Dog Dawson was demoted from a White Shirt and assigned to the Blue Boys because Coach Norton thought he was goofing off. When Dog reported to the Blue Boys, Bubba said, "Listen, you big so-and-so, if you can't make Coach Norton's team you sure as Hell can't make mine. Now go back and tell him I don't want you."

It was hard to tell who was the more surprised, Dog or Coach Norton when the message was delivered. Dog was switched back to the White Shirts and from then on he never had to face Bubba again. He put out to his full extent from then on.

Bubba also was very unselfish. He asked Coach Norton to take him off the traveling squad for a West Coast game and instead take Howard Shelton in his place. "You aren't going to need me, but you might need Howard," he said. Again, Norton was astounded. He was even more so when it turned out that Shelton was needed when the other centers were injured. All Bubba would have done was sit on the bench.

Although Bubba was only 5-7 and weighing but 173 pounds, Bones Irvin had recommended that his San Antonio Thomas Jefferson product be given a scholarship. Even at his size, Bubba had won All-District and All-City honors twice. In addition, he was Texas State High School diving champ. Lil Dimmitt bought the deal and never regretted it. At A&M, Bubba was invaluable as a leader and won two football and two swimming letters.

Lester Richardson, guard, sophomore

Les got to Texas A&M via Houston's Milby High School and Marshall Junior College, where he was All-Conference. A foulup in the transfer of his credits kept him from playing in 1939 although, as it turned out, he was eligible, and this cost him a year of eligibility.

That year, however, he was one of the starting guards on Bubba's Blue Boys. He was a standout in the 1942 Cotton Bowl (Alabama), where he was sworn into the U.S. Navy Seabees at halftime. But for the clerical error it is quite likely that he would have become the fourth All-America product of Uncle Bill James.

Les made chief carpenter's mate in the Seabees while serving in the Pacific. Once back from service, he returned to Texas A&M to get his degree in Industrial Education. While coaching and serving as principal at A&M Consolidated High School, he completed his work for a Masters of Education degree. Then by commuting to Houston at night and on weekends he finished the work to earn his doctorate from the University of Houston

Les served as Superintendent of Schools for the A&M Consolidated School District and at Cuero and Brazosport for over 20 years. He also taught at the University of Houston and became a full professor at Texas A&M in 1966.

William Edward "Ed Robnett, back, sophomore

Ed, brother of Marshall, was a double duty player working at guard and as blocking back on the 1939 National Champions to win his letter. At 5-9 and weighing 190 pounds, he had to be great to be Number 2 at both spots.

Although the family lived at Klondike, he came out of Cooper High School with three letters each in football and basketball. He won his freshman numeral as a blocking back. Although eligible, he dropped out of school in 1940 to take a job.

He did not reenter college until after the war, when he attended Texas Tech and won two letters as a fullback. He received his degree from Tech in 1947 and then played one season pro football with the San Francisco '49ers.

Marshall Foch "Foxey" Robnett, guard, junior

It has been said of Foxey that he could have made the 1939 team at any position and been an All-American doing it.

Marshall came to Texas A&M out of Cooper High School, although his home was in nearby Klondike, where he now is buried. In high school and as a freshman he was a crashing fullback, but Uncle Bill James made a guard of him in 1938.

He majored in physical education in the hopes of becoming a coach, but he never was able to finish the work toward his degree. A 1941 marriage ended in divorce, the only one among the 1939 players who wed.

He played center for the then Chicago Cardinals in '41 and was named the NFL's Rookie-of-the-Year. He then entered military service, but just before he was to enter Officers Training School a knee injury from the Fordham game led to his medical discharge. He rejoined the Cardinals and played two more years before his other knee was torn up, ending what promised to be a brilliant professional football career.

He settled down in Bryan as a brick and masonry contractor, before moving to Dallas. where he was stricken with lung cancer in the mid-1960s.

When surgeons removed one lung and told him his chances were less than one in three of living more than six months, he replied that he was the one. He made good that bet for he lived two more years. After attending a 1939 Team reunion at the 1967 Baylor game, he lived to see the Aggies beat Texas on TV. A few days later, he passed on. The Reverend Joe Boyd conducted his funeral services and 19 of his old teammates were there. To them he was the greatest.

In 1969 he was elected to the Texas A&M Athletic Hall of Fame.

Cullen "Slick" Rogers, back, sophomore

Slick was the third of the Rogers family to win their letters at Texas A&M. Uncle "Lefty" won his as a baseball pitcher in 1923-25. Brother Owen won his football letters in 1936-38, and Cullen got his two in football in 1941-42 and three in baseball in 1941-43. He made Class B All-State as a Mart High School quarterback, but had the misfortune to reach varsity eligibility only to find Price, Pugh, and Jeffry all stacked up ahead of him, so he was held out in 1939.

He did quarterback the Blue Boys and each week took a beating as the next opponent's signal caller. In 1942 he received his BA degree in Liberal Arts and shortly afterwards went on active military duty.

From 1948 to 1958, Slick had a wholesale gasoline distributorship, but decided to switch to insurance. He owned a general insurance business at Marlin and developed a sizable agency.

Martin Ruby, tackle, sophomore

When Martin Ruby failed to make the starting team in 1939, everyone should have known that the Texas Aggies were national title contenders. It was hard to realize that this future All-America and all-pro tackle couldn't move Ernie Pannell or Joe Boyd out of those spots. Any team that Ruby couldn't make just had to be great.

Rube was a product of Waco High School, where he won his letters in football, basketball, and track, making the All-America teams in both of his main sports twice. At Texas A&M, he was the standout freshman lineman in 1938 and, in the '39 spring practice the coaches couldn't see how he would miss being a starter. What they overlooked was that Ernie and Joe had different ideas.

So Ruby had to be content to back up Pannell at left tackle. In 1941, he not only moved in but ended up being named to the All-Southwest Conference team, received some All-America mention and was voted the most valuable lineman in the SWC. The team elected Ruby and Marshall Spivey as co-captains.

After his great college career, he joined the Air Force and played for the Randolph Field Flyers, making All-America for the first time. He played for Randolph in the 1943 Cotton Bowl tie with Texas. He was named to the all-time Cotton Bowl team and later starred and made All-America again at March Field.

When he left the service, he signed to play pro ball with the Los Angeles Rams, but later went to Canada to play for Edmonton. He retired there and made his home in the land of the Maple Leaf.

J. Howard "Pard" Shelton, center, sophomore

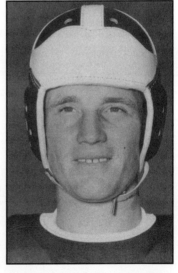

An outstanding center at Hillsboro High, Shelton arrived at A&M when all-staters were available at nearly every position. Most of his first year was with the Blue Boys as the center on "next week's" opponent.

He took his lumps, then moved up to win his letter. In his senior year he served as president of the "T" Association.

A brilliant student, he had extra team value as a tutor in tough math courses. He received his degree in electrical engineering in 1941, and headed for active duty. When he came back he was a lieutenant colonel with the Bronze Star, Combat Infantryman's badge and several Battle Stars for his service in Europe.

Howard entered the banking field with the Federal Land Bank in Hillsboro and Houston. In 1959, he became a vice-president of the Bank of the Southwest in Houston, and later served as president of banks in Temple and Fort Worth.

"Pard," as his teammates called him, was president of the 1939 National Champions group from its inception until he passed away in February 2006.

Earl "Bama" Smith, back, sophomore

Many players make the All-America teams, but how many can you name who cause the Football Rules Committee to rewrite their rule book?

Bama did just that when he was the receiver on the hideout play that Texas A&M pulled on the Longhorns in the 1939 game. It was the play that was the turning point in a game that was scoreless at the end of the half.

Standing just inches from the sideline, Smith caught a pass from Cotton Price for 56 yards to the Texas 26, setting up the first of three Aggie touchdowns.

Herbie came to A&M from Frisco City, in Alabama, recruited by a friend of Coach Norton when he saw some of Bama's great play there. At A&M, he won two football letters and added three more as a sprinter in track.

In 1941, he received his degree in physical education, but was off to the war before he could take a coaching job. He was an infantry lieutenant when the war ended. He came back to Bryan and, after other jobs, in 1951 opened his own Phillips 66 service station.

Herbert Everett Smith, end, senior

Team historians have called Herbie "pound for pound the greatest end football ever saw." In his final game, against Tulane on January 1, 1940, his performance earned him a spot on the all-time Sugar Bowl team.

Although his program weight listed him at 173 pounds, Smitty never topped 160 and went on the field at closer to 150 after a bout with food poisoning. He stood only 5-10, small for an end even in that era.

Facing him on offense was Tulane's 6-5, 235-pound All-America tackle, Harry McCollum, who had boasted all week about how he would pulverize "that little guy." After Dog Dawson kicked off, Smitty subbed in for him and played the remaining 59 minutes of the game.

After the first few plays, Herbie turned to Ernie Pannell and said, "Ernie, you get that linebacker. I can take care of this big SOB all by myself," and he did. McCollum was so helpless that the Tulane coaches jerked him from the game and he played only 22 minutes.

Smith caught four of the five passes thrown to him for 37 yards and three first downs; recovered a blocked Tulane punt, returned a kickoff 30 yards and blocked Tulane's try for the extra point after its second touchdown, thereby avoiding what could have been a tie game.

His final pass reception for 11 yards was lateraled off to Big John Kimbrough, who went the other 16 yards for the tying score. The successful conversion by Cotton Price made the winning score, 14-13, and cinched the Aggies' Number 1 ranking.

Smith was a product of San Angelo High, where made all-district twice and in 1935 made the all-state team. He lettered three years at A&M and was tri-captain of the 1939 team, earning a spot on the All-Conference team that same year.

He received his degree in physical education in 1940 and went on active duty at once. He transferred to the Air Force to become a fighter pilot, but was killed when his training plane, which had been disabled in the air, crashed within a few hundred yards of the landing strip at a Pennsylvania air base, on September 22, 1942. He lies buried in San Angelo, where the American Legion post is named in his honor.

Marshall Spivey, back, sophomore

An all-state, blue chip back from Lufkin, Marshall chose A&M over a number of schools. Coach Norton held him in such high regard, he assigned Dick Todd's Number 25 jersey to him.

Before he finished his career, he had justified that early judgment, winning three football and one track letter as a sprinter. Although not a 1939 starter, he did break in to understudy the Moser and Conatser combination at wingback and lettered. In 1941, he and Martin Ruby were voted co-captains.

He received his degree in agricultural economics in 1942, along with his commission in the army. He went directly to active duty, served in Europe and rose to the rank of major before his discharge in 1946.

Marshall enrolled in the University of Texas law school after the war, and earned his law degree in 1948. He first entered practice with State Senator Bill Moore, in Bryan, moved to Tyler and became a partner in his own firm.

James Sterling, end, sophomore

The coaches saw such promise in Jim that they moved him up to a starting end over several more experienced players. From the 1939 Villanova game, no one was about to take his job away. Proof is that he made the all-conference teams in 1940 and '41.

Jim came to A&M with high credentials from Panhandle High School, where he had been a five-sport man, lettering in football, basketball, baseball, track and tennis, and making all-state in football in 1937. At A&M, he concentrated on football.

He and Derace Moser were the only sophomores to make the 1939 starting team, although there were several on the squad who lettered.

Sterling received his degree in animal husbandry in 1942 and planned on becoming a county farm agent. But the war changed his ambition, and he served with the First Cavalry Division in the Philippines and the occupation of Japan. He was a major when he came home, well decorated.

Jim Thomason, back, junior

After Lil Dimmitt signed Jim Thomason out of Brownwood, he became a key man in recruiting the rest of the Aggie blue chip list. His pitch was: "Let's all go to Texas A&M, where they have nothing. If we stick together, we can win the Southwest Conference championship."

With such help, A&M landed 37 of the 40 players they sought. Those who came aboard did even better than Jim had predicted. They won the National Championship in 1939, and the SWC title in '39 and '40.

Jim wound up in the all-conference backfield both years, was rated the top blocking back in America, and was co-captain of the 1940 team with Tommie Vaughn.

As a sophomore, he won the SWC crown as a shot putter. Homer Norton called him one of the greatest athletes he had ever seen. He could have made any team as a runner, punter, or linebacker, but his great value to the Aggies came in his role as a devastating blocker.

Jim received his accounting degree in 1941. As an Air Force bomber pilot, he flew 62 missions in Europe and the Pacific. He came home as a captain with the Purple Heart, Air Medal with six clusters, among many other ribbons.

He played one year of pro football with the Detroit Lions, but quit to start his careers in insurance and accounting. He did graduate study in accounting at the University of Houston.

Tommie Vaughn, center, junior

Another prized Brownwood product, he became the quarterback and sparkplug of the Aggie defense. Ranked on the depth chart as the third string center in his sophomore season, Vaughn climbed into a starting berth after three games, displacing two seniors.

Tommie diagnosed plays and called the proper alignments so effectively the Aggies set a national record in 1939, allowing opponents just 1.7 yards per running play.

Legend has it that Thomason had to plead for a scholarship for Vaughn so he and his Brownwood buddy could stay together. That was another contribution Jim made to the championship team.

Vaughn's favorite historical figure was Napoleon. He weighed only 165 as a freshman—Tommie, not Napoleon—but he made up for it with sound and fury. His nickname was "Noise."

He picked up his diploma in marketing and finance in 1941, then accepted a commission in the army. Like several Aggies, he switched to the Air Corps and, after five years, much of it spent in the Pacific, he left the military with the rank of captain and a much decorated one.

He opened a Ford dealership in Granbury after the war, spent a few years in Los Angeles, moved back to Texas and became the owner of one of Houston's most popular dealerships.

For more than sixty years, he was a kind of spokesman for the 1939 National Champions, a fixture at their reunions and whatever game the current A&M team would be playing.

Tommie Vaughn passed away in 2005.

ACKNOWLEDGEMENTS

Most books, but especially those dealing with sports, are almost always the purest examples of a team effort—and appropriately.

There was no source of information more rare or valued than the scrapbook kept by Howard Shelton, bound by a cover made of wood, the size of a small suitcase. His collection of clippings and memorabilia stood nearly alone. No member of the 1939 Aggies had kept a journal and you doubt that any had the ego to consider writing a biography. Nor was this magnificent team the subject of national magazine articles. There were no slick sports publications until Sport made its debut in 1950 and Sports Illustrated in 1954.

But beyond the players, and those who kept the flame, the author is hard-pressed to give a proper thanks and credit to Rusty Burson, an Aggie grad and published author (who co-wrote the Dat Nguyen story.) Rusty dug through the decades to provide basic research, conduct interviews and download faded, fragile clippings into computer files. The photography of the times did not lend itself to drama or clarity, but he helped find what was there.

Kathy Capps, of the A&M Lettermen's Association, was another valuable contributor, who kept current the thinning roster of the surviving members of the '39 national champions. Others who lent moral or more tangible support were Alan Cannon, the assistant athletic director, and Homer Jacobs, editor of the 12th Man Magazine.

As indicated earlier, Jack Rains and John Lindsey gave the project its wings, while here on earth Tom Wisdom and Jerry Atkins hauled it across the finish line. Their several roles are not easily defined - fact checkers, cheerleaders, marketing and legal advisors.

Other Aggies offered encouragement, among them former players such as John David Crow, Ray Childress, Charley Milstead, Buddy Payne and Joe Munson. An apology to the many we know we have overlooked.

There were writers whose phrases made the job easier and more interesting, notably the brilliant Dan Jenkins and Blackie Sherrod. A large chunk of gratitude is due Harold and David Raley, father and son, founders of Halcyon Press, for believing in the book and its potential.

Of course, the project would never have been started, or finished, without the support of an array of Aggies, including most of the Class of 1960, whose names appear below:

CONTRIBUTORS PROJECT '39

Allen, Robert H. '50
Atterbury, John '70
Baggott, Bob '69 & Terry '69
Barber, Harwell, '47
Bell, Charles '60
Bourgeois, Gladys '78
Breen, Walt '60
Bryant, Terry '75
Bukowski, Lucian '97
Childress, Ray '85
Clinton, Daniel '52
Cone, Mike '60
Cook, Debra '77
Cooke, Mike '60
DeCluitt, Doug '57

DEVELOPMENT FUND '60

Faulk, Carolyn
Faulk-Clapp, Katie '98
Faulkner, James '60
Feinberg, Hill
Foster, Joe B. '56
Fraga, Steven '97
Graves, Dick '51
Griffin, Gerry '56
Hagler, Jon '58
Harrison III, Dick '47
Heldenfels IV, Fred '79
Huffines, J.L. '44
Krebs, Arno '64

Letbetter, Ronald S. '70
Lindsey, John '44
Little, Jack '60
Lusk, Ron
Marshall, Gene '60
McGee, Ken '60
Milstead, Charles '60
Mims, Percy '60
Murski, Ray '60
Natho, Bernard '60
Nelson, Scott '86
Nye, Erle '59
Oliver, Gale '60
Oxford, Hubert '60
Payne, Buddy '60
Prewitt, Buck '60
Rains, Jack '60
Rains-Waters, Misti '85
Rains, Tom K.D. '90
Rains-Whitus, Sherri '81
Ray, Gerald '54
Schiller, John '81
Schneider, Marvin '60
Shaw, Mike '68
Simmen, Franc '51
Slone, Adonn '60
St. Clair, Carolyn
Sullivan, Steve '72
Townend, Terry '87
Vasovski, Dan '79
Walker, Shawn '84 & Shea '86
Wisdom, Tom '60
Wooley, Lynn '60

INDEX

꿍